Samuel Beckett and the Pessimistic Tradition

Samuel Beckett and the Pessimistic Tradition

By Steven J. Rosen

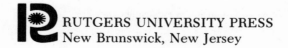

RUTGERS UNIVERSITY PRESS
New Brunswick, New Jersey

First Printing
Copyright © 1976 by Rutgers University, the State University of New Jersey
Manufactured in the United States of America

Library of Congress Cataloging in Publication Data

Rosen, Steven J   1944–
    Samuel Beckett and the pessimistic tradition.

    Bibliography: p. 237
    Includes index.
    1. Beckett, Samuel, 1906–   —Criticism and interpretation.   2. Pessimism in literature.   I. Title.
PR6003.E282Z796   848'.9'1409   76-2506

In memory of my father

Contents

Acknowledgements   ix

Part One: The Function of Meaning in Beckett's Aesthetic

Chapter 1. Incurious Search   5

    2. Against Consolation   19

    3. Pessimist and Skeptic   37

    4. Blathering about Nothing in Particular   57

    5. Failed Sages   71

Part Two: Beckett's Thought in *Proust*

Chapter 1. Approach to *Proust*: Nihilism, Spite, and Misanthropy   123

    2. Beckett, Proust, and Schopenhauer   137

    3. Relativism   153

    4. Time and Habit   173

    5. Problems and Solutions   199

Notes   221

Bibliography   237

Index   243

Acknowledgements

I should like to thank Professors Julian Moynahan and Paul Fussell of Rutgers University for their very helpful encouragement in the undertaking of this study. In a more general way, I am deeply indebted to Professors Marshall Cohen and Richard Poirier, who tried to teach me how to study philosophy and literature creatively.

Perhaps a dog, shortly before it falls asleep, or a drunken elephant has ideas which would not be unworthy of a master of philosophy. But these are of no use to them.

Lichtenberg

Samuel Beckett and the Pessimistic Tradition

Part One: The Function of Meaning in Beckett's Aesthetic

Chapter 1

Incurious Search

There was nothing to assure me that the vagueness of such states was a sign of their profundity rather than of our not having learned to analyze them.
—*Proust*

Seduced and disturbed by the attitudes of Beckett's characters, I have found it only natural to wonder about the mentality that motivated their creation; and to account for the haunting appeal of Beckett's writing, in terms of what it reveals about man's shared psychic life, has been the inevitable if elusive objective of all his critics. For Beckett's art is nothing if not a repository of unconventional attitudes: infantile, narcissistic, nonproductive, spiteful, futile, dangerous unhappiness. Still more remarkable than these attitudes, however, is the reader's provisional acceptance of them—a bemused acceptance of feelings he would normally dismiss as outrageous and absurd.

In other words, despite their absurdity, Beckett's books successfully claim attention as a vision of life. The world his characters inhabit is, the reader knows, merely a limited abstraction, an ordered selection of experiences drawn from a much wider range of possibilities. But it is precisely as such, that is, as a curiously restricted, bizarre, and yet persuasive selection of experiences, that his art engages us. If we are moved by Beckett's works and find them significant, it is because we have been led to think about the value of their odd outlook on life, wondering if this view can give us access, like some religious mystery, to the qualities of grace and wit we admire in Beckett's writing.

In an altogether distinctive way, however, Beckett's works not only nudge the mind but numb it as well, producing an

5

attitude which, while puzzled, remains peculiarly quiescent—the very outlook his hero Molloy described as
"incurious search" (p. 64; by permission of Grove Press, New
York, 1965). Accordingly, most discussions of Beckett's work
begin by admitting that it discourages interpretation, for this
discouragement, in fact, is a large part of Beckett's meaning.
And Beckett's few admiring analyses of other writers' works
voice quite insistently the same kind of protectiveness. This
youthful defense of Joyce, for example, proposes that obscurity
is essential to art:

> The time is perhaps not altogether too green for the vile suggestion
> that art has nothing to do with clarity, does not dabble in the clear,
> and does not make clear.[1]

It is not that Beckett confesses an inability to interpret
Finnegan's Wake. He is claiming that it is beyond interpretation:

> [Joyce's] writing is not *about* something; *it is that something
> itself.*[2]

Furthermore, as if to confirm his early commitment to this
aesthetic, the development of Beckett's own fiction and drama
appears to have been determined by attempts to get further
and further from meaning, closer to an ideal meaninglessness.
A poem appended to *Watt* states what has often seemed the
goal of his subsequent works: "Nothingness in words enclose"
(p. 247; by permission of Grove Press, New York, 1959). "This
is becoming really insignificant," says Vladimir, in and about
Waiting for Godot; still, Estragon replies, "not enough" (p. 44;
by permission of Grove Press, New York, 1954). Comparing
Waiting for Godot to such later works as *Come and Go* or
Imagination Dead Imagine, we are struck by Beckett's aban-
donment of a philosophical content once relatively dense and
explicit, his development away from externalizing references
towards a more absolutely hermetic arbitrary presentation. And
while refusing to elucidate his writing, he has repeatedly insisted upon its simplicity and self-containment:

> I feel the only line is to refuse to become involved in exegesis of
> any kind. . . . My work is a matter of fundamental sounds (no joke
> intended) made as fully as possible, and I accept responsibility for

nothing else. If people want to have headaches among the over-tones, let them. And provide their own aspirin.[3]

So we are not surprised to learn that "Crritic!" is Estragon's worst term of abuse; this hostility to interpretation is not sheer comical self-assertion, but a warning consistent with the basic principles of Beckett's art (p. 48). The aesthetic attitude his works so carefully stimulate, even explicitly recommend, is violated by neat and final solutions to what Beckett poses as insoluble problems. These should be felt to resonate end-lessly, if only because "the end"—as the narrator remarks in *Murphy*—"degrades the way into a means, a sceneless tedium" (p. 188; by permission of Grove Press, New York, 1957). Then who is Godot? A specific answer to that question, while depriving Beckett's writing of its characteristic wit and charm, also distorts the play's deliberate vagueness. Perhaps Beckett had that sterile controversy in mind when he was asked about *Endgame*, "What did it mean for Hamm's and Clov's faces to be red, while Nagg's and Nell's faces were white?" He replied: "Why was Werther's coat green? Because the author saw it that way."[4]

But a complication arises here. While Beckett's impatience with such a question is understandable, his answer invokes a misleading analogy. Indeed, such a question should never be asked about *Werther;* on the other hand, Beckett's works actu-ally provoke such guesswork. When Krapp angrily switches the tape past his recorded revelation, this effort of avoidance draws attention to a meaning not otherwise evident and pro-vokes curiosity about it. And Beckett's refusal to supply the usual dose of details throws those few which he does offer into suggestive prominence. Thus the teasing recurrence he estab-lishes among certain banal particulars has led one critic to propose that those bicycles and bowlers, for example, might be symbols.[5]

Now if, as I think, that kind of interpretive approach is mis-directed, it is nonetheless the case that Beckett seems to in-duce such considerations, not rarely but regularly, and natu-rally we wonder why. Confronted with the puzzles overtly characteristic of Beckett's writing, we learn in time to shift our investigation, but without abandoning it; for if the proper question to ask is not "Who is Godot?" we still want to know why Beckett should choose to confront us with such insoluble problems. The answer that directly suggests itself is this: to make us experience the indeterminability of such issues and thus become aware of our ignorance. But why should the experience of ignorance seem necessary or valuable—at least preferable to the conviction of knowledge? That is the question which brings us to the core of perplexity, the real difficulty, which is so essential to Beckett's art.

If an absence of meaning seems preferable to Beckett, it may be that an unwanted meaning presses itself upon him. Such a mentality would not find itself without a meaning, but rather, meaning-haunted. And thus Beckett characterizes himself, in the dialogues with Duthuit, as *"obliged* to write" (italics mine); that is to say, I suggest, that he feels compelled to deliver a certain message, while averse to its content.[6] And without speculating, in the manner of depth psychology, about specific obsessional pressures at work in Beckett's writing, we can point to his harsh and sweeping pessimism as that unwanted but inevitable message. Furthermore, if the difficulty of Beckett's art sometimes serves to obscure its pessimistic meaning, it is Beckett's pessimism which also leads him to require that art be difficult in order to be authentic. Life is a punishment, he feels, and so it ought to be with literary composition.

> For some authors writing gets easier the more they write. For me it gets more and more difficult. For me the area of possibilities gets smaller and smaller.[7]

Thus, throughout his critical writing, Beckett virtually elevates the difficult to an aesthetic principle, appreciating art in the same terms his fictional characters use to speak about life; each is a series of troubles to be endured, or more perversely, enjoyed as such. He values Proust's writing for straining him to "exhaustion";[8] the painter Bram Van Velde is recommended in terms of total bafflement:

> For what was this coloured plane, that was not there before? I do not know what it is, having not seen anything like it before.[9]

This connection posited between art and inaccessible meaning can also be discerned as the basis of *Watt,* a story about an unhappy hero whose troubles derive from his need to "saddle with meaning" incidents of "great formal brilliance and indeterminable purport" (p. 74). Beckett consistently suggests that beauty and indeterminable purport are inseparable, but such a view is neither obvious nor universal. And to reflect that this version of beauty, like all others, lies in the eye of its beholder, is to realize with Nietzsche that

> *The* beautiful exists just as little as *the* good or *the* true. In every case it is a question of the conditions of the preservation of a certain type of man.[10]

To better understand what type of man is preserved by finding inaccessible meanings beautiful, we can turn to an incident from *Molloy,* where some of the concomitant values implied by Beckett's aesthetic become more than usually explicit:

> I had stolen from Lousse a little silver [among which were] small objects whose utility I did not grasp but which seemed as if they might have some value. Among these latter there was one which haunts me still, from time to time. (P. 63)

Molloy continues with a protracted description of this particular object; suffice it to say that, like the stage of *Happy Days,* the thing exhibits a "maximum of simplicity and symmetry" (p. 7; by permission of Grove Press, New York, 1961). Its apparent inutility evokes some uncharacteristic tenderness from its equally useless owner:

> This strange instrument I think I still have somewhere, for I could never bring myself to sell it, even in my worst need, for I could never understand what possible purpose it could serve, nor even contrive the faintest hypothesis on the subject. (P. 63)

Some critics have plausibly suggested that the object is a knife-rest;[11] but, significantly, Molloy's ignorance of that classification allows him to see the thing as unique. As early as *Proust,* Beckett posited a necessary connection between the perception of uniqueness (guaranteed by ignorance) and what he called "enchantment."

But when the object is perceived as particular and *unique* and not merely as a member of a family, when it appears independent of any general notion and detached from the sanity of a cause, *isolated and inexplicable in the light of ignorance,* then and only then may it be a source of *enchantment.* (P. 69, italics mine)

This "enchantment" is simply Beckett's version of the aesthetic attitude and consistently seen as a function of ignorance or confusion; similarly, Arsene explains humor as an "excoriation of the understanding."[12] And such an ignorance is, clearly, a kind of "higher" ignorance; let us remember that Bram Van Velde's paintings, receiving the ultimate tribute, were found to be like nothing ever seen before. Similarly, the unique little object, as if it were a model work of art, can provoke Molloy to rapt, disinterested contemplation:

And from time to time I took it from my pocket and gazed upon it with an astonished and affectionate gaze . . . for a certain time it inspired me with a kind of veneration . . . (p. 64).

Here we find nothing very unusual, a modern aesthetic pose much like Schopenhauer's or Stephen Dedalus'—simple, elevated but dispassionate, above all without practical, social, or moral consequences. But Molloy gives the posture a distinctive Beckettian twist. For he does not, like the conventional aesthete, assume that the object is practically useless; rather, he thinks that it must have a purpose (or in that sense, meaning) but that its purpose is undiscoverable. Thus he can succumb to the delights of boundless confusion:

for there was no doubt in my mind that it was not an object of virtu, but that it had a most specific function always to be hidden from me. I could therefore puzzle over it endlessly without the least risk. For to know nothing is nothing, not to want to know anything likewise, but to be beyond knowing anything, and to know that you are beyond knowing anything, that is when peace enters in, to the soul of the incurious seeker. (P. 64)

In response, we ought to note that we really cannot know we are beyond knowing anything, for then we know *that;* but Beckett surely wants us to appreciate this paradox, for it typifies the sort of futile aspiration his heroes always suffer. And the futility of a goal need not, for Beckett, diminish its value—it may well increase it; in any case, a goal, even if impossible to realize, does indicate a value and supply a direction. When Moran, towards the end of his journey, remarks of a puzzling intricacy, "with rapture, Here is something I can study all my life and never understand," he has clearly moved both in the direction of Molloy and towards an enlightened kind of ignorance (p. 169).

I say enlightened, because Molloy's and Moran's remarks place Beckett's thought in a long philosophical tradition stemming from Socrates, who also claimed to know that he knew nothing; and as with Socrates, the conscious ignorance Beckett proposes is meant to be a sign of wisdom and spiritual refinement, a condition to be relished and a point of pride. If Molloy's words lead us into the void, to nothingness, then (as Kierkegaard observed of Socratic ignorance) "it is not the nothingness from which one begins, but the nothingness which one arrives at through the perplexities of deliberation."[13] And thus understood, the passage from *Molloy* does not, as we might first think, damn intellectual activity; on the contrary, Molly is attempting to retain the delights of thought by never coming to conclusions.

It is also important to realize that Molloy's contemplation is an aesthetic experience, inasmuch as his rapture is prompted by an object that is unique, carefully patterned, but of no apparent use (its literary equivalent might be exemplified by Beckett's *Ping*). For what is distinctive about Beckett's thought is not that he should find meaning inaccessible (a common enough condition) but that he proposes to prefer this ignorance and to substantiate it through his art. For Beckett, the purpose of art is to propel its beholder towards the sort of endless intellection Molloy describes—a stabilized confusion. The reader (or listener, or viewer) should be led to recognize that he is caught up amongst infinite or irresolvable considerations, but, and this is somewhat odd, he should enjoy that. That is not to say that art alone has such an effect, or that it always succeeds as such, but that ideally such an effect remains art's end.

By comparing Molloy's reflections with a somewhat similar scene, a very well-known dramatization of absurdist realiza-

tion, a clearer understanding of Beckett's distinctively aesthetic concerns will emerge. In Sartre's *Nausea,* the hero, Roquentin, also contemplates an object, in this case a tree root,
and like Molloy he realizes that he cannot comprehend it.
What follows is something like a religious conversion,
specifically a revelation of existence, followed by resolutions
for self-improvement. Roquentin reflects that he "had never
noticed the *existence* of objects before," not until the root, "a
soft, frightful obscene mass" "pressed itself up against [his]
eyes."[14] And what he discovers is that to exist is to be a "fundamental absurdity," that is "irreducible . . . below all explanation" (p. 174). As in the scene from *Molloy,* the question of
function is raised, but here it is dismissed as irrelevant, for
"function would explain the general, but not *that* root" (p.
174); again, bafflement is related to the perception of uniqueness. (Italics mine)

Like Molloy, Roquentin finds himself beyond knowledge,
even beyond ignorance, and feels that his response is sound;
"faced with that great wrinkled paw, neither knowledge nor
ignorance was important: the world of explanations is not the
world of existence" (p. 176). But he does not find this pleasant.
Roquentin does not have anything like what could be called
an aesthetic experience; it is not peaceful; it is less of a trance
than a shock, rendered by Sartre as a melodramatically lucid
vertigo. But the tree root, of course, is not a work of art and,
furthermore, it is explicitly distinguished from that category;
for art, exemplified by *"bars* of music" (italics mine), and
compared to perfect circles, is characterized by symmetry,
formal patterning, and, likewise, nonexistence. It is because
our existence is "amorphous, vague, and sad" (p. 177), that
Roquentin turns to art, resolving to write a book that would
suggest

> something which would not exist, which would be above exis-
> tence. A story, for example, something that could never happen, an
> adventure. It would have to be beautiful and hard as steel and
> make people ashamed of their existence. (P. 237)

Art then is essentially unlike life—orderly, a fiction, and an
ideal—and its thrust is moral. Roquentin will write to remind
"those bastards [who] . . . try to hide from themselves with

their idea of their rights"[15] (like Beckett's bourgeoisie, "baying for their due")[16] that their slack existence is no less gratuitous than his beautiful fiction; then they will realize that their social arrangements are arbitrary creations for which they must bear responsibility.

How far this vindication of rationalist aesthetics, a kind of poetic justice, is from Beckett, however, and at bottom, how utterly conventional and reassuring a view it is. No doubt it is best to guard against slipping into the void. But Sartre makes this stance seem easy, for the absurdity his hero confronts is ugly; though the reader may detect something like sexual fascination elicited by the "soft, frightful, obscene mass," it also presents the sort of vision from which he would naturally recoil. Beckett speaks to another side of our sensibility—to that within us which finds absurdity beautiful and does not want to bear responsibility. The difference involved can be described in terms of high absurdity and low absurdity. The tree root, a strikingly shapeless mass, is "below all explanation"; Roquentin realizes his ignorance, properly stops, changes direction, and shifts into moral gear. Molloy's little object, which is strikingly patterned, is above explanation, so he cultivates his ignorance as an aesthetic sensibility. The interesting implication of this is not that we ought to seek out strikingly patterned little objects; for the sensibility can be trained to view all things, including human situations, in that manner, by avoiding emotional aspects and focusing on matters of form. The anaesthetized, mechanical view of life that inevitably emerges yields the kind of comic sadism so characteristic of Beckett's writing—as when, for example, Molloy exquisitely describes the symmetrical way he goes about a murder, making no reference whatever to the moral issues involved (pp. 83–85).

But let us not exaggerate the nihilism of Beckett's stance. Alain Robbe-Grillet, one of Beckett's more interesting but extreme interpreters, finds him striving to create a "literature of non-meaning"—one that is "free" and a "theatre of presence"; accordingly, he blames Beckett for lapsing at times into detectably humanistic meanings. In other words, Robbe-Grillet would like Beckett's art to solicit the sort of attention Roquentin gives to his tree root; he would like us to be fascinated with its meaninglessness. And his own fiction, of course,

reflects this orientation; objects in Robbe-Grillet's novels, like
Sartre's tree root, evoke a paranoid trance, tinged with something like sexual terror (though not accompanied, as in
Nausea, with lucid reflection). Now whether Beckett should
be doing this or not is a question of taste, but to suppose that
he has this objective in mind is to misread the dominant
character of his work. Moran's bees' dance, Molloy's
knife-rest—which I take as deliberate emblems of Beckett's
art—are not perceived as meaningless objects but rather as
objects whose structures imply an inaccessible meaning. The
distinction is important, because mere meaninglessness could
not sustain the aesthetic response of incurious search that
Beckett's art so deftly solicits. When a meaning is suggested,
one is impelled to search; but if the inaccessibility of that
meaning is also suggested, he searches incuriously. And yet,
he does search or, to employ another formulation of Beckett's,
go on. Whether this oddly paradoxical, suspended condition
lies closer to the reader's own experience of life's absurdity
than the absurdities evoked by Sartre and Robbe-Grillet is a
matter each will have to determine for himself. It seems to me
that much of the haunting power of Beckett's works derives
from their seductive articulation of that attitude. That is, while
accommodating the ugly facts of life, the structures of his art
crystallize life's absurdity—the inaccessibility of its meaning
—and by their stylization, make that absurdity seem somehow
more appealing. It is, above all, this stylization which, as
Molloy puts it, brings peace to the heart of the incurious seeker.

What relation has this version of aesthetic speculation to
previous views? Schopenhauer's aesthetics, as is clear from
Proust, were certainly well known to Beckett, and, in a sense,
Beckett's aesthetic can be understood as a reply to Schopenhauer's. For that philosopher, the end of art is knowledge of
reality, itself conceived as corresponding to the Platonic ideas:

> Its [Art's] one source is the knowledge of Ideas; its one aim the
> communication of this knowledge.[17]

> The objects of genius are the eternal Ideas, the permanent essen-
> tial forms of the world and all its phenomena.[18]

Because "genius" is also "the faculty of suppressing the

will,"[19] the knowledge gained through aesthetic contemplation is commensurate with inner peace; and that is the value of art. Very similar notions are voiced by Joyce through Stephen Dedalus. With statements directly paralleling Schopenhauer's, the young artist proscribes excitation of the will by improper art (pornographic or didactic); the proper end of art, he asserts, is a static contemplation of essential reality (*quidditas*). We might note that Joyce's reality is explicitly distinguished from the Platonic ideas; it is also more limited, concrete, and immediately accessible than the philosopher's. Still, there is an essential agreement here: art supplies a knowledge of reality which brings peace. And the kind of knowledge sought is metaphysical; but, significantly, the kind of questions Beckett's heroes pose, like those of the common man, are naively teleological. Molloy wants to know what purpose his little object can serve, while Moran asks similar questions about the intricate dance of his little bees—to be similarly rewarded with ravished confusion (p. 169). Beckett's version of aesthetic contemplation is then essentially a frustrated teleology, triggered by perception of patterning. As such, it differs significantly from Schopenhauer's and Joyce's aesthetic in that it does not lead to knowledge, except in the sense of realized ignorance.

Not to exaggerate the novelty of Beckett's view, we need only reflect that, if the major movements of modern thought have had one common thrust, it is exactly this: to evoke a reluctance to assign meaning to things. The complexities of Continental existentialism have been reduced, in most readers' minds, to the fundamental tenet that we are put on earth for no purpose; to shrink from this realization, to find reassuring meaning in some preconceived order, is accordingly regarded as the fundamental act of cowardice. At the same time, British philosophy has been dominated by its own particular fastidiousness about explanation. Ludwig Wittgenstein advised his students to avoid those sentences which say, "This is really this [because] everything is what it is and not another thing."[20] But such a statement is neither a necessary rule of being or a principle of thought; it reflects a temperament which wants to see things in this way—the same urge that finds concomitant expression throughout much of modern poetry. The symbolists, most notably, aspired to create self-contained poems, making, at most, a minimum of references to external reality. For this reason any interpretation of their poetry is liable to seem misdirected, because unsympathetic to the aesthetic of autonomy. Nor is the influence of Freudian thought to be neglected here. The doctrine that our only real motives are unconscious implies that, if we think we have understood ourselves, we are almost certainly wrong. Thus the surrealist poets, seizing upon Freud's authorization of the unconscious, were able to advertise the significance of their writing by claiming not to know what it meant.

But whatever its precedents and analogues, there is something about Molloy's attitude which is disturbing, something which we resist, and of course Beckett knows this. In fact it is typical of him to focus on even the tritest bases of culture, in order to suggest (through exaggeration, juxtaposition, or simply naive literalism) their problematical implications. Some disturbing aspects of Molloy's aesthetic have already been suggested. To name the most obvious, does anyone really want to know (that is, feel) that he knows nothing? Neither instinct nor culture would seem to recommend this; indeed, one would expect that sort of recognition to be felt with anguish. The narrator of Keats's "Ode on a Grecian Urn," confronting an abyss of infinite regression, quite naturally draws back—it "tease[s] him out of thought;" but Molloy, under similar circumstances, asking unanswerable questions about a work of art, is happily teased into it. Perhaps Molloy is more philosophically inclined than Keats's speaker, but it is a premise and convention of philosophy itself that argument in a vicious circle amounts to error; to point this out in the arguments of others constitutes sufficient criticism. Such a procedure stems from the natural—it is tempting to say universal—repugnance of mankind to intellectual futility. Hegel's phrase, "bad infinity," makes the same assertion with perfect concision.[21] But Beckett is suggesting an alternative valuation.

Molloy's remarks reflect another problematical theme, one which runs throughout Beckett's works: the necessary solitude of thought, its asocial, or even antisocial consequences. From *Murphy* through *Molloy*, Beckett's heroes turn to reflection as a means of avoiding the world; their thought is indeed solipsistic, if not in actual content, then in effect. And clearly, such thought as Molloy's—that is, thought without conclusions—is useless, in a narrowly practical or social sense; to cultivate an attitude of incurious search is thus, in effect, somewhat socially irresponsible. Beckett may have intended to imply the conflict between social obligations and his hero's contemplative inclinations by basing the means to Molloy's rapture on a theft.

And, regardless of its immoral or amoral implications, the passage from *Molloy* is charged with a spiritual intensity disturbing in itself. Molloy is proposing nothing less than a spiritual program: one should experience ignorance, "for that is when peace enters in." But do we really want "peace?" At that price? Do we really want peace under any conditions or is this yet another one of our platitudinous delusions?

It is not like Beckett to commit himself to one mood without qualification; nothing is sacred, including incurious search, and Molloy's remarks are qualified in various ways. I have already noted the paradoxical or simply contradictory nature of his desideratum—knowing that one knows nothing. And Molloy's unfortunate condition naturally renders his values suspect. To say the same thing, the book's predominantly humorous tone functions as a qualifying context for its weightier remarks. Molloy's statements are also qualified by the reader's allowance for exaggeration and shock value. Similarly, when the Unnamable asserts, "Deplorable mania, when something happens, to inquire what" (p. 296), that sweeping statement takes account of our firm belief that normal curiosity is anything but a "deplorable mania." Furthermore, incurious search is explicitly disavowed in some of Beckett's later works. Malone lists "incurious wondering" amongst the types of "earnestness" he now intends to eschew (p. 120). The Unnamable vents some sarcasm on a related practice, deliberate literary obscurity:

But the discourse must go on. So one *invents* obscurities. Rhetoric. (P. 296, italics mine)

Yet ignorance and incuriosity seem to remain for Beckett essentially valuable conditions, somehow more authentic than their opposites. The Unnamable later imagines a more advanced inner being, Worm, of whom

> to say that he does not know what he is, where he is, what is happening, is to underestimate him. What he does not know is that there is anything to know. His senses tell him nothing, nothing about himself, nothing about the rest, and this distinction is beyond him. Feeling nothing, knowing nothing, he exists nevertheless . . . (p. 346).

Then what, at this point, can be concluded? First, that by posing explicit questions about the value of meaning Beckett's art provokes a reconsideration of values generally and at the deepest level. Furthermore, the aesthetic inferred from Beckett's works—as articulated by Molloy, Moran, and others—is meaning-centered; for Beckett, aesthetic experience requires the stimulation (plus the frustration and, to some degree, suspension) of a rather philosophical curiosity. Thus general questions about Beckett's meaning are wholly legitimate, in fact, inevitable. And yet, though such questions are provoked, they are also undercut. For, as we have seen, one of the things Beckett repeatedly calls into question is the meaning of meaning itself, or, what amounts to the same thing, the value of that heavily loaded concept. This being the case, questions about Beckett's meaning entail a sort of logical circularity—the term employed is itself the point of the dispute. Such a difficulty is typical of Beckett's art. But that is not all, nor is the matter thus to be resolved. For we are nonetheless led to wonder, as I have said, what would make such a view of meaning develop as incurious search suggests? Which traditional meanings, being judged inappropriate or unpleasant, motivate Beckett's skepticism? Worm's is a condition whose advantages are not immediately seen. Why is such an ignorance preferable to knowledge or more authentic? Beckett has not only raised these questions; his art suggests some answers to them as well.

Chapter 2

Against Consolation

And lamentations that inspire my strain
Prove that philosophy is false and vain.
—Voltaire

The enigmatic ideal of incurious ignorance that so distinctively characterizes Beckett's heroes becomes a little less puzzling when seen in relation to its alternatives and consequences. While relishing their incurious ignorance, Moran and Molloy are conscious, necessarily, of having rejected the need to know. The satisfaction and peace they connect with confusion derives from their feeling of freedom from this need, in its purest form a need for healing knowledge or consoling explanations. And when it is said that Beckett's works offer no meaning, this is what is really meant: that they offer no consoling explanations. Rather, he insists upon presenting life as he sees it—nasty, brutish, and long. Perhaps, as Moran is told, things "might have been worse" (p. 175); but in his view, as in Beckett's, they more obviously might have been better.

In itself, this view of things is far from strange, for every age has associated pessimism with wisdom, so much so that Nietzsche, in derision, could call this sentiment the *consensus sapientium:*

> In every age the wisest have passed the identical judgement on life: it is worthless. Everywhere and always their mouths have uttered the same sound, a sound full of melancholy, full of weariness with life, full of opposition to life.[1]

But in Beckett's case the tone of this judgment is far from tiresome. Not the least of his accomplishments consists of hav-

ing retrieved so many pessimistic clichés, rescuing them from
banality and making them available to literature again by in-
congruous placement or witty alteration. Thus, to quote from
Murphy, "the sun shone, having no alternative, on the nothing
new" (p. 1; by permission of Grove Press, New York, 1957),
"the next best thing to never being born" (p. 44), and "how
can he be clean that is born" (p. 71).

The conjunction of this playfulness with such bleak convictions results in what everyone would probably like to produce,
a really entertaining complaint about life. So if this complaint
were to be called Beckett's "message," it would have to be
added that the texture of his prose is far from simply didactic,
that it reflects a wide range of moods and, of course, considerable emotional complexity. In *How It Is,* for example, the
fragmentation of pessimistic dicta gives them a highly poetic
tone:

> man his days as grass (p. 78; by permission of Grove Press, New
> York, 1958)
>
> my life as nothing man a vapour (p. 79)

And against this lilting poetic drone, a more learned language
of complaint seems to mock its own insufficiency:

> some reflections while waiting for things to improve on the fragility
> of euphoria among the different orders of the animal kingdom be-
> ginning with the sponges. (P. 38)

Often the unexpected extremity of Beckett's pessimism, the
insistence of its generality, strikes with a comic shock:

> use your head, you're on earth, there's no cure for that.[2]
>
> Christ, what a planet.[3]

Perhaps most frequently the lamenting voice expresses hesita-
tion or embarrassment or confusion, as if its artistic sensibility
shrank from the banal language of pessimistic generalization:

> Life has taught me that, life, I suppose there is no other word . . .[4]
>
> grope in a panic in the mud for the opener that is my life but of
> what cannot as much be said.[5]

Clearly, Beckett's philosophical interests shape the style of his writing as well as its content. In spite of this, some of his critics have argued that we ought to ignore these concerns. John Fletcher asserts that

> If one distils a philosophy of life from Beckett's writing, it reveals itself as remarkably uninteresting. . . . His themes are very simple and very ancient, going back to Ecclesiastes at least. Beckett's extraordinary power cannot lie in what he says, and so it must lie in the way he says it.[6]

I do not understand why the antique origin of Beckett's themes should deprive them of interest, as Fletcher implies; whatever their origin, adapting to the disappointment of life remains a modern concern as well. And morbid depression is as far from being understood as sexuality, violence, or the other basic and timeless human tendencies.

In any case, Fletcher's reference to Ecclesiastes is apt. Beckett's works contain a number of allusions to that text (and also to its harsher Christian successor, the *Imitation of Christ*); and these allusions reflect the basic similarity of spirit between Beckett and the "Preacher" (the nominal speaker and author of Ecclesiastes). Each of their voices conveys the same essential tone, the tone of persisting in speech while convinced of its futility. And in each case this rhetorical stance corresponds to a more general attitude about life: a dazed sense of arbitrary, compulsive obligation, surviving despite fundamental disillusionment. Lamenting the inexplicably absurd and dolorous spectacle of life, the Preacher concludes that man must, nonetheless, persist in dutiful observances. Beckett's trilogy, which ends with the words, "You must go on, I can't go on, I'll go on," expresses much the same attitude.

The significant difference between Beckett and the Preacher is that the traditional consolations which enable the latter to face the "going on" are remarkably absent from Beckett's works. And it is the absence of these solacing maxims that gives Beckett's writing much of its distinctive shock effect. He strives to remain unconsoled, to retain the integrity of a basic bitterness. Murphy, the hero of Beckett's most explicitly philosophical novel, is distinguished from his fellows in precisely such terms:

Wylie in Murphy's place might have consoled himself with the
thought that the park was a closed system in which there could be
no loss of appetite; Neary with the unction of an Ipse dixit; Tickle-
penny with reprisal. But Murphy was inconsolable . . . (p. 184)

Beckett's refusal to employ the standard rationalizations of
philosophical and religious tradition—indeed, his overt hostility to these doctrines—has led the critic Michael Robinson
to classify Beckett's works as "anti-theodical" literature.[7] For
Beckett (to borrow another phrase from Nietzsche, his inver-
sion of Leibniz) seems to think this "the worst of all possible
worlds."[8] Since "there's nothing funnier than unhappiness,"[9]
and the highest form of laughter is directed "at that which is
unhappy,"[10] it is at least bad enough for his literary purposes,
which of course are predominantly comic. Some of Beckett's
best jokes take the form of a triumphant unhappiness asserting
itself against specious consolation:

Mr. Rooney: Who is the preacher tomorrow? . . . Has he an-
              nounced the text?
Mrs. Rooney: "The Lord upholdeth all that fall and raiseth all those
              that be bowed down." (*Silence. They join in wild
              laughter*).[11]

Perhaps a good part of Beckett's distinctive appeal can be
attributed to his hostility to such cant as is mocked above.
Whether his art is called pure or harsh, something that is not in
it is being referred to; and Beckett's alienation from formal
religious or political doctrines need not be cited to make this
point. Still more significantly absent from his works is the cant
of the common man, the nearly universal reflex action of the
mind which leads the sufferer to conclude, after each misfortune, that it really was a benefit. "I'm so glad I broke my leg,"
such reasoning goes: "I got so much reading done." Or, "I'm
so glad I lost my genitals; it brought me much closer to God."
Of course this sort of rationalizing inevitably attracts suspicion; if not actually insincere, it still seems unauthentic. Montaigne, himself a master rationalizer, once mocked that kind of
facility in the following passage:

'tis for my good to have the stone: . . . the structure of my age must
naturally suffer some decay, and is it not time it should begin to

disjoin and confess a breach? 'tis a common necessity, and there is
nothing in it either miraculous or new; I can therefore pay what is
due to old age, and I cannot expect a better bargain . . . society
ought to comfort me being fallen into the most common infirmity of
my age; I see everywhere men tormented with the same diseases
and am honored by their fellowship, forasmuch as men of the best
quality are frequently afflicted with it; 'tis a noble and dignified
disease . . .[12]

Similarly, when this sort of ingenuity appears in Beckett's
works, it is presented only to reveal its obvious insufficiency.
Winnie's thankfulness in ghastly adversity, her spate of inappropriate, unjustified consolations, makes *Happy Days* seem
perhaps Beckett's bitterest work. In *The End*, Beckett's starving hero attempts to suck the udder of a cow, "covered with
dung," and then to milk her more conventionally, only to be
dragged and kicked about. His subsequent reflections, which
are reflex consolations, are made to appear especially ridiculous by this slapstick context:

The milk fell to the ground and was lost, but I said to myself, No
matter, it's free.

. . . I reproached myself with what I had done. I could no longer
count on this cow and she would warn the others. More master of
myself I might have made a friend of her. She would have come
everyday, perhaps accompanied by other cows. I might have learnt
to make butter, even cheese. But I said to myself, No, all is for the
best.[13]

The less naive Malone rephrases the *carpe diem* attitude, adding a macabre twist:

Come on, we'll soon be dead, let's make the most of it. (P. 226;
by permission of Grove Press, New York, 1965)

And when the Unnamable seems to indulge in a plausible, if
somewhat melancholy consolation, he also goes on to point
out its dire implications:

It is true that one does not know one's riches until they are lost and
I probably have others still that only await the thief to bring them to
my notice. (P. 314)

Here Beckett is playing with the inherent ambiguity of the language of consolation. Consoling saws presume a dialectic; that is, their appropriateness depends entirely upon their having an effective relationship to the particular situation, audience, and mood at hand. What is consoling to some may not be consoling to others but merely a more damning reformulation of the nagging problem. The thought that all must die, for example, might console someone feeling the isolation or injustice of his approaching death; but it becomes a shocking thought in other contexts.

Despite these circumstantial complexities, however, it is legitimate to speak of a logical system underlying consolation or at least a considerable consistency and its crystallization through influential texts into a definite art or tradition. It will be useful to bring these standard tactics of relief to mind, for, although they are largely absent from Beckett's works, their presence is anticipated, and he anticipates that anticipation. Conveniently, the mentality Beckett so militantly opposes has its own *locus classicus* in Boethius' *Consolation of Philosophy*. Having fallen from the height of good fortune to an arbitrary imprisonment and death sentence, Boethius composed an argument between his complaining self and an allegorical figure, Lady Philosophy. A universally recognized voice, that of the older, conventional, female relative, emerges in its purest, most exasperating form; a look at Lady Philosophy's arguments will provide examples of exactly the sort of thought Beckett is combatting:

> (1) You have not been driven out of your homeland, you have willfully wandered away.[14]

This can be called the voluntaristic consolation. Demonstrate to the sufferer, especially when it is not at all obvious, that in some sense, however remote, he "chose" and is thus "responsible" for his condition. This will silence him, for no one has the right to complain about chosen results. And oddly enough, it seems that most people would rather feel guilty than impotent. Thus the rejected lover who proclaims his guilt is usually masking a more disastrous and accurate fear: that he was powerless from the start; and thus he consoles himself. For there is something consoling in the memory of power,

however deluded, perhaps because it implies an ultimate release from present sufferings. "If I got myself into this," the
feeling is, "I ought to be able to get myself out of it." But did
he get himself into it? Does it really make sense to regard a
man as responsible for the conditions of his misery? As Beckett would ask, did he choose to be born? Or to have a human
nature?

Sartre, although a rigorous pessimist, in many ways re-
sembling Beckett, has stooped to this voluntaristic consolation. His diatribes upon man's freedom and consequent responsibility would sound like delusions of grandeur to
Beckett's heroes, who prefer to cultivate delusions of impotence. Anything, admits Moran, even his paranoid obsessions,
is preferable to admitting he is "solely responsible for [his]
wretched condition" (page 107). Similarly, the narrator of the
Texts for Nothing can imagine no greater happiness than to
have

> a nanny, I'll be her sweet pet, she'll give me her hand, to cross
> over, she'll let me loose in the garden, I'll be good, I'll sit quiet as a
> mouse in a corner and comb my beard, I'll tease it out, to look more
> bonny . . . *I'll have no responsibility*, she'll have all the responsibil-
> ity . . . (P. 86, italics mine)

Indeed, Beckett's later heroes are so far from affirming their
situation, as Lady Philosophy recommends, that they will not
even affirm their thoughts—traditionally, the unfortunate's
only refuge; rather, they report a voice suffered inside the
head. Few men regard themselves as masters of their fates, but
who does not think himself the master of his soul? The answer
is, Beckett's heroes, who seem to be the cabin boys of their
souls. Nor is their stance to be dismissed as merely comic
exaggeration. For Beckett's own public statements insist upon
the necessary passivity of the artist. He asserts in *Proust* that
"the will is not a condition of the artistic experience" (p. 69;
by permission of Grove Press, New York, 1960). And twenty-
five years later he adds this logical extension: "I am working
with impotence, ignorance."[15]

The next of Boethius' consolations is that

> (2) God assigns to every season its proper office. (P. 17)

This, the holistic rationale, is perhaps the most widely used technique of consolation in literature. It is found in Ecclesiastes, where the conviction that all is "vanity and vexation of spirit" is countered with the following reassurance:

> To every thing there is a season, and a time to every purpose under the heaven . . . (3: 1)

Similarly, in Marcus Aurelius,

> the lion's gaping jaws, and that which is poisonous, and every harmful thing, as a thorn, as mud, are after-products of the grand and beautiful.[16]

The same tactic can be found in a host of major works, including those of such apparent polarity as Pope's *Essay on Man* and Blake's *Marriage of Heaven and Hell*. The trick lies in taking a sufficiently distant and inclusive view, simulating the divine perspective, which inevitably produces an impression of order. The passage of the seasons and strife in nature—to take the more commonplace topics of the argument—are thereby seen as systems of perpetual renewal. In this way present woes, like the cold of winter or being eaten, appear part of a justified cycle. But all this is parodied and exploded by Arsene's monologue in *Watt*. Natural cycles are cited *ad nauseam*, leading to "the celebrated conviction that all is well, or at least for the best." And then this is deflated: "Am I not a little out of sorts? . . . He has learned nothing" (p. 42). Nor will Molloy allow himself the holistic consolation: "For the particulars . . . there is no need to despair. It's for the whole there seems to be no spell" (p. 27).

Boethius' next consolation is that

> (3) No man can ever be secure until he has been forsaken by fortune. (P. 17)

The quest for emotional "security" underlies stoicism and other ascetic philosophies; the hope they offer is to minimize anxiety by renouncing goods subject to fortune's disposition. There is no doubt that Beckett finds this spirit attractive, and once he might have thought it a very possible course. In *Proust* he affirmed the "wisdom that consists not in the satisfaction, but in the ablation of desire" (page 7) a point often made again in *Murphy*. But in *Murphy* Beckett's pessimism asserts itself against even this bleak hope: we learn that the complete apathy Murphy desires is reserved for the insane. And if in *Murphy* insanity itself suggests an escape, this is not the case in *Watt*. For there the subject is mentalities sufficiently deranged, yet still insufficiently detached. As Arsene explains,

> it is useless not to seek, not to want, for when you cease to seek you start to find, and when you cease to want, then life begins to ram her fish and chips down your gullet until you puke, and then the puke down your gullet until you puke the puke, and then the puked puke until you begin to like it. (P. 42)

The quest for apathy is nonetheless a quest, and thus doomed like any other to futility; so Arsene concludes that the "glutton castaway, the drunkard in the desert, the lecher in prison . . . [are] the nearest we'll ever get to felicity" (p. 42). On the other hand, Beckett's later heroes do achieve a spirit of renunciation comic in its extremity. Consider Molloy, "poking about in the garbage . . . bent over a heap of muck, in the hope of finding something to disgust [him] with eating forever" (p. 57). And yet Molloy continues to confess a residual anxiety (the term recurs throughout Beckett's writing), as if this anxiety were the inescapable condition of humanity. Moran's breakdown (or conversion, or enlightenment) hinges upon this admission:

> The colour and the weight of the world were changing already, soon I would have to admit I was anxious. (P. 96)

The point is that he has always been anxious, but only now is ready to admit it. Similarly, the Unnamable, who has lost everything a man can lose, grants

> I have no cause for anxiety. And yet I am anxious. (P. 302)

His plight suggests what the common man already knows — that although no man will be secure until he has been forsaken by fortune, he will only be more insecure afterwards.

Boethius next reasons that

(4) Now it pleases me [speaking here as Fortune or Fate] to withdraw my favor. You should be grateful for the use of something which belonged to someone else. You have no legitimate cause for complaint. (P. 23)

This attitude is also common to most systems of consolation. It appears in Diogenes the Cynic,[17] in Seneca,[18] and again in Lucretius:

Why not depart from life as a sated guest from a feast?[19]

Because man has no right to life and happiness, he should gracefully accept misfortune. But, as Beckett would no doubt note, the argument works just as well the other way; that is, man has no right to life, nor has death any right to him. He has no contract with the cosmos, and the application of legal analogies (such concepts as "rights" and "justice") to explain man's radical misery is merely ridiculous. This sort of critique can be detected in *How It Is*, whenever the hero naively insists on the "justice" of life as reciprocated torture (page 117).

Nor is life, furthermore, to be properly characterized as a "feast." Malone's sardonic gratitude for living makes this plain enough:

Be born, that's the brainwave now, that is to say live long enough to get acquainted with free carbonic gas, then say thanks for the nice time and go. (P. 225)

Boethius continues,

(5) No man can be rich who cries fearfully and considers himself to be poor. (P. 25)

This suggests that mind be put over matter. But what, then, shall be put over mind? The Unnamable, a "head abandoned to its ancient solitary resources" (p. 361), is nonetheless sorrowfully situated. A confidence in the mind's power to view any condition favorably is a conviction common to all systems of consolation, necessary as an operational principle; but it is especially well developed in the stoicism of Marcus Aurelius:

I can have that opinion about anything which I ought to have. If I can why am I disturbed? The things which are external to my mind have no relation at all to my mind. Let this be your conviction and you stand erect. To recover your life is in your power. Look at things again as you used to look at them; for in this consists the recovery of your life.[20]

The naive optimism of these brave words is what separates Beckett so sharply from stoicism, some affinity notwithstanding. Next Boethius points out that

(6) If you possess yourself, you have something which . . . Fortune cannot take away from you. (P. 29)

This sentiment is typical of classical philosophers. "When asked what advantage had accrued to him from philosophy," Antisthenes the Cynic replied, "the ability to hold converse with myself."[21] And why is this held to be advantageous? Because, by virtue of self-sufficiency, misfortunes can be transcended; or, as Boethius more modestly puts it, we can be consoled for them. Similarly, Rousseau defended his egocentricity—an influential model for many modern literary voices —as a necessary consolation:

Alone for the rest of my life, because I cannot find except in myself *consolation,* hope and peace, I ought not, and do not wish to occupy myself any longer save with myself. . . . Let me devote myself entirely to the sweetness of speaking with my own soul, because that is the only thing of which men cannot rob me.[22] (Italics mine)

Now this is not the view of Beckett's heroes, who find speaking with their own souls a pathetic futility (in the case of Krapp) or a kind of obsessive torment (in the case of the Unnamable). Of course, the sort of self Rousseau had in mind is a thickly textured web of idiosyncrasies, which in his *Confessions* and *Reveries* he sought to correlate and justify; Beckett's concept of the self does not support or reflect this kind of social and moral interest. As man withdraws from the world and approaches the self, Beckett's trilogy suggests, the self becomes successively emptier, even finally without distinct identity at all. Furthermore, as vacant and uninteresting as this self is, it still resists real possession. In *Film,* for example, Beckett's theme is the mind's bifurcation into perceiving subject and perceived object; subject and object can never be united, and thus the hero's self-consciousness effects an anxious and perpetual self-estrangement.

Boethius continues:

> (7) Earthly rewards are, in any case, finite and temporal, hence paltry in connection with infinity and eternity. (P. 38)

This argument, by definition, is indisputable, but Beckett can more easily imagine infinite and eternal punishments than rewards. Thus he has Moran wonder, "Might not the beatific vision become a source of boredom, in the long run?" (P. 167) For infinity and eternity are likely to seem torments in themselves.

Furthermore, according to Boethius:

> (8) Philosophy argues that misfortune is more beneficial than good fortune, for good fortune deceives, but misfortune teaches. (P. 56)

Here the philosopher's reasoning does violence to ordinary language and common sense. If misfortune is really more beneficial than good fortune, then it is not misfortune—in fact, there can be no such thing. It is towards this extremity that the arguments of optimists ultimately tend, while pessimists like Beckett are determined to insist that misfortune does exist, as such.

As to the more limited claim here, that misfortune teaches, Beckett's works indeed acknowledge an intimate connection between knowledge and suffering. Since reality is fundamentally evil, pain is inevitably instructive. But as Arsene would have it, this is "useless knowledge, dearly won."[23] The Unnamable also expects to learn:

> Let them scourge me without ceasing and evermore, more and more lustily. . . . In the end I might begin to look as if I had grasped the meaning of life. (P. 353)

Of course the knowledge thus acquired is not worth its cost and is no effective consolation. Rousseau, to whom Beckett alluded in *More Pricks than Kicks,* (p. 24) has also criticized this familiar rationalization.

it is a very sad knowledge, this, which experience has made me acquire for twenty years; ignorance is still preferable. Adversity without a doubt is a great master; but this master makes his lessons cost dearly, and often the profit that one obtains from them is not worth the price one has paid.[24]

Beckett would go even farther, finding knowledge not only too costly but, in some cases, intrinsically undesirable. There are certain things most people would rather not know, such as the hour of their death. And since precisely such things are the objects of Beckett's constant attention, the attitude that emerges most consistently from his writing is that of an ironic but aesthetically intensified agnosticism.

Boethius' argument continues,

(9) I can see clearly the consequence of your reasoning. For it follows that the good are powerful and the wicked are impotent. (P. 79)

This rationalization of apparently triumphant evil goes back to Socrates and Plato. It is explained in *The Republic* that wicked tyrants are "slaves" to their passions and, consequently, "impotent," while the *Apology* asserts that a "worse man cannot harm a better." Beckett takes a sardonic view of the resentment which must motivate such desperate intellection. Hence his mordant description of Murphy's mind, lower chamber, where continuous rearrangements of the worldly power structure are performed:

Here the pleasure was reprisal, the pleasure of reversing the physical experience. Here the kick that the physical Murphy received, the mental Murphy gave.... Here the whole physical fiasco became a howling success. (P. 111)

Boethius' equation of power and pleasure with virtue was also preceded in the writings of Marcus Aurelius, who asked, "How many pleasures have been enjoyed by robbers, patricides, tyrants?" Beckett might actually attempt the calculation. The conclusion of *How It Is* envisions a logarithmic expansion of masters and victims, spiralling out towards infinity.

Boethius' next and final argument is also so remote from the actual experience of life as to seem, whatever its logical coherence, simply false. Accordingly, it evokes what Beckett calls the "hollow laugh."[25]

> (10) Look here . . . since all fortune, whether sweet or bitter, has as its purpose the reward or trial of good men, or the correction and punishment of the wicked, it must be good because it is clearly either just or useful. (P. 98)

The specious ease with which Boethius disposed of apparent evils proceeded from this fundamental faith:

> You believe that the world is not subject to the accidents of chance, but to divine reason. Therefore you have nothing to fear. (P. 19)

Beckett, of course, would reject this premise; even accepting it, however, he would not draw Boethius' conclusion. That is, if a divinely ordained system (as Moran believes) does govern human affairs, it might really mean trouble.

I have been looking at something that is not in Beckett's writing, a set of consoling rationalizations, because his thought takes shape through contention with this mentality. As Paul Kristeller has observed,

> The views against which a thinker reacts mark also the starting point for his own thought, determine the range and direction of his ideas, and often constitute the necessary complement to his own system. . . . Ideas lose their force when the conditions against which they were conceived disappear, just as a man leaning against a wall will collapse when the wall is suddenly taken away.[26]

Thus without reference to the more normal sentiments that Beckett mocks or deliberately avoids, his meaning might be missed, since it is largely reactive and contentious. But if Beckett's pessimistic drift can usually be inferred from the absence of consolation in his writing, there are also certain moments when his hostility to delusive rationalizing becomes plain and explicit. At the conclusion of "Dante and the Lobster" (in *More Pricks than Kicks*), the hero is given some fatuous assurances that the animal, about to be boiled alive in the usual way, will not suffer. The squeamish Bellacqua, unlike his crueler and more appealing successors, must console himself; so he reflects that "It's a quick and painless death."

But then a voice suddenly answers, "it is not" (p. 22; by permission of Grove Press, New York, 1957). These words are not assigned to any of the characters present. It is Beckett speaking *in propria persona*, but without the usual formalities of introduction; the effect produced is one of disturbing authority.

In this passage there is a contentious and didactic pessimism; the real cruelty of the case—and by implication, of life in general—is explicitly asserted. Such allusions to animal suffering figure frequently in arguments against the optimistic outlook. For the suffering of humans can be explained by their guilt; an individual's sins seem usually sufficient, or, lacking them, he can invoke the sins of his father. But of what are animals guilty? Or their fathers? Hence the powerful motif of animal slaughter recurrent in *Watt, Molloy,* and *Malone Dies.* Schopenhauer also referred to animal pain in pessimistic contention:

> The pleasure in this world, it has been said, outweighs the pain; or at any rate there is an even balance between the two. If the reader wishes to see whether this is true, let him compare the respective feelings of two animals, one of whom is engaged in eating the other.[27]

And here there is a kind of rhetorical sensibility often associated with assertive pessimism. The tension that inheres between the elegant symmetry and unexpected violence of such language produces a cruel humor, characteristic of such works as Schopenhauer's essays, *Gulliver's Travels, Candide, The Secret Agent,* and most of Beckett's writing; on the other hand, this tone is absent from those pessimistic works, like Hardy's, which do not directly combat optimism.

Given the thorough and combative nature of Beckett's pessimism, however, some important questions about its motives remain to be considered. Apart from the rich vein of humor it provokes, what makes this stance so appealing to Beckett? Why does he so insistently reject consolation? And is that simply the case? There is no doubt a line of thought in Beckett's works and a mood as well that are similar to the pessimism of Swift, Voltaire, Schopenhauer, and Conrad. But these authors are more or less clearly ironic, while in Beckett's writing something else can be detected, a response to human sufferings and their corresponding rationales that goes beyond bitterness and wit towards a different perspective, even, perhaps, a kind of solution. And this is both puzzling and strange.

In the scene from *Molloy* involving Gaber and Moran in the forest, a full page of dramatic delay and circumlocution precedes Gaber's recollection of a remark by Youdi:

> He said to me, said Gaber, Gaber, he said life is a thing of beauty, Gaber, and a joy for ever. . . . [Moran replied,] Do you think he meant human life? (P. 134)

In the context of Moran's experience, it seems that Youdi's Keatsian remark is surely false; that is, of course life is bad. But can this be Beckett's point? If so, the ironic machination at work here seems strangely crude and tedious. The reader might suppose that Beckett is investigating the aesthetic possibilities of the bad joke, perhaps because he finds that life is a bad joke. And what is a bad joke? Essentially, a tasteless anticlimax, an anticipation without reward, a statement which comes too arbitrarily to its conclusion, or perhaps to no real conclusion at all. But if this is the normal experience of life, that it is a bad joke, who is then to say that life is "bad?" By what criterion? Life is not required to be a good joke. I am saying, in other words, that the object of Beckett's ridicule in this passage, is not "life," but the tendency to formulate judgments about life's quality, whether affirmative or negative. It is also true that such judgments, particularly pessimistic ones, are at the basis of Beckett's art; but in going on to ridicule this judgmental tendency, I suppose he was attempting to exorcise from within himself what he came to regard as a fatuous compulsion.

The ending of *Watt*, in the same way as the scene considered above, is at once haunting and hard to take. The weary hero, unhappy as well as deranged, overhears some smugly satisfied remarks:

> All the same, said Mr. Gorman, life isn't such a bad old bugger. He raised high his hands and spread them out, in a gesture of worship. He then replaced them in the pockets, of his trousers. When all is said and done, he said. (P. 244)

Are we to understand that Mr. Gorman is simply dead wrong?—that is, that the opposite of his remarks is true? In fact, the idyllic aspect before him would seem to justify his sentiments:

> the sky falling to the hills, and the hills falling to the plain, made as pretty a picture, in the early morning light, as a man could hope to meet with, in a day's march. (P. 245)

Yet, here, as throughout the book, Beckett's language is alienating, addressing readers as if they were children and thus repelling belief—which is not to deny its mesmeric effect. The only thing to be concluded here, I think, is this: Beckett is saying that life is neither a good nor a bad old bugger, that such statements are meaningless or at least without authority apart from the purely subjective moods they attempt to substantiate. Of course, as Beckett knows, these moods cannot be escaped; inevitably, man lives by them. And with remarkable obsessiveness and complexity they have remained the focussing motive of his art.

Chapter 3

Pessimist and Skeptic

*Who is unhappy at having only one mouth? And who is
not unhappy at having only one eye?*

—*Pascal*

To what extent and for what reasons does Beckett reject
consolation? There is nothing remarkable about an aversion to
clumsy attempts at consolation. Montaigne, who constantly
sought to find consolations and to express them gracefully,
took note of this danger.[1] As Calderón, an author cited by
Beckett in *Proust*, observed:

> To seek to persuade a man that the misfortunes which he suffers
> are not misfortunes, does not console him for them, but is another
> misfortune in addition.[2]

At best, a consolation is something less than a full and direct
compensation for suffering; when entirely relieved, a person
doesn't claim to be consoled but rather rewarded or recovered.
In other words, consolation does not bring eyesight to the
blind; it only improves their hearing. Similarly, imagine that
basic and original lament of the child crying for his mother's
breast; suppose she approaches and, instead of nursing the
infant, remarks that suffering brings knowledge or that others
are no better off. Would this be expected to satisfy him?

No. To accept consolation is, in reality, to accept defeat. And
the classic rationalizations of misery are easily open to objection by one not in a mood to be consoled. Consider the
strategies of solace suggested in Boethius' *Consolation of
Philosophy:* (1) the *volitional* (it's your own fault), (2) the
holistic (it's part of a master plan), (3) the *stoic* (it's a blessing

37

in disguise to be relieved of superfluities), (4) the *legalistic* (no one has a right to happiness), (5) the *mentalistic* (put mind over matter), (6) the *egoistic* (you can always withdraw to an undamaged aspect of self), (7) the *limitational* (your suffering is finite), (8) the *educational* (suffering brings knowledge), (9) *the equation of power with virtue* (a worse man cannot harm a better), and conversely (10) *the equation of unhappiness with virtue* (suffering is a sign of election, a trial of the righteous). Now this array can be reduced to two essential approaches: the sufferer is asked to simply ignore his misery or to shift his perspective in a way that will minimize and justify it. These consolations do not replace a loss, then, but redirect the sufferer towards something secondhand, a substitute, a convenient fiction, something thought about as an alternative to dwelling on immediate need and pain.

But seen in this light, what body of literature or system of thought is not at bottom a system of consolation? Any literary vision, including pessimism, can be understood as a cultivated alternative to some more distressing realization. Every book, in other words, implies an antitruth, an opposite meaning, which its function is perhaps to obscure. In Beckett's case this silent alternative is nothing other than the cruel, clear, adolescent expectation everyone strives in later years to forget he had: that real joy is indeed available, but only through social status, wealth, beauty, the sex life these former benefits make available, the destruction of one's enemies, a clear conscience, and heirs to pass it all on to. What better way to negate this hideous realization than through the pessimistic conviction that all men must be essentially miserable at all times? As such, extreme pessimism functions the way the Adlerian inferiority complex does: it is an excuse for failure and thus nothing but a kind of shallow optimism.

That pessimism is not so much the opposite of consolation as a kind of consolation in itself becomes clear when we consider the dramatics of those situations in which solace is proposed. Often when consolation is offered, it is not so much to comfort a complainer as to silence him. For complaints are annoying in their implicit claims to sympathy; no one really wants to share the feelings of a sufferer. The tone of Boethius' consolations makes this motive, that of silencing complaint, entirely clear:

Now it pleases me [Fortune, Fate] to withdraw my favor. You
should be grateful for the use of things which belonged to someone
else. *You have no legitimate cause for complaint.*[3] (Italics mine)

Of course no one needs to listen to complaints, but neither
must he stop complaining. Clearly, much of Beckett's verbal
energy derives from the spirit of complaint, so he would
naturally regard consolations as, in effect, threats to stifle him.
Complaint itself consoles his speakers, and they cling to that
along with the solitude it entails, since complaints are socially
unacceptable.

Let us not conclude that Beckett altogether rejects consolation. Rather, he rejects the consolations offered by others; as
for himself, he takes comfort in complaint and in complaint
rationalized through pessimism. A similar temperament was
displayed by Huysmans' Des Esseintes, whom Beckett mentions in *Proust:*

To console himself, he [Des Esseintes] recalled the comforting
maxims of Schopenhauer, and repeated to himself the sad axiom of
Pascal: "The soul is pained by all it thinks upon."[4]

At first, it may be difficult to see how such reflections could
bring comfort. Of course, Des Esseintes is supposed to be
perverse, but his perversity, like Beckett's, is well grounded
in traditional literary postures. And in fact, the maxims of
Schopenhauer and Pascal's dictum may well console some
persons for a number of reasons.

First, pessimism offers certain literary and intellectual advantages. Like all obsessive dispositions, it precludes careful
thought and the painstaking examination of details; the
scrutiny of particular cases may be reasonably avoided if "for
the whole there is no spell." Thus pessimism serves a defensive function: it wards off annoying and distracting trivialities.
And in most respects, Beckett's art has moved towards radical
simplification, his severe pessimism ordering and confining its
materials. The levelling and simplifying effect of a pessimistic
attitude is displayed in *Waiting for Godot.* Here Vladimir's
annoying curiosity about details is swept aside by Pozzo's pessimistic (and poetic) generalities:

Vladimir: Dumb! Since when?
Pozzo: (*suddenly furious*). Have you not done tormenting me
            with your accursed time! Its abominable! When!
            When! One day, is that not enough for you, one
            day he went dumb, one day I went blind, one day
            we'll go deaf, one day we were born, one day we
            shall die, the same day, the same second, is that
            not enough for you? (*calmer*) They give birth astride
            of a grave, the light gleams an instant, then it's night
            once more. (P. 57; by permission of Grove Press, New
            York, 1954)

To consider some of pessimism's more general benefits,
uses unrelated to literary values: the diminution of hope limits
disappointment, thus keeping a moody temperament evenly
balanced, and Beckett's hatred of oscillating moods was made
clear as early as *Proust*. Furthermore, the characterization of
life as evil can console a morbid temperament such as
Beckett's for its loss, that is, for impending death. Why cry
over spilled excrement? And this works both ways. Molloy
affirms life because his intimations of afterlife are inevitably
pessimistic:

Yes, the confusion of my ideas on the subject of death was such that
I sometimes wondered, believe me or not, if it wasn't a state of
being even worse than life. So I found it natural not to rush into
it . . . (P. 68; by permission of Grove Press, New York, 1965)

Thus, in general, pessimism affords a means of better enduring present suffering. Schopenhauer declares that "unless suffering is the direct and immediate object of life, our existence
is the most purposeless thing in the world."[5] Thus, in spite of
its bleakness, his philosophy supplies a consoling sense of
purpose.

Furthermore, like the very consolations it rejects, pessimism offers some temperaments a means (as Moran says) of
"gilding [their] impotence" (p. 105). Restrict a man sufficiently
and, paradoxically, he gains a certain dignity. So Schiller observed when speaking about fate in classical tragedy: it "elevates man when it crushes man."[6] The reason for this is not
hard to detect: just as many an underling will associate himself
with the glory of his charismatic leader, so any sufferer can

imaginatively participate in the power oppressing him. In this sense, if man is contemptible because of his heavy burden, he is also admirable because of that burden. That Beckett's writing does in fact console by virtue of its very bleakness was asserted by Karl Gierow, the Swedish Academy's Nobel Prize spokesman:

> the writing of Samuel Beckett rises like a miserere from all mankind, its muffled minor key sounding liberation to the oppressed and comfort to those in need.[7]

That it is a miserere from all mankind brings up another one of pessimism's benefits. As Pascal's dictum, cited above, indicates, Pessimism generalizes one individual's difficulties. "The soul," he says, not merely my soul, "is pained." Misery loves company, and the complaints of the miserable, if properly phrased, postulate cosufferers. Montaigne availed himself of this consolation, though ironically:

> society ought to comfort me, being fallen into the most common infirmity of my age; I see everywhere men tormented with the same disease and am honored with their fellowship . . . [8]

And Moran employs the same desperate tactic in imagining himself and Gaber part of a vast network; for, as he admits, "the feeling that we were the only ones of our kind would, I believe, have been more than we could have borne" (p. 107). Pozzo's speech, cited above, performs the same generalizing function, as indicated by the transition from singular to plural pronouns:

> one day *he* went dumb, one day *I* went blind, one day *we'll* go deaf, one day *we* were born, one day *we* shall die, the same day, the same second, is that not enough for you? (Calmer). *They* give birth astride of a grave, the light gleams an instant, then it's night once more. (P. 57, italics mine)

Of course the will to generalize our own difficulty, if only imaginatively, can indicate a cruel disposition. But Beckett's writing indeed often focuses upon cruelty, particularly in *Molloy,* Part II, and *How It Is.* And unless the reader is prepared to acknowledge a sadistic component in himself, as well as in Beckett, it is difficult to explain the appeal of his gloomy art. As Schopenhauer observed,

> the most effective consolation in misfortune or affliction of any kind is the thought of other people who are in a still worse plight than ourselves; and this is a form of consolation open to everyone.[9]

Indeed, there are so many ways to become consoled that it seems impossible, in the end, to avoid it altogether. Thus those literary voices which base themselves on a refusal to accept consolation progress almost inevitably towards a somewhat different position, in which they declare that there is pleasure in their pain and no such condition as a complete dissatisfaction, thus testifying to the fathomless complexity and resilience of the human spirit. The classic statement of such a sensibility is surely Dostoevsky's *Notes from the Underground,* and a look at that book, together with some of its successors, will help to reveal what is distinctive about Beckett's more puzzling spitefulness.

Early in his monologue, Dostoevsky's quintessential anti-hero rejects the two basic arguments of consolation: that his suffering is inevitable (which is no consolation) and, on the other hand, that it is his own fault (which is not strictly true):

> Merciful heavens! but what do I care for the laws of nature and arithmetic, when, for some reason, I dislike those laws and the fact that twice two makes four? Of course I cannot break through the wall by battering my head against it if I really have not the strength to knock it down, but I am not going to be reconciled to it simply because it is a stone wall and I have not the strength.
> As though such a stone wall really were a consolation, and really did contain some word of conciliation, simply because it is as true as twice two makes four. Oh, absurdity of absurdities! How much better it is to understand it all, to recognize it all, all the impossibilities and stone walls, not to be reconciled to one of those impossibilities and stone walls if it disgusts you to be reconciled; by way of the most inevitable logical combinations to reach the most revolting conclusions on the everlasting theme that even for the stone wall you are yourself somehow to blame, though again it is as clear as day you are not to blame in the least, and therefore grinding your teeth in silent impotence to sink voluptuously into inertia, brooding on the fact that there is no one even for you to feel vindictive against.[10]

As the Underground Man observes here, there is a "voluptuous pleasure in such frustration, even "an enjoyment which sometimes reaches the highest degree of voluptuousness" (p. 35). Or if such suffering is not actually satisfying (which, after all, is a clear contradiction in terms) then it is still valuable nonetheless, for

> man will never renounce real suffering, that is destruction and chaos. Why, suffering is the sole origin of consciousness. Though I did lay it down at the beginning that consciousness is the greatest misfortune for man, yet I know man prizes it and would not give it up for any satisfaction. (P. 54)

What Dostoevsky means by "consciousness" is, essentially, the opposite of mathematical certainty, a progressive uncertainty, an incessant mulling over of paradoxes. At first the Underground Man asserts that such confusion—confusion about the source and purpose of one's pain—is painful itself:

> it is simply a mess, no knowing what and no knowing who, but in spite of all these uncertainties and jugglings, still there is an ache in you; and the more you do not know the worse you ache. (P. 35)

But later on he speaks of this condition as the goal of all human endeavor:

> And who knows (there is no saying with certainty), perhaps the only goal on earth to which mankind is striving lies in this incessant process of attaining, in other words, in life itself, and not in the thing to be attained, which must alway be expressed as a formula, as positive as twice two makes four, and such positiveness is not life, gentlemen, but is the beginning of death. (P. 52)

This passage approaches Beckett's ideal of incurious search but with an essential difference: whereas Molloy finds "peace" in the realization of his ignorance, the Underground Man, perhaps more understandably, finds his confusion torturously exciting and vivifying; he even equates incessant uncertainty with "life itself." And, by equating torturous uncertainty with life itself, he is able to vaunt his superiority over those who console themselves with specious rationales:

> As for what concerns me in particular I have only carried to an
> extreme in my life what you have not dared to carry halfway, and,
> what's more, you have taken your cowardice for good sense, and
> have found comfort in deceiving yourselves. So that perhaps, after
> all, there is more life in me than you. Look into it more carefully!
> (P. 140)

Thus in his spite and willful misery, his refusal to be consoled,
the Underground Man styles an affirmation of life itself, but at
others' expense. It is apparent that, for this hero, the real consolation that lies in rejecting consolations is sadistic or, at
least, sadomasochistic; for he feels most alive when insulting
those less masochistic than he. And this is what the narrative
section of Dostoevsky's book is meant to show; the Underground Man feels compelled to make the officer, his old
schoolmates, especially the innocent prostitute, bear witness
to his suffering, in order to make them realize their own re-
pressed unhappiness.

A similar set of attitudes, somewhat simplified and exaggerated, appears in Céline's *Journey to the End of the Night*.
Again the refusal to accept consolation is central and insistent;
for instance, Céline goes out of his way to have his hero discover and denounce a letter of Montaigne's, consoling the
latter's wife for the loss of their son.[11] And, as in the *Notes
from the Underground,* the insistence that unconsoled suffering is mankind's only authentic reality is connected with misanthropy. This misanthropy gives meaning to life and, as such,
is consolation in itself:

> The greatest defeat, in anything, is to forget, and above all to forget
> what it is that has smashed you, and to let yourself be smashed
> without ever realizing how thoroughly devilish men can be. When
> our time is up, we people mustn't bear malice, but neither must we
> forget: we must tell the whole thing, without altering one
> word,—everything that we have seen of man's viciousness; and
> then it will be over and time to go. That is enough of a job for a
> whole lifetime. (Pp. 20–21)

Whereas Dostoevsky's hero suffers from the indifference of
his fellow men, Céline's Barmadu suffers from their actual
hostility; hence the latter's more intense misanthropy. And
when Dostoevsky connects unconsoled dissatisfation with vi-

tality and the will to live, the reader feels that the connection is metaphorical; Céline seems to mean this literally. One had better watch out:

> There is nothing you can explain. The world only knows how to kill you. . . . To trust in men is to let oneself be killed a little. (P. 176)

This set of emotions is dramatized throughout the book's successive episodes. At the outset the hero is resisting the rationalizations of military death—honor and patriotism—with an iconoclastic cowardice. Later on, in medical practice, he is consulted about an old woman who "complains about everything." Her daughter-in-law offers consolations ("you have your ailments like all old people have"), but the old one vociferously rejects them:

> "Old yourself, you little slut! . . . Lies and trickery! . . . She struck out against the contact, the fates, the resignation of the outside world . . . (p. 251)

Two points emerge from this configuration. First, the bitter complainer, though aged and reclusive, is uniquely vital:

> a bright expression danced in [her eyes] . . . a lively glance which you noticed at once and which made you forget all the rest, because it was light and youthful and gave you a feeling of pleasure . . . (p. 252)

And second, it develops that those who offer her consolation are literally trying to murder her. Essentially the same situation emerges again at the book's conclusion. The consolation offered here is love, and it is explicitly rejected as such:

> Why it's every darn thing that repels me and disgusts me now. . . . Do you have to make love in the middle of all that's going on? And seeing the things one sees? Or maybe you don't notice anything? . . . You don't mind eating rotten meat? Helping it down with that Love sauce of yours? That's good enough is it? Not for me it isn't. (Pp. 497–98)

This disconsolate stance provokes the murder of the speaker (the alter-ego Robinson) at the hands of his would-be wooer and consoler.

Céline and his hero are doctors by profession, expert at detecting life signs. And what emerges in his writing, even more directly than in Dostoevsky's, is an equation of the forces of consolation with the forces of death. Thus, the refusal to accept and come to terms with the inevitable conditions of life indicates a greater capacity for living, but it is a dangerous liveliness, the sort that can get a person killed. Still, the whole business of keeping people alive is more or less a futility anyway. And, if that is so, does it matter if the victim, once sucked into the maelstrom, hollers out or shrugs? For Céline, it certainly does. If freedom is confined to a matter of gestures and attitudes, then those gestures and attitudes are all that matter.

And that is precisely the message of Camus' *The Stranger,* a book which might well have been subtitled *The Anticonsolation of Philosophy.* As in Boethius' text, an imprisoned hero considers traditional consolations while awaiting execution. At first Meursault would like to be consoled, but he finds the familiar rationalizations ineffective:

> I made the most of this idea, studying my effects so as to squeeze out the maximum of consolation. Thus, I always began by assuming the worst. . . . That meant, of course, I was to die. Sooner than others, obviously. "But," I reminded myself, "it's common knowledge that life isn't worth living, anyhow." And, on a wide view, I could see that it makes little difference whether one dies at the age of thirty or threescore and ten — since, in either case, other men and women will continue living, the world will go on as before. Also, whether I die now or forty years hence, this business of dying had to be got through, inevitably. Still, somehow this line of thought wasn't as consoling as it should have been; the idea of all those years of life in hand was a galling reminder![12]

A priest enters, analogous to Boethius' Lady Philosophy, and observes that "every man on earth [is] under sentence of death" (p. 146). But the hero points out that this "could be no consolation" (p. 147). Then, literally driven to the wall, the priest asks, "Do you really love these earthly things so very much?" (P. 149) Meursault's answer, if not in so many words, is quite clearly, "Yes." The reader learns that this priest, dispensing traditional solace, lives "like a corpse" and can't "even be sure of being alive" (p. 151). The condemned man, on the other hand, loves life so much that he feels "ready to start [it] all over again" (p. 154). And while refusing to be consoled for his death, Meursault paradoxically accounts himself "happy still" (p. 154), justified in his lifelong conviction that "nothing has the least importance" (p. 154) because everyone will have to die one day.

Dostoevsky's Underground Man, Céline's Barmadu, and Camus' Meursault are successive figures in the tradition that has established the current conventions of unconventionality. And they all refuse to be consoled at the moment of death or reconciled to the inevitable conditions of life; but as we have seen, this stance has its own inner logic and compensation — the sense of vitality intrinsic in a rebellious posture. In the case of Beckett's heroes, however, the benefits of pessimism are somewhat more difficult to detect. These characters are somewhat misanthropic, to be sure, but they do not trouble to justify their misanthropy; their hate lacks the consistency, the intensity, and the nobility that is to be found in the feelings of other misanthropes. In fact, theirs is a comic misanthropy, and in these ridiculous remarks of Malone, Beckett seems to be mocking that whole posture:

> Let me say before I go any further that I forgive nobody. I wish them all an atrocious life and then the fires and ice of hell and in the execrable generations to come an honoured name. Enough for this evening. (P. 191)

Nor do Beckett's heroes claim a superior vitality; they don't even desire it. Indeed, Moran's postulated ideal is that of the least possible life:

> To be literally incapable of motion at last, that must be something! My mind swoons when I think of it. And mute into the bargain! And perhaps as deaf as a post! And who knows as blind as a bat! And as likely as not your memory a blank! And just enough brain intact to allow you to exult! And to dread death like a regeneration. (P. 140)

In short, Beckett seems to be working from a more thoroughly pessimistic position than his literary predecessors (as, in fact, he has always claimed); for he rejects not only the traditional consolations, but also the consolations ordinarily derived from making that rejection. And yet, if the materials and energy of his writing do derive from pessimistic complaint, Beckett's later works are also remarkable for their tone of resignation. While he has remained hostile to optimistic rationalizing (most clearly in *Happy Days*), alterations in the later writing indicate Beckett's own attempts, by various shifts, to make the best of life's bad bargain. It seems as if, like most pessimists, he has found that not only is suffering inevitable but that consolation is too.

This effort to adjust reveals itself most prominently through Beckett's changing treatment of futility. Futility is obviously an evil, an integral topic of the standard pessimistic lament from which all of Beckett's writing develops; nonetheless, Beckett has also tried to view this condition from more salutary perspectives. For the experience of futility presupposes an individual consciousness with a goal or value thwarted; but generalized, emotionally neutralized, and depersonalized, the prospect of futility becomes one of simple recurrence. This shift of perspective, allowing for a reinterpretation and acceptance of what once seemed "futile" actions, informs the course of Beckett's general development. The change is reflected in his critical writing, as the moral fulminations against habit in *Proust* give way to praise of futile persistence in the dialogues with Duthuit. Similarly, describing what Michael Robinson has interpreted as an analogue for writing, Moran speaks of his search for Molloy as something done

> neither for Molloy, who mattered nothing to me, nor for myself, of whom I despaired, but on behalf of a cause which, while having need of us to be accomplished, was in its essence anonymous, and would subsist, haunting the minds of men, when its miserable artisans should be no more. (Pp. 114–15)

The task is impersonal and unending; thus conceived, its futility becomes a sublime global recurrence.

Beckett's acceptance of futility or investigation of its usefulness is also indicated in other ways. While his early hero Murphy, a determined nonworker, drew such pleasure from his lazy contemplations that "pleasure was not the word" (p. 113), Beckett's later writing has moved to a concern with futile efforts: contemplation conceived as such or such themes as "going on" and "obligation." To use Freud's terms, Beckett discarded the pleasure principle, finding it (as Moran says) "the fatal pleasure principle," and subsituted for this Freud's "reality principle" of repetition or incessant striving (p. 99). And this development is common to the literature of complaint and consolation. The same progression shapes Ecclesiastes: having renounced pleasure ("I said in my heart . . . enjoy pleasure: and, behold, this also is vanity"), one is naturally driven to duty ("Fear God and keep his commandments: for this is the whole duty of man.") Similarly, the heroes of Beckett's later books ponder whether life might be endurable or even attractive as a perpetual frustration, whereas the spirit of the early books did not move past resentment (or "kicking against the pricks"). And his strange appreciation of the beauty of fruitless labor can also be discerned through the repetitive structure and style of his later writing. Clearly, he has determined to "reject the plane of the feasible,"[13] in order to see if futility might provide a more satisfying aesthetic. What prompts this direction is his conviction that all activities are inevitably futile but that art can reconcile mankind to this futility.

For Beckett, as for Camus, a reinterpreted myth of Sisyphus provides an appropriate model here. "If Sisyphus thinks each journey is the first," says Moran, that "would keep hope alive, would it not, hellish hope? Whereas to see yourself doing the same thing endlessly over and over fills you with satisfaction" (p. 133). Camus' remarks may seem similar:

> If this myth is tragic, that is because its hero is conscious. Where would his torture be, indeed, if at every step the hope of succeeding upheld him? . . . [But] the lucidity that was to constitute his torture at the same time crowns his victory. There is no fate that cannot be surmounted by scorn.
> If the descent is thus sometimes performed in sorrow, it can also take place in joy. The word is not too much. . . . Crushing truths perish from being acknowledged.[14]

But some differences are worth noting. For Camus, the myth has political implications ("Sisyphus, proletarian of the gods, powerless and rebellious"), and these are wholly absent in Beckett (p. 89). Again, Camus' reinterpretation leads toward a strenuous humanitarianism and the striking of rather noble postures:

> He is superior to his fate. . . . It makes of fate a human matter, which must be settled among men." (P. 90)

It is hard to see how these meanings are derived, but in fact Camus' myth really means to do away with futility altogether:

> It teaches that all is not, has not been exhausted. It drives out of the world a god who had come into it with dissatisfaction and a preference for futile sufferings. (P. 90)

Moran, as we have seen, asserts a real preference for futility—a bizarre hedonism without moral implications.

This is a statement more extreme than Camus' but also more ironic and complex, less purely didactic in tone. Camus also speaks of pleasure ("joy. The word is not too much."), but this is not a pleasure taken in futility as such; rather it is a joy felt in mastering and appropriating his fate ("His rock is his thing"—p. 90). In short, Camus' approach to futility is just another case of mind over matter. "There is no fate that cannot be surmounted by scorn," he says; and this offers no new interpretation of futility. Beckett is attempting a more ambitious and specific reordering of values—not surmounting futility but retaining its experience while enjoying it. This is perverse, as is Moran's designation of hope as "hellish." (Camus admits that hope is encouraging: "Where would [Sisyphus'] torture be," he says, "if at every step the hope of succeeding upheld him," p. 90). But Beckett's revaluation of futility and hopelessness is not unprecedented; it is to be found in Nietzsche's endorsement of eternal recurrence and also in the wit of such introspective pessimists as Leopardi ("To enjoy life, a state of despair is necessary")[15] and Jules Renard ("I am a happy man for I have renounced happiness").[16] Beckett's art rests upon this kind of emotional paradox, sustaining a confusion of mood difficult to describe without such unsatisfactory terms as masochism. If it is very striking, it is also not quite credible; that is, when Moran and Molloy assert their bizarre preferences, it is natural to suspect them of seeking effects. Is their endorsement of futility to be regarded as a real transcendence of resentment, or merely a spiteful approval of situations which ought to be improved? Surely, Beckett cannot wholly subscribe to these attitudes and sometimes, in stating them, he must be simply engaging in sheer wit. But if that is so, what motivates this wit and why does he express the same sort of perverse revaluations so consistently?

It should be added here that, if these problems provoke confusion, the graceful rhythms of Beckett's prose induce a poised and stable bafflement. And this very bafflement reflects another of Beckett's attempts to deal with life's insuperable difficulty: his increasing emphasis upon skepticism, as exemplified in Molloy's incessant "it seems to me." I am saying that along with his impulse to judge life and judge it harshly, Beckett seems to have developed an alternative conviction, that as Nietzsche said, "one cannot make such a judgement, because one is party to the dispute" (though that is exactly why one wishes to make a judgment).[17] This shift towards skepticism is markedly dramatized in Moran's development and in the transition from Moran to Molloy. Back from his journey, Moran is confronted with his neighbors' optimistic platitudes. He rejects them, to be sure, but with a skeptical rather than an assuredly pessimistic tone:

> The winter had been exceptionally rigorous, everybody said so. We therefore had a right to this superb summer. I do not know if we had a right to it. (p. 188)

But his conversion to indifferent ignorance is still incomplete, for he looks forward to enlightenment: "They will be happy days. I will learn" (p.188). Molloy, on the other hand, admits at the outset, "The truth is I don't know much" (p. 7); nor does this matter to him: "and how can you want to know? No, all that is not worthwhile bothering about" (p. 46).

My point here is not that Beckett is skeptical, which is obvious, but that his skepticism serves to balance and offset his pessimism. This statement may seem odd because, from one perspective, skepticism is merely a logical extension of pessimism, the result of minimized expectations applied to the goal of knowledge. In this sense, a pessimistic doctrine is incomplete without skepticism, and Ecclesiastes, one of the earliest pessimistic complaints, is the lament of a disappointed sage (someone particularly concerned about the futility of searching after wisdom). But skepticism is also apt to become the last refuge of a pessimist, for if it is believed that knowledge entails pain (reality being intrinsically evil) then it follows that it is better not to know. Ignorance becomes bliss. Thus in "Whoroscope," Beckett's Descartes asks not merely for another hour of life, but for another "inscrutable hour."[18] And this is what the critics have often overlooked about Beckett's skepticism—that it is consciously motivated and regarded as soothing, seen as a balm, not a burden. For skepticism brings peace of mind. At least, as Lichtenberg affirmed, it is supposed to do so:

> Nothing can contribute more to peace of soul than having no opinion at all.[19]

The common misinterpretation of Beckett's skepticism, devised, perhaps, in order to make him seem "relevant," is that his doubt (like the Underground Man's) is tortured and proceeds from his modernity; he is anguished because he cannot but would like to accept the old verities.[20] But Beckett's skepticism is not properly viewed as a particularly contemporary trait nor as an anguished doubt.

In examining Kafka, Ionesco discovered a cultivated ignorance, characterized it acutely, and thought it the spirit of the time:

> The theme of man lost in a labyrinth, without a guiding thread, is basic . . . in Kafka's work. Yet if man no longer has a guiding thread, it is because he no longer wants one. Hence his feelings of guilt, of anxiety, of the absurdity of history.[21]

But Nietzsche also thought a cultivated skepticism the distinguishing mark of his own generation, due (yes) to racial mixing:

> there is *today*, according to common consent, no better soporific and sedative than skepticism, the gentle, fair, lulling poppy of skepticism; and even *Hamlet* is now prescribed by the doctors *of the day* against the "spirit" and its underground rumblings. . . . For the skeptic, being a delicate creature, is frightened all too easily; his conscience is trained to quiver at every No, indeed even at a

Yes that is decisive and hard, and to feel as if it had been bitten. Yes and No—that goes against his morality; conversely, he likes to treat his virtue to a feast of noble abstinence, say, by repeating Montaigne's "What do I know?" or Socrates' "I know that I know nothing." . . .

Thus a skeptic *consoles* himself; and it is true that he stands in need of some consolation. For skepticism is the most spiritual expression of a certain complex physiological condition that in ordinary language is called nervous exhaustion and sickliness; it always develops when races or classes that have long been separated are crossed suddenly and decisively. In the *new generation* that has, as it were, inherited in its blood diverse standards and values, everything is unrest, disturbance, doubt, attempt . . .[22] (Italics mine)

Yet Nietzsche's own references to Montaigne, Shakespeare, and Socrates suggest that the deliberate cultivation of skepticism, in quest of inner peace and consolation, cannot be confined to any "new generation." It is more characteristic, perhaps, of some generations than of others, but it is certainly characteristic of some temperaments in every generation. In fact, the emotional advantage of skepticism, its consoling power, was recognized in antiquity; that doctrine's authoritative spokesman, Sextus Empiricus, declared that

the originating hope of skepticism . . . is the hope of attaining quietude.[23]

And that is how it is with Beckett. His skepticism is classical; there is no reason to regard it as the product of a particular historical situation. Like the ancient skeptics and many others since, he is looking for peace; as Molloy remarked,

to know that you are beyond knowing anything, *that is when peace enters in*, to the soul of the incurious seeker. (P. 64, italics mine)

When he is not glad to be unhappy, Beckett can turn from pessimism to skepticism as a healing alternative, from the notion that reality is evil to the view that it is merely unknowable, or as Heraclitus said, "accustomed to hide itself."[24] From the precise laws determined in *Proust*, which prove that unhappiness is inevitable, Beckett can turn to the notion that reality is really chaos, an unorganized plenum, or as he says in *Murphy*, "a great blooming buzzing confusion" (p.112). This view is maintained by means of a moralistic epistemology, originally Hindu and Buddhist, which Beckett probably derived through Schopenhauer. Here perception is held to be a function of attention, which organizes a visual field by bringing into focus a figure upon a ground; but attention, in turn, is determined by need. When the subject is properly returned to indifference (e. g., when Neary falls out of love with Miss Counihan), the ground becomes "mercifully free of figure" (p. 245). And so Murphy's beatific vision, entertained in the third or top zone of his mind, is found to feature "a flux of forms, a perpetual coming together and falling asunder . . . nothing but commotion and the pure forms of commotion" (p. 112). The connection of such a consoling vision with classical skepticism was pointed out by Hegel, who saw both as a means to a poised self-assertion:

> Sceptical self-consciousness thus discovers in the *flux* and *alternation* of all that would stand secure in its presence, its own freedom, as given by and received from its own self. It is aware of being this ataraxy of self-thinking thought, the unalterable and authentic certainty of self.[25] (Italics mine)

Beckett's skepticism is generally conveyed through his attention to the absurd, that is, whatever is unintelligible, arbitrary, or unjustified. His rhetoric cultivates skepticism by frustrating rational anticipation, employing such devices as extreme repetition and non sequiturs. At the same time, these elements of stylistic disorganization are offset by a tendency to extreme symmetry, at the expense of a more rational and conventional content. This drive towards sheer balance is also anticipated in Sextus Empiricus' paradigmatic definition of skepticism:

> Skepticism is an ability, or mental attitude, which opposes appearances to judgements in any way whatsoever, with the result that, owing to the *equipollence* of the objects and reasons thus opposed, we are brought firstly to a state of mental suspension and next to a state of unperturbedness or quietude.[26] (Italics mine)

Beckett is addicted to "equipollence"; as Molloy puts it, he has a "mania for symmetry" (p. 85). And what might underlie this urge? It projects a world in which decision becomes impossible because alternatives are equally weighted. As an illustration, Beckett has not been able to resist citing the old scholastic chestnut of Buridan's ass, who cannot choose between equidistant bales of hay. And his own heroes often find themselves so situated:

> The part of him [Murphy] that he hated craved for Celia, the part that he loved shrivelled up at the thought of her.[27]

Of course one would not expect Murphy to find "peace" in this situation, and he doesn't; but Murphy is not the speaker of this sentence. The narrator is the one who entertains this vision, and his voice reveals a rather pointed "unperturbedness."

Beckett's most frequently cited remark about style displays the complex and interesting connection among the issues discussed here:

> I am interested in the shape of ideas . . . even if I do not believe in them. There is a wonderful sentence in Augustine. I wish I could remember the Latin. It is even finer in Latin than in English. "Do not despair; one of the thieves was saved. Do not presume; one of the thieves was damned." That sentence has a wonderful shape. It is the shape that counts.[28]

This remark has been cited by Hugh Kenner to demonstrate Beckett's aversion to meaning, his replacement of intellectual with aesthetic values.[29] Beckett's words here certainly do lend themselves to that interpretation. But Augustine's sentence (which appears, reformulated, in most of Beckett's works) also suggests Beckett's most compulsive themes. For Beckett is drawn, first of all, to the calm the saint is recommending and also to the explicit skepticism which the formal symmetry of the sentences in turn reflects. That skepticism, I submit, is a "meaning" in itself. In other words, it is an interpretation of life and a strategy for living, a tactic of consolation. In fact, some of Beckett's many references to Augustine's remark (such as the Unnamable's "don't be discouraged, one of the thieves was saved") focus on its consoling function (p. 308). But then its reliability must be disputed:

> Vladimir: . . . of the four evangelists only one speaks of a thief being saved. The four of them were there. . . . One out of four.

> Of the other three two don't mention any thieves at all
> and the third says both abused him . . . . only one speaks
> of a thief being saved. Why believe him rather than the
> others? (P. 9)

Skepticism, calm, symmetry, consolation, pessimism—
Beckett's themes relate through an obsessive circularity, successively invoking and cancelling one another out. Still we
can safely say that skepticism and pessimism are the dominant
and ordering tendencies of his art, that they precede his more
particular formulations. In the words of Unamuno:

> It is not usually our ideas that make us optimists or pessimists, but
> our optimism or our pessimism, of psychological and perhaps
> pathological origin, that makes our ideas.[30]

Chapter 4

Blathering about Nothing in Particular

*At times, as the proverb says, one remains a philosopher
only because one says —nothing!*
                                                    —*Nietzsche*

To draw out a further implication of what has already been
observed about Beckett's meaning, it is general. Beckett has
narrowly limited his focus to the universal, only the universal;
and it is this commitment to generality which often effects the
wide-ranging and striking ambiguity so characteristic of his
writing. Consider the generic title of Beckett's *Play*. Here a
conceptual ambiguity is implied in the term's double meaning
(dramatic work and game). This in turn sets up a significant
emotional ambiguity: it establishes the contrast between
amusement (as expected of games) and the bleak world *Play*
actually sets forth; similarly, we do not know whether to take
the title as a modest gesture—it is merely a play, any old
play—or an audacious one—it is *the* play, the essence of
plays. Language of the utmost generality accommodates a great
diversity of emotional responses, including the response that
such language reflects a touching poverty of feeling.

Also, as has been seen, Beckett frequently employs unexpected generalizations, referents of shocking scope, for purely
comic effect:

> And if there were two things that Watt loathed, one was the earth
> and the other was the sky. (P. 36; by permission of Grove Press, New
> York, 1959)

The formula so distinctively employed here is wonderfully

effective, but Beckett's generalizations are no mere rhetorical trick. Style, he says in *Proust,* is "more a question of vision than technique" (p. 67; by permission of Grove Press, New York, 1960), and another one of his remarks suggests that he is actually looking for some final statement that will be unlimited in its validity.

> Being has a form. Someone will find it someday. Perhaps I won't but someone will.[1]

Perhaps he has found it, "for esse," according to Nietzsche's etymological speculation, "basically means to breathe."[2] It may be that Beckett's *Breath* is actually based on this etymological connection. In any case, that work and other recent efforts (e. g., *Come and Go, Imagination Dead Imagine*) reveal a decisive effort towards all-inclusive suggestiveness, a search for some image that says it all. There is, as Heidegger observed, something essentially philosophical about this attempt "to think a single thought about beings as a whole"; Periander of Corinth, one of the archetypal Seven Sages, is supposed to have enjoined it, saying "Take into your care beings as a whole."[3] Unfortunately, the art that is thus produced is apt to seem hopelessly abstruse or insignificant.

Beckett's finest works also result from the generalizing impulse; but in them universal attitudes, not images, are voiced with a comic and uncanny authenticity. In fact, Beckett's trilogy strikes the common chord with such authority that Jean-Jacques Mayoux remarked, "le son de sa voix dans nos oreilles, c'est notre propre voix, enfin trouvée."[4] Hugh Kenner has also commented on the remarkable psychic realism of Beckett's writing: "its eerie fidelity to the movements of a mind that has noted itself in motions, [is] the point where his highly specialized, self-immolating art impinges on our sense of the familiar."[5] Even Northrop Frye, whose critical approach is based upon principles of detachment and objectivity, was uncharacteristically moved to find the Unnamable's voice "like our own subconsciousness if we acquire the trick of listening to it."[6]

If Beckett has achieved the most convincing interior monologue to date, it is interesting to note that he has achieved it by abandoning its pretense; that is, his fictional voices admit to giving their monologues a minimum of authorial direction, while occasionally acknowledging the tediousness of their tasks, in a manner typical of introspective diarists. They are not listening to something subconscious, which is impossible by definition. What Frye and the other critics are suggesting is that Beckett voices a kind of consciousness which, when it is entertained, *seems* to have always been there, unacknowledged. Certain characteristics of this consciousness lead one to ascribe to it, rightly or wrongly, a more profound reality. And what are these characteristics? Its principle features are indicated in another one of Frye's observations, where he describes a different aspect of Beckett's realism—the cataloging of actions in *Watt*:

> The most trivial actions of *Watt*, most of which are very similar to those we perform ourselves every day, are exhaustively catalogued in an elaborate pretense of obsessive realism, and we can see how such "realism" in fiction, pushed to so logical a conclusion, soon gives the effect of living in a kind of casual and unpunishing hell. Watt finally decides that "if one of these things was worth doing, all were worth doing, but that none was worth doing, no, not one, but that all were inadvisable, without exception."[7]

The important terms here are "trivial" and "hell." Beckett's monologues oscillate between these two dominant modes, each of which involves a high degree of generalizing. The former, based on the model of mathematics, can be termed absurdity, because, as in mathematics, alternatives are listed without preference, though in situations where the reader would expect preference to be indicated. Thus when Molloy vaguely recalls an act of sexual intercourse, he indifferently exhausts the set of its logical possibilities. The consequences are comic and realistic:

> I toiled and moiled until I discharged or gave up trying or was begged by her to stop. (P. 56; by permission of Grove Press, New York, 1965)

A tendency to introspection reduces interest in distinctions of content by bringing the recurrent forms of consciousness to attention. The mysterious conclusion of *Molloy*, where Moran asserts a flat contradiction without acknowledging its tension, can be explained as a result of this development; that is,

Moran's remarks are meant to indicate a milestone in his progression towards introspective passivity. The words in question are

> It is midnight. The rain is beating on the windows. It was not midnight. It was not raining. (P. 176)

As it happens, there are a number of phrases made about midnight in the second part of *Molloy,* and they form a definite series. The section begins with Moran straightforwardly asserting that "It is midnight" (p. 92). Subsequent episodes repeatedly characterize him as a man who "enjoyed dotting [his] i's" (p. 117). Later on, when Moran actually sets off towards Molloy, he observes with uncharacteristic approximation that "It was nearly midnight" (p. 127). A few pages further, we find him entirely indifferent to such specifications:

> Midnight struck, from the steeple of my beloved church. It did not matter. (P. 130)

The book's conclusion, a flat assertion of contradictory alternatives, is the most direct and immediate expression of this indifference available: it either is midnight or it is not, but in either case, it doesn't matter.

This paradoxical juxtaposition of alternatives, a wonderfully mysterious moment of levity, freedom, and irresponsibility, provides a hint of release from time itself, an effective sense of being above it all. Perhaps if it is realized, as Moran says, that everyone is right, then the reader will feel liberated from judging and allowed to simply experience the concrete. But the implications of Moran's apathy are not only comic and aesthetic; they are also pessimistic. By insisting that his particular misery is inevitable and universal, the pessimist is often making an interested generalization, one necessary to authorize the apathy a life of contemplative detachment entails. In the following remarks, Molloy simply goes through the changes of this progression; he realizes that all that can be known through introspection is the recurrent forms of consciousness (or "laws of the mind") and proceeds to offer a pessimistic assertion as the plainest, simplest truth available:

And once again I am I will not say alone, no, that's not like me, but, how shall I say, I don't know, restored to myself, no, I never left myself, free, yes, I don't know what that means but it's the word I mean to use, free to do what, to do nothing, to know, but what, the laws of the mind perhaps, of my mind, that water rises in proportion as it drowns you and that you would do better, at least no worse, to obliterate texts than to blacken margins, to fill in the holes of words till all looks like what it is, senseless, speechless, issueless misery. (P. 13)

What Molloy thinks he is describing here is not a self-critical mood in the life of a decrepit writer but "Life" itself, or "Life and Death", for nothing, as Malone said, "was ever about anything else, to the best of my recollection" (p. 225). And Beckett is always writing, though by no means uncritically, about the mind's tendency to want to understand its experience in terms of the largest abstractions possible. As Estragon remarks, the art of *Waiting for Godot* is "blathering about nothing in particular," that is, striking general attitudes, almost but not quite devoid of specific referents (p. 42; by permission of Grove Press, New York, 1954). Furthermore, pessimism attaches itself naturally to this generalizing urge. In a critical article describing the painter Jack B. Yeats, Beckett called the painter "great" because he made a general and essential statement, ignoring the accidental, and this must be pessimistic:

> Mr. Yeats' importance is elsewhere to be sought than in a sympathetic treatment (how sympathetic?) of the local accident, of the local substance. He is with the great of our time . . . because he brings light, as only the great dare to bring light, to the issueless predicament of existence.[8]

There is nothing strange in this connection. No one who wins a lottery has the nerve to say, "that is life"; if one wants to characterize "life" in general, it is only safe to describe it as a futile struggle to assuage the fear of death, or something of the kind. But if everything is the same because it's all bad, what follows is that it can't be judged at all; the most generalized focus leaves the judge without a criterion—something outside of the subject at hand which can be used as a basis for comparison.

Thus Beckett's writing oscillates between pessimistic complaint and skeptical detachment as a result of his commitment to discussing life in the most fundamental and general terms. For that matter, his two mime plays, the *Acts Without Words,* offer unmistakably plain emblems of these same attitudes. In the first a man is apparently thrown onto a stage and proceeds to reach, like Tantalus, for ever receding containers labelled "Food" and "Water." This action has the generalizing, didactic effect of a parable; one easily recognizes "life," rather than some particular set of circumstances, in this model of continuous frustration. This is the pessimism of Ecclesiastes: "the eye is not satisfied with seeing, nor the ear filled with hearing." The second play, which suggests an even broader view, consists of two men, quite different types, issuing in turn from sacks, performing brief gestures, and returning to them. The pantomime proceeds across the stage, suggesting the pointless but not otherwise painful succession of generations. This detached view is not far from the reassuring consolation of Ecclesiastes:

> To every thing there is a season, and a time to every purpose under the sun.

These are the themes, or meanings, that always emerge when local problems and circumstances are dismissed: the sad futility of individual lives, the emotionally more neutral cyclicity of larger patterns. And when Beckett seems to be avoiding meaning, these most fundamental meanings still come forth. In *Watt,* for example, a hostility to meaning is quite insistent, and at several points the narrator describes a discovery of meaninglessness, or nothing; still, the themes of futility and cyclicity emerge at precisely these points. In one instance, the hero witnesses an event—the visit of the piano-tuning Galls—which the narrator calls "an incident of great formal brilliance and indeterminable purport." Later on, the narrator speaks of this episode as a "nothing that had happened":

> What distressed Watt . . . was that nothing had happened, that a thing that was nothing had happened. (P. 74)

This appears to be deep stuff, but in fact the Gall's message is plain enough and simply pessimistic:

> The piano is doomed, in my opinion, said the younger. The piano-tuner also, said the elder. The pianist also, said the younger. (P. 76)

Further on, Watt becomes entranced by Mr. Knott's apparently senseless speech, but in fact this talk is not entirely insignificant. Its formal pattern, according to the narrator, suggests the endless cyclicity of natural process:

> a wild dim chatter, meaningless even to Watt's ailing ears . . . [like] rain on the bamboos, or even rushes . . . [like] the land against the waves, doomed to cease, doomed to come again. (P. 72)

In these examples from *Watt* Beckett characteristically adopts an assertion of meaninglessness and nothingness to emphasize a meaning that is actually at hand, stripping it of irrelevant qualification and lending it a mysterious amplification. It should be added, however, that Beckett's writing also makes vacuity itself felt as a presence, and does this so often that Northrop Frye finds the purpose of his art to lie in nothing other than the restoration of silence.[9] Nearly all the different strategies for evoking the void pointed out in R. M. Adams' *Nil* (e.g., non sequiturs, irrelevance, contemplative fixation) are employed at one time or another in Beckett's writing.[10] The most direct of these, the hiatus in manuscript, is used in *Watt.* Several times Moran explicitly asserts, "I'll tell you nothing" (e.g., on p. 134). Filling out a complete set of alternatives, such as saying that it either is or is not midnight, is another way of saying nothing. We also feel confronted by a vacancy when Molloy's treasured piece of silver is presented as an object without a concept. To similar effect, whenever Molloy or Moran use the word "free" they are voicing a concept without an object. There is no such thing as freedom, Beckett implies, because the limited and obsessive routines of consciousness prevent one from ever experiencing it.

What all these separate little vacancies probably stand for is death, a topic Beckett has been treating continuously since *Proust,* where he stated that

Whatever opinion we may be pleased to hold on the subject of
death, we may be sure that it is meaningless and valueless. (P. 6)

Lacking firsthand information, our assertions about death are
merely another instance of claiming to know what we do not;
this is the starting point of Socrates' classic discussion of death
in *The Apology,* and Beckett also likes to strip away conventional and illusory consolations, while taking pride in knowing
that he knows nothing. He may also find that agnosticism
about death is the surest means man has of giving life a sense
of value. For our lives not only seem meaningless when we
reflect upon the finality of death; life would also seem de-
prived of significance if it were learned that it went on forever.
In this respect, we are safe only as long as we don't know.
Thus Moran, while desiring the least possible life, equally
dreads death and regeneration:

> To be literally incapable of motion at last, that must be something!
> My mind swoons when I think of it. And mute into the bargain!
> And perhaps as deaf as a post! And just enough brain intact to allow
> you to exult! And to dread death like a regeneration. (P. 140)

Molloy perfectly voices the timid pessimism of the common
man (and Hamlet) on this point. Let everything stay as it is, not
because life is good, but because it is only possible to imagine
a change would be for the worse:

> Yes, the confusion of my ideas on the subject of death was such that
> I sometimes wondered, believe me or not, if it wasn't a state of
> being even worse than life. (P. 68)

Consequently, Beckett's eschatological works (*The Unnamable, How It Is, Play*) imagine an afterlife essentially like life
itself but a little more painful, that is, a condition in which
solitude, failure of communication, futility, torture, and uncertainty are all the more sharply felt. It can be said, then, that
Beckett uses the situation of death to focus in another way on
what he considers the essential characteristics of life. But he
also wants to talk about death itself, I think, and in effect, to
deny it, or at least deny its existence as an absolute. Without
ignoring the bleakness of Beckett's afterlife milieus, the

reader can still detect the motive of consolation behind them, for they offer a kind of immortality. Pim, the Unnamable, and the characters of *Play* are not dead, in the strictest sense; their consciousness functions and, unlike the living, they are spared the pain and fear of dying. Socrates' treatment of death also concludes on this note:

> For among the advantages which those in Hades have over us is the fact that they are immortal for the rest of time, if what we are told is true."[11]

Thus, in Beckett's treatment of death his levelling impulse is again at work; it's all the same, he tells us, even life and death do not essentially differ. Values are flattened to indifference, moods to a uniform calm, and hope is pointless, since a change or exception is all that can be hoped for, and there are no exceptions. And if death is like life, it follows that life is also like death. They are inextricably associated for, as it is observed in *Endgame,* life is a process of decay:

Hamm: Nature has forgotten us.
Clov: There's no more nature.
Hamm: No more nature! You exaggerate.
Clov: In the vicinity.
Hamm: But we breathe, we change! We lose our hair, our teeth! Our bloom! Our ideals!
Clov: Then she hasn't forgotten us. (P. 11; by permission of Grove Press, New York, 1954)

The Lost Ones is entirely about this perception: that living is gradual dying. One of Beckett's favorite conceits is the birth into death—"giving up the ghost, be born at last," as the Unnamable puts it (p. 335). What is perhaps his most famous image falls under this category:

Vladimir: Astride of a grave and a difficult birth. Down in the hole, lingeringly, the grave-digger puts on the forceps. (P. 58)

"It's vague, life and death," Malone admits, and I do not suggest that Beckett means to offer final formulations on the subject. But surely significant tendencies can be discerned in his treatment. That he chooses to talk about life and death betrays a generalizing, homiletic impulse that is of interest in itself; he wants to remind his readers that we all must die, whatever that means. Coping with that awareness entails coping with ignorance, for no one really knows anything about death. In all, death is the perfect topic for Beckett's temperament; were he not at all morbid, his pessimism and skepticism would still find a natural outlet in dealing with a matter both inevitable and mysterious. His works describe a quest for effective calm, an acceptance of life's inevitable sorrows which remains realistic by falling well short of *amor fati* and continuing to pay tribute to the problems (such as death) it would also like to transcend.

To secure this peace of mind, it is necessary to maintain that all efforts are futile, because all conditions of life are essentially similar. Distinctions of milieu are not only irrelevant to this sort of vision, but, as local accidents suggesting irrelevant meanings and explanations, contraindicated; hence the general lack of concrete details in Beckett's writing. His characters too are deliberately similar—"Living souls," says the hero of *The Expelled*, "you will see how alike they are."[12] For the complaint of Beckett's characters is general, nonspecific, and that is its point. As Molloy puts it:

> I know that I know nothing, am only crying out as I have always cried out, more or less piercingly, more or less openly. (P. 25)

Thus Beckett's critics distort the spirit of his writing when their interpretations confine his lament to a particular intellectual system or psychological condition.[13] To this sort of analysis, Beckett might reply in the words of his spiritual precursor Leopardi:

> It is through necessity that men are wretched, but they are determined to believe that they are so by accident.[14]

Still further from the point are those who think that Beckett is complaining about capitalism or modern mass society.[15] Beckett is especially skeptical of political solutions to human unhappiness, and this avoidance of the political perspective is symptomatic of the introspective and pessimistic tempera-

ment his art so authoritatively expresses. Leopardi evinces the
same attitude:

> You know that I abhor politics, because I believe, indeed I see, that
> men are unhappy under any form of government, which is nature's
> fault for having created men to be unhappy; and I smile at the
> happiness of the crowd, for my little brain cannot conceive a happy
> crowd made of unhappy individuals.[16]

Along the same lines, Nietzsche asserted that

> He who has the *furor philosophicus* in him will have no time for
> the *furor politicus,* and will carefully avoid reading the papers
> every day, or serving a party.[17]

He distinguishes

> Journalism versus philosophy: Every philosophy which believes
> that the *problem of existence* has been set aside, or even solved, by
> a political event, is a comic pseudo-philosophy.[18] (Italics mine)

Proust's writing also contains several statements of this sort, in
an uncharacteristically proud, assertive vein:

> Those who have created for themselves an enveloping inner life
> pay little heed to the importance of political events.[19]

But Proust did treat political material in *Remembrance of Things
Past,* and Beckett has severely blamed the author for those
lapses,

> passages dealing with the war, when for a space he ceases to be an
> artist, and raises his voice with the plebs, mob, rabble, canaille.
> Tragedy is not concerned with human justice. Tragedy is the
> statement of an expiation, but not the expiation of a codified breach
> of a local arrangement, organized by the knaves for the fools. The
> tragic figure represents the expiation of the original sin, of the
> original and eternal sin . . . of having been born.[20]

This opaque and vehement assertion requires some elucida-
tion. The "sin of having been born" alludes to a line in
Calderón's *La vida es sueño.* But why this complete and
unqualified identification of "art" with "tragedy," especially

concerning a work so full of humor as Proust's, which, furthermore, ends on such an affirmative note? It is necessary to understand the pessimistic assumptions in Beckett's writing to fill in the gaps of his sometimes confusing assertions. The passage will become clearer if one of Schopenhauer's statements is considered:

> Because a genuine enduring happiness is not possible, it cannot become the subject of art.[21]

Given that sort of conviction, all art must be tragic. And if we think in such panoramic concepts as "the human condition" or "the problem of existence," the "local arrangement" of politics will indeed seem altogether trivial.

Actually a political note intrudes once into Beckett's fiction; however, this rather interesting exception reveals why such themes are generally absent. The nameless hero of *The End* passes a political orator:

> He was bellowing so loud that snatches of his discourse reached my ears. Union ... brothers ... Marx ... capital ... bread and butter ... Love. It was all Greek to me. The cab was drawn up against the kerb, just in front of me. I saw the orator from behind. All of a sudden he turned and pointed at me, as an exhibit. Look at this down and out, he vociferated, this leftover. If he doesn't go down on all fours, it's for fear of being impounded. Old, lousy, rotten, ripe for the muckheap. And there are a thousand like him, worse than him, ten thousand, twenty thousand—a voice, thirty thousand. Every day you pass them by, resumed the orator, and when you have backed a winner you fling them a farthing. Do you ever think?—The voice, God forbid. A penny, resumed the orator, tuppence,—the voice, thruppence. It never enters your head, resumed the orator, that your charity is a crime, an incentive to slavery, stultification, and organized murder. Take a good look at this living corpse. You may say it's his own fault. Ask him if it's his own fault.—The voice, ask him yourself. Then he bent forward and took me to task. I had perfected my board. It now consisted of two boards hinged together which enabled me, when my work was done, to fold it and carry it under my arm. I liked doing little odd jobs. So I took off the rag, pocketed the few coins I had earned, untied the board, folded it, and put it under my arm. Do you hear me, you crucified bastard! cried the orator. Then I went away, although it was still light. But generally speaking it was a quiet corner, busy but well-frequented.

He must have been a religious fanatic. I could find no other explanation. He had a nice face, a little on the red side.[22]

The orator's speech is, of course, somewhat implausible.
His energetic invective betrays a considerable misanthropy at
the root of professedly humanitarian concerns. In fact—the
hero is not altogether wrong—his language is generally closer
to religious than political oratory. And to the extent that he is
regarded as a fanatic, he becomes just another one of Beckett's
appealing eccentrics. But the author takes care to give him
some strictly political language as well ("charity is a crime"),
and this sort of speech, juxtaposed with the ensuing comments
of the narrator, seems stale, silly, and flat.

As I interpret this unique interlude, it dramatizes a conflict
between rival approaches to life; specifically, it invites us to
feel the irrelevance of politics. For the hero of *The End*
demonstrates a certain spiritual superiority over the orator. He
is not merely naive; he has a sort of higher ignorance. His
indifference to insult, much like Molloy's imperturbability
("Insults, abuse, these I can easily bear"—p. 22) is comically
extreme; nonetheless, he retains a saintly poverty of spirit or
sage dignity and effectively transcends the orator's fury.

Beckett's portraits of bums derive from the perceptive, sympathetic observation that such people develop a pervasive indifference as a matter of principle and a means of maintaining their dignity. However, his heroes are only incidentally
impoverished; they are also decrepit, senile, insane, homi-
cidal, and consequently social outcasts, men whose mode of life
makes the notion of human "rights" seem a wholly ludicrous
fiction. That no one really has any rights (only privileges) is a
natural consequence of the cosmic, ultrageneralized focus
Beckett brings to bear upon reality, but it is perhaps one of the
defects of that perspective too. In any case, no one can doubt
that starving people would really be benefited by a more
equitable distribution of wealth, and Beckett's writing will
always be faulted by some for its refusal to address, as such,
the problems that arise from economic irrationality and injustice.

This is not to say that the value of Beckett's art is purely
literary. He requires that political explanations and proposals
to cure unhappiness be discredited because, like the political

orator cited above, Beckett also wants to use his heroes "as an exhibit," but of another idea: that the nature of consciousness, under any circumstances, dooms man to misery. That mankind is only united by the common sense of impending separation is a truth with pathological implications, and hence one from which it is necessary to take a certain distance. Consequently, Beckett's suave exaggeration of the miseries and limitations of life suggests, by the blandness of its overstatement, just the opposite: that man can really take just about anything and retains, however constrained his circumstances, a considerable and fundamental inner worth. Nor is that all. Having realized that everyone is dying little by little every moment, Beckett resolved to spend the rest of his life making jokes about it, and this focus can liberate his readers to deal with their fears of death and aging less painfully. Such encouragement, of course, is available from innumerable sources. What is more pointedly and distinctively humane about Beckett's writing is its tolerant, while probing, presentation of human inconsistency. The amazing thing about Moran is not that he tortures his son or that he does this while rationalizing it or that he sometimes doesn't take the trouble to rationalize it; what is amazing and shockingly persuasive as a generalized portrait of humanity is that all of these things are true of him. Perhaps the more mankind realizes that such inconsistencies typify us, the more we will be drawn to share our minimized shame in a community of laughter. But it has to be doubted.

Chapter 5

Failed Sages

> ... *The wisdom of all the sages, from Brahma to Leopardi, the wisdom that consists not in the satisfaction but in the ablation of desire.*
>
> —*Proust, p. 7*

Throughout his career, Beckett has written about and with the voice of a recurrent literary type: the cranky, misanthropic individualist, who endeavors to speak with authority about the whole human condition. The more socially isolated and introspective Beckett's heroes become, the more they feel burdened by a universal consciousness and obliged to talk about what they think should be obvious to everyone. According to Arsene, "the same things happen to us all ... if only we choose to know it."[1] That is certainly a levelling statement, but it also implies a distinction: some of us don't choose to know it—which is apparently why the statement is worth making. Clearly, this rhetorical posture is grounded in irony and paradox, because the same things can't be true of us all if only some of us know it. Their relative consciousness of the human condition is what makes people different; but, according to Beckett, it is a difference that makes no difference. The basic and inevitable problems of life are not really altered by becoming conscious of them.

So, as they readily acknowledge, Beckett's heroes are the type of outcast intellectual whose claim to spiritual preeminence tends to discredit itself. Beckett's term for such a figure is "the Sage," and, "from Brahma to Leopardi," as Beckett points out in *Proust*, sages have rationalized their sense of failure by teaching the same pessimistic doctrine—that every human effort is doomed to futility. In quest of inner peace and enmeshed in frustration, they conclude that "wisdom consists

71

not in the satisfaction, but in the ablation of desire."[2] In quest of certain knowledge and caught in contradictions, they conclude that skepticism is man's fullest understanding. When it is added that such a temperament tends to be amoral and cosmopolitan as well as passive and irresponsible, the major characteristics of the type have been indicated.

Beckett's concern with the sage mentality as a fundamental and recurrent type underlies and links what might otherwise appear to be random philosophical allusions strewn throughout his works. The function of these allusions is to supply Beckett's writing with a reverberatory background of intellectual history as seen from his particular perspective. All his learning is marshalled to remind the reader that there is indeed a tradition of sages, consisting of men who sat alone in their rooms or wandered about in woods, recording their contemplative pursuit of inner peace, while mindful of the efforts of their predecessors; and as Beckett views this history, it is a succession of failures. He has Molloy remark that

> there seem to be two ways of behaving in the presence of wishes, the active and the contemplative, and though both give the same result it was the latter I preferred, matter of temperament, I presume. (P. 52; by permission of Grove Press, New York 1965)

On the one hand, Molloy's rather quaint philosophical terminology dignifies his apathy, because contemplation is traditionally the philosopher's *summum bonum;* but at the same time he deflates the pretensions and ideals associated with such terms by telling us that contemplation and action give the same, that is, futile, result.

The sage acting in the world is almost always treated comically or tragicomically, and by the time of *Murphy,* if not sooner, Beckett had also decided to treat his sages as comic figures. In that book the narrator's tone leaves the least pretentious character (Celia) almost entirely unscathed, while the professional sage (Neary) is ironically abused. Later on, in Beckett's trilogy, the sage mentality is directly voiced and to finer comic effect. At one point, Malone calls himself "the sage," then makes a modest retraction. His topic here is apathy, in other words the "ablation of desire" that Beckett associates, more consistently than any other trait, with sage-consciousness:

> It is true that I have *no wish* to leave my bed. But can *the sage* have
> no wish for something the very possibility of which he does not
> conceive? I don't understand. The *sage* perhaps. (P. 254, italics
> mine)

In *How It Is*, the narrator recalls another sage:

>   that extreme eastern
> sage who having clenched his fists from the tenderest age
> it's vague till the hour of his death it is not said at what age
> having done that
>
> the hour of his death at what age it is not said was enabled
> to see them at last a little before his nails his death having
> pierced the palms through and through was enabled to see
> them emerging at last on the other side and a little later
> having thus lived done this done that clenched his fists all
> his life thus lived died at last saying to himself latest breath
> that they'd grow on (p. 53; by permission of Grove Press, New York,
> 1958).

In that gruesome little scene, all the essential ingredients of
the sage's mentality according to Beckett are gathered together. A perverse self-mortification, here suggesting a sort of
crucifixion, views itself with comically extreme detachment,
obsessively vows to go on, but is also deluded. And in *The
Lost Ones*, Beckett distinguishes the sedentary and apathetic
members of a fictional realm by calling them "semi-sages." (P.
28; by permission of Grove Press, New York, 1972)

As literary fashions change, the sage's didactic impulse
speaks through different forms and conventions, such as the
modest *pensée*, personal journal, or discursive philosophical
treatise. It is clear that Beckett's fictional writing has been
influenced by various kinds of philosophical prose, to no small
degree. In *Molloy*, for example, didactic terms are sometimes
used as transitional phrases:

> Do I have to go on? No, for it is clear . . . (p. 73)

> Let us try to get this dilemma clear. Follow me carefully. (P. 72)

But the interesting thing about this stylistic influence is that

Beckett's prose incorporates the tone of archaic didactic literature as well as that of more sophisticated philosophy. Arsene's monologue in *Watt*, a nearly incoherent cascade of *exempla*, approaches a parody of the medieval didactic manner. And Beckett is decisively influenced by still more ancient styles of teaching. He seems especially attracted to the vagueness or oracular language, in which an abundance of demonstratives and pronouns serve to give statements their widest possible reference as, for example, in this speech of Malone's:

> This time, then once more I think, then perhaps a last time, then I think it'll be over, with that world too. Premonition of the last but one but one. All grows dim. (P. 203)

The sage tradition to which Beckett's allusions refer originated in Indian religious literature, the wisdom books of the Bible and other Near Eastern texts, and pre-Socratic Greek philosophy. The sage's attitudes of independence and apathy received their classic articulation from Socrates, and those of his successors who focussed on spiritual (rather than more technically philosophical) concerns; these were the cynics, stoics, and skeptics. Then Christian ascetics, like St. Augustine and Thomas á Kempis, absorbed the sage tradition and gave it a masochistic turn, rationalizing misery as suffering for Christ. With Montaigne, succeeded by Pascal, Descartes, Geulincx, Rousseau, Baudelaire, Proust, and amongst Beckett's contemporaries, Céline and the surrealists, a secular sage tradition established itself in French meditative and confessional literature. Of course, Beckett has referred to other sages as well, such as Leopardi and Schopenhauer.

What all these figures have in common is their search for inner peace, attempted through detachment from worldly pursuits and endorsement of the inner life—"where all I need," according to Moran, "is to be found."[3] It is at this point, alas, that their troubles really begin. If, like Plato's Socrates, one assumes that the mind is a repository of superior reality, the knowledge of which is bliss, such knowledge generally turns out to be impossible to grasp or incommunicable or impractical or simply unpleasant. Nonetheless a sage will persist in his role, afflicted with the need to impart what he knows to be useless knowledge. This despairing view of the contemplative enterprise is nothing new to the tradition itself. Beckett's critique of the sage mentality offers no alternative for those who, like himself, are permanently saddled with apathy and convinced that neither facing reality nor avoiding it is effective. An examination of the sage tradition shows that these figures pride themselves on demolishing the consolations of their predecessors and posing ever more pessimistic views of life; their claim to success lies in their acknowledgement of failure, and they protect themselves from ridicule by inviting it.

The most ancient source of the sage's outlook that is cited by Beckett is the biblical book of Ecclesiastes. The pessimistic verse, "the eye is not satisfied with seeing, nor the ear filled with hearing," turns up in *The Unnamable* as "the eye is truly hard of hearing."[4] If the parody indicates hostility, it is not difficult to understand Beckett's malice. The chief function of biblical wisdom literature is to counsel prudence and rationalize human suffering by assigning it some sort of "meaning." The Hebrew word used for meaning in these texts (*yithron*) also has the connotation of profit;[5] consequently, these works tend to exhibit a tone which naively blends practical and contemplative orientations. The same is true of Moran, the least spiritually developed of Beckett's sages, as can be seen when he remarks:

> Not one person in a hundred knows how to be silent and listen, no, nor even to conceive what such a thing means. Yet only then can you detect, beyond the fatuous clamor, the silence of which the universe is made. I desired this advantage for my son. (P. 121)

The prudent, antihedonistic attitudes which dominate biblical wisdom literature are simply the attitudes of the aged, necessarily authoritative in a feudal, patriarchal economy in which old men monopolized power. Having all the wealth and women available, they promulgated a spiritual training designed to discourage others from taking these things from them; at the same time, their doctrines sincerely reflected the inability of the infirm to enjoy themselves under any circumstances. However well the wisdom texts may succeed in explaining human suffering, they address themselves to a nihilism and pessimism that sometimes breaks through to the surface. This is not only true of Ecclesiastes and Job. In a little known Egyptian wisdom text, a slave answers his master's earnest question "What, then is the good?" with the following reply:

> To have my neck broken and your neck broken and to be thrown into the river.[6]

Because wisdom literature is so directly the expression of a certain social order, the quaint didactic tone taken by Beckett's philosophical vagrants is more nearly resembled in the writing of the pre-Socratic philosophers, a bunch of quirky individualists. Beckett's own works allude to Pythagoras, Democritus, Zeno, Empedocles, and Heraclitus by name. In certain cases, Beckett has concerned himself with pre-Socratic ideas, but more important is his artful assimilation of the pre-Socratic spirit, its social detachment, vatic rationalism, and wry naivete. This autobiographical fragment of Xenophanes suggests the exhausted, self-deprecatory tone of the trilogy:

> Already there are seven and sixty years tossing my thought up and down the land of Greece; and from my birth there were another twenty-five to add to these, if I know how to speak truly of these things.[7]

The witty remarks attributed to these sages are all of a kind; their absolute brevity and paradoxicality reflect the independence and calm characteristic of the philosophical temperament. For example, "when [Thales'] mother tried to force him to marry, he replied it was too soon, and when she pressed him again later in life, he replied that it was too late."[8] "When he was asked why he had no children of his own, he replied, 'because he loved children.' "[9] This sally would not be at all out of place in a monologue of Beckett's, where it would be written out straight, so as to read:

> I never wanted to have any children. Because I loved children.

Of course it is Heraclitus, the weeping philosopher, whose tone and thought more consistently suggest Beckett's than do any of the other pre-Socratics'. And here is a sage if there ever was one:

> He grew up to be exceptionally haughty and supercilious, as is
> clear also from his book, in which he says: "Learning of many
> things does not teach intelligence; if so it would have taught
> Hesiod and Pythagoras, and again Xenophanes and Hecataeus'. . . .
> Finally, he became a misanthrope, withdrew from the world, and
> lived in the mountains feeding on grasses and plants. However,
> having fallen in this way into a dropsy he came to town and asked
> the doctors in a riddle if they could make a drought out of rainy
> weather. When they did not understand he buried himself in a cow-
> stall, expecting that the dropsy would be evaporated off by the heat
> of the manure; but even so he failed to effect anything and ended
> his life at the age of sixty.[10]

Considering this legend, we might recall Beckett's reclusion
in the Atlas Mountains after winning the Nobel Prize; and we
understand why the hero of *The Expelled,* lies down in the
gutter and wryly adds, "without thinking for a moment of
Heraclitus."[11] With Heraclitus the sage of comic tradition—
embittered, incompetent, obsessively misanthropic—is already essentially developed. He might remind us especially of
Molloy, who also withdraws from the world, eats grass, and
gravitates to excrement.[12] The comic legends about Heraclitus
are now supposed to be largely fictitious, but it is easy to see,
from his first fragment, why they were invented. They simply
should have happened:

> Of the Logos which is as I describe it, men always prove to be
> uncomprehending, both before they have heard it, and when once
> they have heard it. For although all things happen according to this
> Logos, men are like people of no experience, even when I distin-
> guish each thing according to its constitution and declare *how it is;*
> but the rest of men fail to notice what they do when they wake up
> just as they forget what they do when asleep.[13](Italics mine)

The difficulties of the sage's situation, consistently ex-
ploited in Beckett's novels, are all manifest here. Heraclitus'
Logos denotes the common, underlying, universally effective
principle of order—something like the "Form of Being" Beckett speaks of seeking. And Heraclitus' famous irony reflects,
among other things, the tension between the general scope of

this intuition and his solitary acquaintance with it. His first
fragment can be paraphrased as "I and only I know that everything is the same"; this is merely a more extreme version of
Arsene's claim that "the same things happen to us all . . . if
only we choose to know it." What is difficult to reconcile here
is the knower's privileged claim to knowledge and the levelling implications of that knowledge; if the Logos is universally
effective, then why doesn't everyone know about it?

Another problematical implication of Heraclitus' position is
the futility of knowledge. What value lies in knowing the
Logos if, in any case, it is unalterable? In other words, what
value lies in knowing the inevitable? Arsene's remark contains the same implication. Since the "same things happen to
us all . . . if only we choose to know it," then they will con-
tinue to happen to us, although we know it. Knowledge is
useless under such conditions, and Arsene actually draws this
conclusion:

> And if I could begin it all over again, knowing what I know now,
> the result would always be the same.[14]

Nor is that all. Heraclitus, like Beckett, felt obliged to tell us
"how it is "; "but men always prove to be uncomprehending."
Hence the irascible note of frustration in his fragments, much
like the splenetic tone of Beckett's early works. The sage's
knowledge, then, is incommunicable, ineffective, and impossible, and this is the situation Beckett affirms in his maturity:

> there is nothing to express, nothing with which to express, nothing
> from which to express, together with the obligation to express.[15]

There are other analogies between Beckett and Heraclitus.
In spite of his sweeping claim to knowledge, Heraclitus retained a naive astonishment at man's self-deception and futile
resistance:

> Therefore it is necessary to follow the common; but although the
> Logos is common the many live as if they had a private understand-
> ing.[16]

So his prose projects a strange blend of assurance about the human condition and social bewilderment, a juxtaposition of tones that Beckett's trilogy fruitfully develops. Finally, Heraclitus admitted that even his philosophical knowledge was incomplete. He found that the quest for knowledge required inner probing:

I searched myself out.[17]

But like Beckett's heroes, he seems to have found it is precisely the self that cannot be known; for

You could not discover the limits of the soul, even if you travelled every road to do so; such is the depth of its meaning.[18]

In recognition of these altogether typical problems, a sage develops some defensive strategies; hence Heraclitus' self-parody—and that of Beckett's characters and Beckett himself. Heraclitus was once found warming himself by a kitchen fire, "not a place where a Greek gentleman normally would have been found."[19] Never at a loss, he replied, "Here too are gods"—a timely allusion to his glorification of fire. The strange allusions made by Beckett's heroes to his previous works perform a similar defensive function; they raise a protective wall around the fictional domain, while mocking its very isolation. The same hermetic device was employed by Blake; it is typical of privileged knowers.

Sages are privileged knowers, and an air of mystery was deliberately cultivated in certain primitive philosophical circles. This is apparently what interests Beckett about Pythagoras, mentioned several times in *Murphy;* his dicta were secrets, transmitted only to initiates. Thus Neary, a Pythagorean, warns Wylie that

betrayal will automatically entail the fate of Hippasos the Akousmatic, "drowned in a puddle for having divulged the incommensurability of the side and diagonal . . ."[20]

When Pythagoras discovered his famous geometrical theorem, he sacrificed an ox.[21] That act would be of little interest if it were performed by a magician, but to the modern mind it is striking and amusing in a mathematician; and it is exactly such tensions that draw Beckett to the sage mentality. The air of mystery that pervades *Waiting for Godot* and *Molloy* has an effect both comic and poetic, because it is juxtaposed against the preoccupations of characters which, in most respects, are remarkably banal.

What makes Pythagoras a thorough sage and not just an occult mathematician is that he also advocated apathy and detachment:

> Life, he said, is like a festival; just as some come to the festival to compete, some to ply their trade, but the best people come as spectators, so in life the slavish men go hunting for fame or gain, the philosophers for the truth.[22]

But Socrates, in this as well as other respects, is the most paradigmatic sage. According to legend, he rationalized passivity with witty assertions of intellectual and moral superiority. Thus when someone expressed surprise at his indifferent response to a beating, he replied, "Shall I take a donkey to court if it kick me?"[23] When Xanthippe told him he suffered unjustly, he said, "Would you want me to suffer justly?"[24] His exhortation to philosophy in the *Phaedo*, based on the premise that worldly activity is futile, set the pattern for subsequent descriptions of the intellectual life:

> Every seeker after wisdom knows that up to the time when philosophy takes over his soul it is a *helpless prisoner*, chained hand and foot in the body, compelled to view *reality* not directly, but through prison bars, and wallowing in utter ignorance. And philosophy can see that the imprisonment is ingeniously effected by the prisoner's own *active desire*, which makes him first accessory to his own confinement. Well, philosophy takes over the soul in this condition and by gentle persuasion tries to set it *free*. She points out that *observation by means of the eyes and ears is entirely deceptive*, and she urges the soul to refrain from using them unless it is necessary to do so, and encourages it to collect and concentrate upon itself . . .[25] (Italics mine)

Time and much repetition have turned these notions into platitudes, but Beckett has shown a remarkable capacity for taking them seriously and literally. In fact, they form the basis, the point of departure, for his artistic vision. Socrates' remarks constitute the whole spiritual and artistic program outlined in *Proust:* the related goals of freedom and reality, the disdain of empirical information, the mind-body distinction, the "contraction of the spirit," and, as always, the condemnation of "active desire." But in Beckett's works this outlook is also defeated; freedom and reality become futile, disastrous ideals—at least, no more attainable through contemplation than by any other means.

Though Socrates is never named in Beckett's works, there are many points in common between the sage paradigm and the typical Beckett hero: their compulsive attention to inner voices, falling into trances (which makes Socrates late for the symposium), the cultivation of tranquillity, eschewal of public concerns, and even dying, as Malone does, feet first.[26] Moran, like Socrates, claims to use the "maieutic" educational method, and one of this character's most sententious remarks seems to have Socratic origin:

> For what I was doing I was doing neither for Molloy, who mattered nothing to me, nor for myself, of whom I despaired, but on behalf of a cause which, while having need of us to be accomplished, was in its essence anonymous, and would subsist, haunting the minds of men, when its miserable artisans should be no more. It will not be said, I think, that I did not take my work to heart. But rather, tenderly, Ah those old craftsmen, their race is extinct and the mold broken. (Pp. 114–15)

The Socratic concept of philosophy as a common pursuit might be of influence here; what is more certainly of Socratic origin is Moran's strange reference to "craftsmen" (in what sense is Moran a craftsman?). As it happened, Socrates told Thrasymachus in the *Republic* that "a craft as such does not seek its own advantage but that of the subject on which it is exercized."[27] Thus Moran explains that his quest is not undertaken for himself, nor for Molloy, but on behalf of the task itself.

Beckett is reported to have left his academic career for literature with a profession of ignorance in the Socratic manner, saying that he "could not bear the absurdity of teaching to others what [he did] not know himself."[28] But that is precisely what his writing does teach—"what he does not know himself" (that is, his ignorance rationalized and affirmed as a sort of dogmatic skepticism). Similarly, Socrates' certain conviction that he knew nothing became the fundamental motive of his vocation, a kind of *raison d'être*. From the discovery of that famous paradox, that his wisdom consisted in knowing that he knew nothing, followed his commitment to the didactic life, examining himself and others, and instructing the latter in their own ignorance. According to Beckett, his own realization of ignorance was the inspiration of *Molloy:*

> I conceived of Molloy and the rest the day I became aware of my stupidity. Then I set out to write the things I sensed.[29]

And the dawning awareness of ignorance is the theme that novel constantly recapitulates. For example, when Moran contemplates the dance of his bees, he reflects upon his superior knowledge in a Socratic fashion ("I alone of all mankind knew this"—p. 168). And it is revealed that what he alone knows about this spectacle is that he will never understand it. This is also Molloy's claim to distinction:

> I know that I know nothing . . . (p. 25)

And his consolation:

> to know you are beyond knowing anything, that is when peace enters in . . . (p. 64)

My intention here is not to assert a peculiar and striking likeness between Beckett and Socrates; the latter is merely the most well known example of the recurrent sage type they both exemplify. Each is chiefly concerned to characterize the value of contemplative life. This is no longer the dominant concern of philosophers, but once philosophy was a spiritual discipline, not merely a particular domain of ideas and methods. Malone retains the archaic though still recognizable sense of the term when he writes that Sapo "submitted with *philosophy* to vexations" (italics mine)—in other words, with cultivated resignation and indifference. As early as Plato and Aristotle, however, the difference between sages and philosophers began to emerge. Plato and Aristotle certainly con-

Failed Sages 83

tinued to praise the contemplative life, as did their predecessors; but in their hands, philosophy became so much more complex and technical that, as a technique, it could be developed apart from spiritual motives. Beckett's interests lie in the more primitive sage tradition and in its modern extensions, such as Schopenhauer's thought—intellectual systems explicitly developed in order to attain tranquility. The philosophers to whom Beckett alludes are all insistently apathetic; Geulincx, one of whose dicta is cited in *Murphy*, perfectly exemplifies their temperament:

Ubi nihil vales, ibi nihil velis. (P. 178)

The sage tradition, then, passed from Socrates not to Plato but to the cynics. These mendicant, antisocial wanderers, distinguished by their hostile verbal facility, might be considered in detail as prototypes of Beckett. Antisthenes, the putative father of the school, developed an eclectic outlook much like Beckett's in its components. He absorbed the asceticism of Socrates:

From Socrates he learned his hardihood, emulating his disregard of feeling, and thus he inaugurated the Cynic way of life.[30]

To this he added the skeptical arguments of Socrates and that of an earlier mentor, Gorgias, whose philosophy has already been mentioned in relation to Beckett's by A. J. Leventhal. It consisted of three propositions:

(1) that nothing exists.
(2) if it existed it could not be known
(3) if it could be known it could not be communicated to others.[31]

Antisthenes buttressed his skepticism with the logical paradoxes of Zeno the Eleatic which, as Richard Coe and other critics have observed, figure prominently among Beckett's life-long preoccupations.

What Antisthenes added to these ideas was a new mood, one of aggressive contempt; the original cynic railed without discrimination against virtually all positive assertions. And his pupil, the more famous Diogenes, broadened his mentor's attack to include not only philosophical doctrines but also social conventions, holding that "Everything is permitted."[32] After him, the cynics practiced a principled indecorum, making a point of being offensive. Like Beckett, Diogenes did this with scatology, nor did he confine himself to offensive language; his public excretions, immortalized in anecdotal lore, were rationalized as "natural" and thus a legitimate expression of his philosophical program of "following nature."[33] Despite that rationalization, of course, there is some simple hostility in Diogenes. The general tone of cynical behavior is perhaps best illustrated by the following anecdote:

> Someone took Diogenes into a magnificent house and warned him not to expectorate, whereupon, having cleared his throat, he discharged the phlegm into the man's face, being unable, he said, to find a meaner receptacle.[34]

It is not easy to understand the cynics. There seems to have been an element of deliberate exaggeration in Diogenes' practices:

> He used to say that he followed the example of the trainers of choruses; for they set the note a little too high, to ensure the rest would hit the right note.[35]

But exaggeration is not the only problem cynicism presents, and the cynics are more apt to provoke an ambivalent than a qualified response. Nietzsche, at different moments, called cynicism "the ultimate which can be attained on earth," but also "the only form in which mean souls touch honesty."[36] This variance is altogether typical and reasonable, for in cynicism the contradictory potential implicit in the sage type becomes most manifest. The cynics looked at Socrates' irony and skepticism, his logic-chopping and controversions of common sense, above all, his principled social detachment, and read there a message of subversion—at least a kind of subversive theatricality. And not without reason. Playfulness was certainly an aspect of Socrates' character; Nietzsche called him "the buffoon who made others take him seriously."[37] And Kierkegaard, whose admiration of Socrates was more ardent and less qualified than Nietzsche's, called him

a "caricature and ideal."[38] The phrase applies perfectly to
the sage type in general and particularly as exemplified by
Beckett's heroes.

A certain disreputability and immoralism—at least an
imaginative or speculative immoralism—tends to go along with
the sage stereotype. Socrates himself was executed for cor-
rupting the youth. And if that charge was not the real reason
for his death, it at least presented itself as a plausible excuse;
he could be seen in that light. The Aristophanic Socrates offers
to teach chiseling.[39] And an anecdote about Aristippus,
another disciple of Socrates and a contemporary of the early
cynics, exemplifies the sort of unscrupulous cleverness com-
monly associated with the sage figure in antiquity:

> When he [Aristippus] asked for money, Dionysius [a tyrant] re-
> plied, "But you said the wise man would never be in want." "Give
> me the money and then we will go into that." Dionysius gave it,
> whereupon Aristippus replied, "You see, I am not in want."[40]

As for Diogenes, he actually had a criminal background; his
father, and along with him, little Diogenes too, were banished
for the former's counterfeiting.[41] In fact, some scholars have
interpreted cynicism as simply Diogenes' rationalization of
his banishment; an impoverished outcast will indeed find
misanthropic asceticism convenient enough. In any case,
Diogenes adopted the metaphor of counterfeiting ("alter the
currency," he said) to describe his assault on all established
values.

I would not offer to explain Pim's torturing, the Unnamable's violence, Moran's murder, or Molloy's assault
and theft as examples of cynical unscrupulousness. But there
is an odd scene in *Murphy* that seems to derive from the
model of intellectualized amoralism. By a complicated series
of maneuvers, Murphy is able to chisel some extra tea at a cafe.
This is not remarkable, but the didactic tone of the narrative
is; the hero's method is described with the functional detail of
a blueprint, and the reader is exhorted to "try it" (p. 84).

It would be wrong, however, to be entirely cynical about
cynicism; routinely cranking out the most misanthropic interpretation available ignores the purpose of the movement,
and its purpose was the source of its potent influence.

Diogenes died, according to legend, by *apnoea* (holding his breath). This is no doubt a source for Beckett's *Murphy,* in which the same fate is anticipated for Mr. Endon, the hero's exemplar of worldly detachment. And this legend points out the positive goal of the cynical movement, a self-control so extreme that it extended, in this case, to the involuntary vital functions. In this the cynics reduced sageness to its essence; without endurance and independence a sage is no longer recognizable as such. Thus even the most negative characterizations of the type retain these characteristics; Aristophanes' Socrates "has endurance and never stoops to flattery."[42] The founding cynic, Antisthenes, asserted that he'd "rather be mad than feel pleasure"[43] and advocated a life of toil (as an anaesthetic), for the goal of self-control involves contempt for all pleasurable sentiment—the "ablation of desire" Beckett insisted upon in *Proust* and has been investigating, through his fictional imagination, ever since. This doctrine is not entirely negative nor to be confused with a death wish, because in knowing that he has no desires, the sage is supposed to retain (as Moran says) "just enough consciousness to let [him] exult" (p. 140). But Beckett's characterizations suggest that the ascetic is just as likely to be embittered as exhilarated by his loss of feeling.

It was under stoicism that "sage" became a technical term and a fully crystallized concept; but because of this clarification, and stoicism's growing influence, the sage ideal began to attract more criticism. In fact, the philosophical school of skepticism arose largely through contesting stoicism's guarantee—that their ideal man, the sage, need only "follow nature" to attain an apathy not unlike happiness.[44] "Following nature" meant limiting needs to natural desires, not sophisticated luxuries, and tending to humane obligations.

Some of Beckett's critics have called him a stoic, and, if loosely enough conceived, the term applies. But "cynic" would be much more appropriate; Beckett's tone, like that of the cynics, is both a good deal more negative and much more playful than that of any of the classical stoics. In any case, like the ancient skeptics, Beckett rejects the more hopeful aspects of both stoicism and cynicism, especially their confidence in the mind's capacity for self-government. This is the very crux of the problem: whether or not freedom and tranquillity are indeed available through contemplation. Marcus Aurelius advised man to "consider that everything is opinion, and that opinion is in your power."[45] Beckett's heroes might agree that everything is opinion but not that opinion is in their power; their thought is not rationally directed but obsessively suffered. Furthermore, a strategy of conscious rationalization, when perceived as such by an observer, always seems illegitimate. Whenever Beckett describes such a moment in fiction, he inevitably commits himself to criticizing it. At one point the Unnamable describes a position in which he cannot move, adding, "I take advantage of this to learn to stay quiet" (p. 332). But no one, the reader thinks, can practice consciously and with success such facile resignation. In this passage the specious manipulations of consolational philosophy are exposed by the sarcastic transparency of Beckett's language. Beckett finds that stoicism doesn't work for the same reasons as those given by Pascal—another ascetic introspective in quest of inner peace, prone to generalizing about the human condition and in these respects a sage (but one with a more pessimistic psychology than the classic sages). I cite Pascal's critique because it is usefully explicit:

> The Stoics say, "Retire within yourselves; it is there you will find rest." And that is not true.[46]

The condition of rest and independence at which the stoic aims is insupportable, given human nature:

> Description of man: dependency, desire of independence, need.[47]
>
> Condition of man: inconsistency, weariness, unrest.[48]

Man is bound in time, he changes, his moods change, and the spiritual advice of the stoics takes no account of these necessities:

> The Stoics: They conclude that what has been done once can be done always.[49]

But in speaking critically of stoics, we should remember that the sage type is one that is prone to accept its failures, maintaining authority by wittily reformulating them as successes.

Socrates' decision to base his claim to wisdom on the fact that he realized his ignorance is the principal instance of this strategy. And the classical skeptics, who criticized stoicism, were just as much rival sages themselves, also seeking quietude through contemplation—contemplation without the need to come to conclusions. They thought they found a tranquilizing assurance in dogmatic disbelief, supposing (in the words of a seventeenth-century French skeptic) that "we possess nothing more certain than doubt."[50] Or consider Einstein, a sage of our own time, looking for a "unified theoretical conception comprising all data"[51] (like Beckett's "Form of Being"?). Where does this lead him? To "an uncertainty concerning the choice of basic theoretical concepts."[52] But this uncertainty, Einstein finds, is something to be cultivated:

> The most beautiful and profound emotion we can experience is the sensation of the mystical. It is the sower of all true science. He to whom this emotion is a stranger, who can no longer wonder and stand rapt in awe, is as good as dead. *To know that what is impenetrable really exists,* manifesting itself as the highest wisdom and the most radiant beauty which our full faculties can comprehend only in their primitive forms—this knowledge, this feeling, is true religiousness.[53] (Italics mine)

As Lichtenberg said, to much the same effect,

> To become wiser means to become increasingly acquainted with the errors to which this instrument with which we perceive and judge can be subject.[54]

Thus those playing the role of the wise man frequently admit their ignorance and defend it by arguments designed to show its righteousness and inevitability. This stance is aptly expressed in Tennyson's poem, "The Ancient Sage":

> Thou canst not prove the Nameless, O my son,
> Nor canst thou prove the world thou movest in,
> Thou canst not prove that thou art body alone,
> Nor canst not prove that thou art spirit alone,
> Nor canst thou prove that thou art both in one.
> Nor canst thou prove that thou art immortal, no,
> Nor yet that thou art mortal—nay, my son,
> Thou canst not prove that I, who speak with thee,

Am not thyself in converse with thyself,
For nothing worthy proving can be proven,
Nor yet disproven. Wherefore thou be wise,
Cleave ever to the sunnier side of doubt,
Cling to Faith beyond the forms of Faith![55]

The point to be understood in connection with Beckett's works is this: the retractions, successive contradictions, and professions of ignorance that characterize the speech of Beckett's heroes are not intended to disqualify their meaning or authority. These devices are the expressions of Beckett's skepticism, an intellectual and spiritual attitude that claims its own sufficiency as a guide to the perplexed and usually characterizes those professing to be very wise.

That is not to say that sages cannot hold religious convictions, and in fact the sage mentality reaches us from antiquity through religious as well as secular currents. Stoicism was absorbed into Christian asceticism by such authors as St. Augustine and, later on, Thomas à Kempis—each of whom is cited in Beckett's works, the former a number of times.[56] We have already observed, through Pascal's critique of stoical self-sufficiency, its incompatibility with Christianity; but these doctrines were also significantly compatible. As A. D. Nock's study of *Conversion* demonstrates, ancient philosophy itself barely differed from religion in tone and purpose; the philosophical life—it was a way of life—attracted converts seeking to renounce the world, much like ascetic Christianity. Boethius, taking no chances, was both a stoic and a Christian, finding their common core, no doubt, in the ablation of desire his Lady Philosophy recommends:

Now the good is defined as that which, once it is attained, relieves man of all further desires.[57]

The attitude Beckett takes toward Christianity is not very easily determined. He blasphemes and is apparently no believer; his allusions to theology in *Watt* and *Molloy* are wholly contemptuous. But the Christian allusions made throughout Beckett's writing suggest that he finds this outlook to be of compelling interest. If he is not attracted to Christian dogma, he is certainly attracted to Christian attitudes, particularly those attitudes which are similar to an ascetic sage's.

It was St. Augustine's *Confessions* that first brought the themes of sage literature—concern for the truth, obsessive introspection—to extended narrative form. Basically, Augustine's book perpetuated the misanthropic voice of prophecy and wisdom literature, but it also turned that voice against itself. After Augustine, self-criticism (as well as self-examination) became part of the sage's program.

Beckett's early poem "Whoroscope" disparages Augustine's conversion, as described in the *Confessions,* by replacing the saint's affirmation of belief with an admission of self-deception.[58] But in spite of this derision, Beckett must have found Augustine's great moment interesting, for it shows yet another sage electing asceticism. Augustine's conversion was effected, he said, when his eye fell upon this biblical verse:

> Let us pass our time honourably, as by the light of day, not in revelling and drunkenness, not in lust and wantonness, not in quarrels and rivalries. Rather, arm yourselves with the Lord Jesus Christ; spend no more thought on nature and *nature*'s appetites.
> (Romans 13:13,14; italics mine)

As with all of Beckett's sages, Augustine's life-long motive was the ablation of desire; in fact, he urged this even more emphatically than the classic sages. The cynics and stoics thought that "nature's appetites" were minimal enough, and blamed civilization for plaguing man with excessive desires. But Augustine's insistence upon the doctrine of Original Sin, stressing the difficulty of asceticism, locates an evil and insatiable need in man's very nature. This theme became a commonplace in such medieval texts as *The Imitation of Christ:*

> The source of temptation lies within our own nature, for we are born with an inclination towards evil.[59]

Thomas à Kempis' book, mentioned in *More Pricks than Kicks* (p. 37), urges us to despise the world, cultivate a spirit of obedience, and hope for inner peace. But, as is sometimes the case with Beckett's heroes, Thomas' asceticism modulates towards masochism. Because its sources are innate, he shows that our unhappiness is incurable and there is really no good hope of finding peace:

There can be no complete security nor perfect peace in this life.[60]

So long as we remain in this world, we cannot remain without trial and temptation. . .[61]

Since the Christian ascetics find that suffering is inevitable, they urge us to suffer for the right reasons. Indeed, this is the only consolation available under such circumstances:

Is there anyone who enjoys anything as he wishes? Neither you nor I, nor anyone else on earth. . . . Whose, then, is the happiest lot? Surely, he who is able to suffer for God.[62]

Yet Thomas admits that this redirection—away from worldly pursuits and towards God—will only intensify the Christian's woes:

The more spiritual a man's desires become, the more bitter does his present life grow for him.[63]

You are greatly mistaken if you look for anything save to endure trials, for all this mortal life is full of troubles, and everywhere marked with crosses. The further a man advances in the spiritual life, the heavier and more numerous he finds the crosses, for his ever-deepening love of God makes more bitter the sorrows of his earthly exile.[64]

To understand the appeal and usefulness of such sentiments, they must be regarded as replies to moments of extreme dejection. Nonetheless, the codification of these attitudes into texts like St. Augustine's *Confessions* and *The Imitation of Christ* promoted and trained a sensibility on the whole more masochistic than ascetic. The world described by Augustine is generally a good deal bleaker and less relieved by incidental pleasures than the one observed by Beckett's heroes. As Gide observed,

Christianity consoles; but there are naturally happy souls who do not need consolation. Consequently, Christianity begins by making such souls unhappy. . .[65]

And by this logic, it has to keep them unhappy, so that Christians will remain in need of their religion's consolation. It is possible to detect a sardonic assessment of Christianity, along

these lines, in *Waiting for Godot.* When the tramps claim to
outdo Christ in their suffering, Beckett is suggesting that
Christianity is an ineffectual system of consolation that actually promotes a culture of suffering and guilt. It is in this way
that the *Imitation of Christ* proposes to keep the spiritual
motor in perpetual motion; the Christian will keep going on,
in quest of peace, towards even greater miseries. And that is
not unlike the paradoxical attitude of Molloy, who remarked:

> Had I been able to conceive of something worse I would have had
> no peace, if I know myself, until I had got it. (P. 46)

Of course, some important differences must be noted between ascetic Christianity and Molloy's mentality. The Christian sage is oriented towards God and "perfectly dead to
self."[66] Molloy's imperative concerns (to see his mother, to
record his experience) are more mundane. More important,
the ascetic Christian seems to cultivate an intensity of feeling;
nothing could be further from Molloy's wishes. Finally,
Thomas praises the ascetic life, finding it a "good and holy
thing to suffer in this way."[67] Molloy admits his asceticism:

> I was bent double over a heap of muck, in the hope of finding
> something to disgust me forever with eating . . . (p. 57)

But his tone does not commend the pursuit. A God who con-
signs unbelievers to Hell cannot be expected to appeal to the
skeptic. Thus, although the apathy of Beckett's heroes at times
seems to have been colored by Christian asceticism or other
doctrines which rationalize suffering as a kind of divine service, they are more often than not inclined to mock this attitude and assert its fictitiousness.

It seems, then, that the secular sage tradition, more self-
oriented and less intense than ascetic Christianity, has more
amply influenced Beckett's writing. Skepticism and stoicism
were revived during the Renaissance by Montaigne, among
many others, and Montaigne's successors in French reflective
literature (e.g., Pascal, Descartes, Rousseau, Constant, Baudelaire, Proust, Breton, Céline, Sartre, Camus) establish the
modern sage tradition leading up to Beckett's works. The
constant pattern that emerges in this body of literature is that

of introspection leading to apathy and skepticism. Montaigne's definition of philosophy as "learning how to die" (through solitary meditation) seems strikingly appropriate to *Malone Dies;* furthermore, he celebrated his discovery of Sextus Empiricus' skeptical compendium by striking a medal. Descartes' radical introspection, coupled with a countervailing tendency to legislate the universal laws of consciousness, places him clearly in the sage tradition. And what is not often remembered about Descartes is that the goal of his *Meditations* was not pure knowledge. Rather, it was "perfect repose of spirit." Like all of Beckett's favorite sages, Descartes based his hopes for happiness on apathetic resignation:

> although I did not pretend to scorn all glory like the Cynics, I yet
> had very small esteem for what I could not hope to acquire.[68]

Rousseau voiced the same attitude, but with characteristic extremity:

> The real world has its boundaries, the imaginary world is infinite;
> since we cannot enlarge the one, let us contract the other.[69]

Rousseau, whose *Confessions* are mentioned in *More Pricks than Kicks*, was perhaps the most influential of modern sages. His celebrated later life, as well as his later writing, was clearly modelled after the sage ideal; the ostentatious worldly retirement, the simple but eccentric "Armenian costume," the pithy misanthropy of his conversation—all these characteristics suggest Rousseau's deliberate emulation of the classic sage figure. Towards more modern sages Rousseau admits some resemblance, but takes a competitive tone.

> I do not go so far as St. Augustine, who was consoled for being
> damned, if that were the will of God.[70]

> I shall carry out the same enterprise as Montaigne, but with a goal
> entirely contrary to his, because he did not write his *Essays* except
> for others, and I do not write my Reveries except for myself.[71]

The reason that Rousseau's *Confessions* and *Reveries* make the sage's stance available to the modern sensibility is that his claims to independence and indifference are so patently insincere; thus Rousseau has none of the specious dignity that estranges us from real stoics. In spite of his superficial suavity, he is too emotional, too apt to fall into alternating moods; and in spite of his claims to social detachment, he is not at all indifferent to his audience. Rousseau's reflective works, though nominally reveries and confessions, are clearly self-justifications. And his continuous need to justify betrays the insufficiency of these justifications; it is as if Rousseau were always apologizing for the wrong crime, his real sin, as Beckett would say, being the sin of his birth. Rousseau's successors in the reflective mode were quick to note his contradictions and futilities. Baudelaire's response is typical:

> "How many men are there in the world so ready as I am to pass judgement on themselves, so severe in self-condemnation?" Thus he at once condemns and glorifies himself. . . . Doesn't all this remind you of Jean-Jacques . . . Making his confession to the universe—not without a certain voluptuous pleasure. . . ?[72]

But a sensible, moralistic criticism of Rousseau is more or less beside the point, and Baudelaire is not really interested in making one. For Rousseau's influence upon this tradition lies in his failure, a failure which his successors need only more directly affirm for themselves to claim it as a good. Having pointed out the contradictions in Rousseau—the persistence of his need despite his claim to indifference, the persistence of his pride in his act of self-abasement—Baudelaire proceeded to base his own claim to spiritual distinction on a sorrow and maladjustment that had value because it was so frankly realized. Sounding a good deal like one of Beckett's heroes here, Baudelaire announces his avowal of ignorance and an unidealized apathy:

> To know nothing, to teach nothing, to will nothing, to sleep, and only to sleep, that today is my vow. An infamous and disgusting vow, but sincere.[73]

Nor is that all. Probing onward to the ultimate paradox, Baudelaire confessed his very insincerity, but at precisely that point found himself in touch with universal human consciousness:

> Hypocrite lecteur, mon semblable, mon frère . . .[74]

And Baudelaire's writing is only one of many such developments; Dostoevsky's *Notes from the Underground* is another. Modern literature abounds with misanthropic, intellectual heroes, claiming a fuller awareness of both ideals and inescapable realities, who reject the social world in order to aim at a sage's honesty, independence, and tranquillity. They fail to achieve this, of course, but manage to exploit the very failure of their emulation. As Goethe said, "the greatest art in life consists of changing the problem into a postulate; in this way one succeeds."[75] Thus when Dostoevsky's Underground Man finds himself enmeshed in successive contradictions, he proceeds to define consciousness as such; he thereby removes the criterion of critical judgment, because no one can be judged to fail in performing a futile act. Similarly, when Camus' Meursault finds himself unable to accept death without fear, he chooses to regard this as a sign that he has "really lived."

The same can be said for most of Beckett's heroes: their consciousness is one continuous effort to rationalize its own failure to attain tranquillity. But, in the case of Beckett's writing, it should be added that the background of tradition that lies behind this mentality is made especially emphatic and explicit. His references to the pre-Socratics, Descartes, and Geulincx keep the sage paradigm in mind; his language, sometimes philosophical in tone, sometimes gnomic, reinforces the sage connection. What suggested this erudite approach to him? We cannot be sure, of course, but Joyce (with whom the younger Beckett was closely acquainted) was well versed in philosophical lore. Richard Ellmann's biography reports him as quoting Parmenides and comparing himself to Diogenes.[76] In *Ulysses*, Stephen Dedalus is compared to the founder of cynicism, in a way that would also apply to a number of Beckett's characters:

> You remind me of Antisthenes. . . . It is said of him that none could tell if he were bitterer against others or against himself.[77]

Then again, Joyce entitled an early lecture "Ireland, Land of Saints and Sages," and the term "sage" crops up quite often in the works of another Irish writer, George Russell ("A. E."), who applied it to a Celtic visionary tradition. Russell's works are cited in *Murphy* and *Watt*, but he styled himself a happy sage, if such can be, and a look at *The Candle of Vision* will

suggest a source for the thin but gushing optimism Beckett
deflates at the end of *Watt*.

Beckett's attraction to the sage type is not to be explained as
an Irish phenomenon; on the contrary, the use of sages indicates a reaction against the limitations of national culture,
through alignment with a cosmopolitan type—Diogenes the
Cynic is supposed to have coined that term—common to all
cultures.[78] The intellectual and moral climate of *Murphy*,
where Beckett's sages, as such, first appear, is more directly
connected with the expatriate milieu in London than with the
specifically Irish characters it describes. An interesting parallel
can be found in the American Nathanael West's *The Dream Life
of Balso Snell*, written in Paris during the same period.

Here the internationalist impulse expresses itself through
the same themes and types found in Beckett's early writing.
West's hero is employed in a library's "philosophy department
. . . patronized by alchemists, astrologers, cabalists, demon-
ologists, magicians, atheists, and founders of new religious
systems."[79] His fantasy commences on a scatological note,
with entry into a Trojan horse through the anus. There he
meets with an eager disciple, who mistakes him for the
"philosopher saint, Apollonius of Tyana,"[80] and later on encounters a mystic, "Maloney the Areopagite."[81] Snell is a pessimist, and most of the book's rhetorical energy seems to derive from what he calls "the natural antipathy pessimists feel
for optimists."[82] He talks sententiously of "Life" and
"Realities" (e. g., "Life is a prison without bars"),[83] he "wal-
lows in discomfort"[84] and consoles himself with the thought
that "all must die," reflecting that thus he can make "death's
victory [his] own."[85] His relations with various women suggest
the Murphy-Celia situation; in each case, the men are "on the
side of the intellect against the emotions, the brain against the
heart."[86] And a short passage in diary form voices the same
complaints that Beckett, with much greater depth and re-
sourcefulness, investigates as affirmations in his later works. I
mean Socratic ignorance and futile persistence:

> I can know nothing; I can have nothing. I must devote my whole
> life to the pursuit of a shadow. It is as if I were attempting to trace
> with the point of a pencil the shadow of the tracing pencil. I am
> enchanted with the shadow's shape and want very much to outline

it; but the shadow is attached to the pencil and moves with it, never allowing me to trace its tempting form. Because of some great need, I am continuously forced to make the attempt.[87]

Among the most prominent literary ideas prevalent in Paris during Beckett's early years there were those of Breton and other surrealists, authors Beckett found sufficiently interesting to translate. And no wonder: in the formulations of Breton, who claimed Heraclitus as a "Surrealist dialectician,"[88] the main thrust of the movement was simply to reaffirm, with extremist enthusiasm, the governing tendencies of the sage mentality. Through the process of automatic writing—that is, writing "without any volitional effort," abandoning the "critical faculty," and in a state of "extreme detachment"—Breton and others endeavored to produce an exact representation of "spoken thought." This is carrying apathetic contemplation to the limit, and its products were found to be characterized

> chiefly by a very high degree of *immediate absurdity*, the peculiar quality of that absurdity being, on a close examination, their yielding to whatever is most admissible and legitimate in the world: divulgation of a number of facts and properties on the whole not less objectionable than the others.[89]

In other words, Breton found that the writing produced under an attitude of indifference quite naturally expressed that indifference. And finding that such writing was at times also obscure, Breton was able to rationalize this obscurity with a sage's typical endorsement of ignorance. The following remarks recall Beckett's early diatribes against clarity in art; according to Breton, the great poets did not perceive their subject clearly, but rather were

> confined in the dark grooves of being to hear the speaking indistinctly and, while they write, to understanding [it] no better than we the first time we read them . . .[90]

It is known that Beckett's trilogy is largely a reworking and arrangement of materials derived from automatic writing. Syntax, thematic development, and plot are ample evidence of Beckett's literary control, but his heroes' increasingly minimal situations (e. g., the Unnamable's jar) are forms designed to "admit the chaos" and "accommodate the mess." Nonetheless, Beckett's critics have tended to minimize the influence of the disreputable Surrealists upon his work. John Fletcher's remarks typify this commonsense bias:

> About the only manifesto [Beckett] has ever signed was published in the same review [*transition*] in 1932. It proclaims the "autonomy of the poetic vision" and the "hegemony of the inner life over the outer life." It is against the reactionary conformity to the classical ideal, and is for an art welling up unbidden from the unconscious. In this, of course, the manifesto reveals the influence of the Surrealists. . . . It is not likely that Beckett took any of this too seriously.[91]

But Beckett does take these issues seriously. His works are precisely about the "hegemony of the inner life over the outer life," together with the manias and other miseries that worldly detachment entails. With the Surrealists, Beckett consistently assigns a superior reality to mental life, a mental life more characterized by psychic automatism than rationality. Their difference, of course, is that Beckett does not describe a person's attunement to his own thought as a benefit, whereas Breton, with incredible optimism, saw the expression of psychic automatism as "the solution of the principal problems of life."

Total contemplative self-enclosure, as Breton and Beckett both realized, is best observed amongst the insane. Breton determined to experiment with automatic writing only after receiving verbatim reports of consciousness from psychoanalytic patients and he generally idealized the insane, because

> Mad persons . . . exhibit *so profound a detachment* from the critical judgements passed upon them and from the various reproofs inflicted upon them, that it is permissible to suppose them so comforted by their imagination and so charmed by the delirious concepts that they cherish the fact that those concepts are only valid for themselves. . . . I could spend my life provoking the confidences of mad persons; for they are persons of scrupulous honesty whose innocence is only equalled by my own.[92] (Italics mine)

Beckett worked for a while in a mental institution, and *Murphy* describes an apathetic intellectual's quest for detachment among the insane. But Murphy also encounters "paranoids, feverishly covering sheets of paper with complaints against their treatment or verbatim reports of their inner voices" (p. 167). Here are the precursors of Molloy's "They," Moran's "fiends," and the Unnamable's "college of tyrants." As William James's studies of religious experience pointed out, automatic writing is an activity frequently governed by a paranoid sense of spiritual presence. The Unnamable will not resist the spirit:

> it's all a question of voices. I say what I am told to say in the hope that some day they will weary of talking to me. The trouble is I say it all wrong, having no ear, no head, no memory. Now I seem to hear Worm's voice beginning. I pass on the news, for what it's worth. (P. 345)

Typically, Beckett offers a version of vatic paranoia that is droll and deflated. And the transition from *Murphy* to *Watt* clearly shows Beckett's growing refusal to glamorize madness of any sort. Céline's *Journey to the End of the Night*, another text in the French introspective tradition, dramatizes the same development. At first, the hero is inclined to social withdrawal, supposing that "One is really quite all right inside."[93] But subsequent experience, including employment in a madhouse, persuades him that

> all that makes up a lunatic is the ordinary ideas of mankind shut up very tight inside a man's head. The outer world held well at bay and that's enough. Then the mind gets like a lake without an outlet; it's a head bolted and barreled, infected, stagnant.[94]

I do not cite Breton and Céline to suggest that Beckett's ideas must have derived from the Parisian milieu of the 1930s; his thought is no more intrinsically connected with that than with any other period. I shall cite one more sage to show that Beckett's meaning is perennial—a more or less inevitable progression through the changes of introspective pessimism. Kierkegaard is interesting in that his *Journals* and other writings present an unusually thorough documentation of the inner life's traditional development, and because Martin Esslin (one of Beckett's foremost critics) has misappropriated the philosopher to support a contention that Beckett's work has "no meaning" whatsoever. Esslin observes that Beckett, like Kierkegaard, deals with "existence," as opposed to "essence;" by this he means that each is attentive to change and concreteness and therefore avoids general formulations. "An artist like Beckett," according to Esslin, "does not concern himself with abstract and general verities."[95] "No universal lessons, no meaning, no philosophical truths could possibly be derived from a writer like him."[96] Such a statement can rest upon only a peculiarly limited definition of meaning. Kierkegaard's *Journals* and Beckett's progression of novels present an altogether parallel and definite development, leading to the sage's obligatory revaluation of futility and doubt.

As his *Journals* frankly confess, Kierkegaard suffered initially from an unhappy social isolation, and this is what motivated his contemplative pursuits. The misery of solitude and social frustration prompted his further withdrawal into the consoling world of thought:

> Inwardly torn asunder as I was, *without any expectation of leading a happy earthly life* . . . what wonder that in desperate despair I grasped at nought but the intellectual side in man and clung fast to it, so that the thought of my own considerable powers of mind was my only consolation, ideas my one joy, and mankind indifferent to me.[97] (Italics mine)

Similarly, Beckett's Murphy turns to

> the intellectual love in which he alone could love himself, *because there alone he was loveable.* (P. 179, italics mine)

At the first stage of the sage's typical development, then, we find a sweeping pessimism and self-disgust, from which, however, his intellectual endeavors are exempted. And another irreducible feature of the type should be noted here: a need to express, strange in combination with social withdrawal, but nonetheless insistent. The young Kierkegaard finds his escape from man insufficiently complete, and yet he wants to communicate too. Since he still requires an audience, he adopts a defensively difficult style:

> I tried to write in such a way that the heretics could not understand it.[98]

Nonetheless he laments their incomprehension, suitably, in a paradoxical manner:

> People understand me so little that they do not even understand when I complain of being misunderstood.[99]

This ambivalence about communication remains a constant trait, together with solitude. As the Unnamable remarks, after what he claims is eons of suffering:

> inability to speak, inability to be silent, and solitude, that's what I've had to make the best of . . . (p. 396)

Obliged to speak, what message do the perplexed sage's words initially contain? He is spitefully negative about everything but contemplation. Because he wants to complain and accuse, he is especially irked by attempts to console him. Hence Kierkegaard's attraction to Job, whom he admires for his persistence in a justified complaint.[100] He denounces man *en masse*, the various classes and sects, and his literary public.[101] He is defiantly unconcerned with efforts toward social and political improvement.[102] In fact, he would like to withdraw not only from social bonds but from even the slightest sensual interruption of his reveries. So the torturous and inexplicable tie of mind to body becomes his frequent lament:

> I am in the profoundest sense an unhappy individuality which from its earliest years has been bordering upon madness, which must have deeper roots in some disproportion between soul and body; for (and this is what is extraordinary) it has no relation to my mind.[103]

These themes all occur in Beckett's early works. The narrative voice of *Murphy* is misanthropic. Murphy himself has high hopes for the inner life, though the narrator's tone is already registering a dissociation from that hope:

> It is most unfortunate, but the point of this story has been reached where a justification of the expression "Murphy's mind" has to be attempted. (P. 107)

In spite of this rather heavy sarcasm, however, the narrator is clearly on the side of Murphy and his intellectualism. The hero is set off from the other characters as (in Kierkegaard's terms) an "unhappy individuality;" we feel he is right not to want to work, and right to prefer contemplation, though this attracts hostility from others, who call him "Thou surd" (p. 77). Then another stage of development ensues: complete disillusionment, not only with active life, but with mental life as well. "To live a life of blessed quiet here on earth," as another sage observed, "either matter or soul is a hindrance."[104] Since we all suffer these impediments, there is no point in stressing individuality, and accordingly the theme fades out of Beckett's works. The surd, always a favorite symbol, is retained, but now it signifies something else: futility. There is no pride in intellectuality, since thought (which never reaches a final conclusion) is as futile as everything else.

Thus Kierkegaard, whose development again parallels Beckett's, finds that knowledge is never immediately or completely available:

> I cannot understand pure revelation—the region of the spirit is intrinsically dialectical.[105]

Nor will the mediation of memory afford a better understanding:

> Life can never be understood in time simply because at no particular moment can I find the necessary place from which to understand it—backwards.[106]

In fact, the very act of remembering seems to entail an automatic disillusionment:

> He was in love, deeply and sincerely in love; that was evident, and yet at once, in one of the first few days of his engagement, he was capable of recollecting his love. Substantially he was through with the whole relationship.[107]

The didactic impulse is retained, in spite of his sorrowful uncertainty:

> Without being able to appeal to revelations, or anything of the kind, I have understood myself in having to stress the universal in a botched and demoralized age.[108]

But here is quite a problem: "obliged to write," as Beckett would say, he has nothing certain to communicate. He fears he will be faulted for unseriousness[109] and wonders if he is not vainly proud.[110]

Then necessarily, at this point, a sort of conversion is achieved. The old difficulties are accepted, in fact embraced; the problem itself becomes the solution. One will always doubt, there are no conclusions; life is nothing but a futile repetition, and this itself has been said before. With the wisdom of Ecclesiastes at his disposal, a sage's literary problems become more manageable; in fact, writing is reduced to a matter of expression:

> What makes the difference in life is not what is said, but how it is said. As for the "what" the same thing has already been said perhaps many times before—and so the old saying is true: there is nothing new under the sun, the old saying that is always new . . .[111]

Thus spoke Kierkegaard, in a development altogether typical of the introspective type. This is also the governing mood of Beckett's *Watt*, particularly Arsene's monologue; life is repetition, the knowledge of which is to no avail, and reason becomes indistinguishable from rhetoric. What next? The adoption of a thoroughgoing skepticism, in the manner of the sage paradigm Socrates, furthered Kierkegaard's development:

> How many of them ever experience the maturity of discovering that there comes a critical moment when everything is reversed, after which the point is to understand more and more that there is something which cannot be understood?
>
> This is Socratic ignorance, and this is what the philosophy of our time requires.[112]
>
> Socratic ignorance . . . is maturity, is intellectually speaking what conversion is morally and religiously, is what it means to become a child again.[113]
>
> Take Socrates for instance! In those days, one sophist after another came forward and showed that the misfortune was the lack of sufficient knowledge, more and more research was necessary, the evil was ignorance—and then along came old father Socrates saying: "no, it is precisely our ignorance which is our salvation."[114]

Just like Kierkegaard and Socrates, Beckett takes on the sage role by insisting that he, unlike most men, realizes his ignorance. As has already been observed, this is the moment of *Molloy:*

> There is no key, there is no problem. . . . I conceived of Molloy and the rest the day I became aware of my stupidity. Then I set out to write the things I sensed.[115]

But this realization need not abolish all criteria of truth. Truth takes on a new meaning, in Kierkegaard's words:

> an *objective uncertainty* held fast in an appropriation process of the most passionate inwardness.[116] (Italics mine)

"Objective uncertainty"—knowing that one knows nothing— is the goal towards which Beckett's novels resolutely move. The concluding contradictions in *Molloy* and *How It Is* indicate the ultimate uncertainty that "passionate inwardness" usually entails.

Then is the quest for certainty doomed to futility, and ceaseless? Excellent! For according to Kierkegaard:

> The ideal of a persistent striving is the only view of life that does not carry with it an inevitable disappointment.[117]

Only an unrelieved repetition, he adds,

> has not the disquietude of hope . . . nor the sadness of recollection; it has the blessed certainty of the instant.[118]

Thus the very futility of intellectual pursuits and the infinite persistence that futility requires gives the sage an opportunity for a certain heroism and satisfaction. Accordingly, Moran imagines a Sisyphus "doing the same thing over and over again . . . with satisfaction" (p. 133) and the trilogy ends with the Unnamable's "I'll go on" (p. 414). It may be difficult to feel this vacant imperative as a message, but it is one and typically sagacious. The last words of the Buddha, it is said, were "All accomplishment is transient. Strive unremittingly."[119] Similarly, a hermit once remarked of Confucius, "Is that not the man who knows that striving is without hope and yet goes on?"[120]

Here then is the typical sage's career in a nutshell: Disappointed with man, he turns to contemplation, the realm of ideas. But thought itself is found to be intrinsically futile. Doubly disillusioned, at an insoluble impasse, he undertakes a necessary transvaluation of values: ignorance and futility must be endorsed. He becomes reconciled, in Kierkegaard's wonderful phrase, to the "delights of Tantalus."[121] This is a definite process, composed of definite ideas, cohering in a definite relation. And Beckett's works reflect the same pattern of concerns: turning away from the world in disgust (*Proust*), discovering the futility of contemplation (*Murphy, Watt*), and then embracing that futility (*Molloy, Malone Dies*). However, Beckett's later works (*The Unnamable, Endgame, How It Is, The Lost Ones*) seem less concerned with sustaining this revaluation, than with underlining the inevitability of suffering, and stressing the pathos of futility. The tendency for pessimism to keep recurring in the detached intellectual was a subject also treated by Kierkegaard; and in *Either/Or* he explained that moral and ultimately religious concerns are required to bring the isolated thinker out of despair. In these maneuvers Beckett cannot follow the Christian philosopher, but neither has he been able to give the way of pure contemplative indifference an unqualified endorsement. In fact, the more completely and resourcefully his prose has reflected a commitment to philosophical detachment, the more it has betrayed an undercurrent of bitter dissatisfaction.

Consider the example of *Murphy*. At this point in Beckett's career the sage ideal still offered him considerable hope, and the book is strewn with didactic endorsements of apathy. Its most abused characters are a greedy landlady and a lecherous homosexual; those least abused are relatively indifferent to worldly desires. The heroine presses the hero to look for a job; they argue; and his assertion of passivity takes the tone of authority:

"Have I wanted to change you? Have I pestered you to begin things that don't belong to you and stop things that do? How can I care what you do?"

"I am what I do," said Celia.

"No," said Murphy. "You do what you are, you suffer a dreary ooze of your being into doing." (P. 37)

Murphy feels "in close sympathy" (p.100) with sheep. His idea of bliss is the "sensation of being a missile without provenance or target" (p.113). And yet, according to the narrator, Murphy is still not indifferent enough. He insists on making willful choices, asserting preferences; for example, he eats his crackers in inverse order of preference, saving the best for last. And merely to withhold gratification is insufficiently sagacious. As the narrator observes:

> this was to violate the very essence of assortment. . . . were he to overcome his infatuation (with certain crackers) then the assortment would spring to life before him, dancing the radiant measure of its total permutability . . . (p.97).

The total ablation of desire, then, makes the experience of "total permutability" available; the latter is the aesthetic correlative and also the reward of practicing the former. Beauty consists in absolute circularity, symmetry, and equalization, but this vision can only be a consequence of indifference; thus the narrator observes one of his characters moving with the "beautiful indifference of a shuttle" (p. 198). Similarly, Murphy's birthmark identifies his charred remains at the coroner's inquest, and the coroner, because he is indifferent to Murphy's death, finds this "beautiful in a way . . . birthmark deathmark I mean, rounding off the life somehow" (p.267). And this sort of vision, apart from its beauty, is also presented as a vision of reality, since life is conveyed as a series of endlessly recurring cycles. That outlook is established at once by the narrator's opening words, which immediately allude to Ecclesiastes:

> The sun shone, having no alternative, on the nothing new. Murphy sat out of it, as though he were free, in a mew in West Brompton. Here for what might have been six months he had eaten, drunk, slept and put his clothes on and off, in a medium-sized cage of north-western aspect commanding an unbroken view of medium-sized cages of south-eastern aspect. Soon he would have to make other arrangements, for the mew had been condemned. Soon he would have to buckle to and start eating, drinking, sleeping and putting his clothes on and off, in quite alien surroundings. (P. 1)

The structural principle of this style is simple mechanical

alternation. The second sentence mirrors the structure of the first, as the fifth repeats the fourth; like the sun, they have no alternative. Murphy's northwestern cage reflects upon many southeastern doubles; we know his activities are a pointless routine, because Beckett lists them ("eaten, drunk . . ."), and exactly repeats the list soon afterwards. Much of this symmetry and repetition seems deliberately pointless; that is, we do not need to know that Murphy puts his clothes on and off in his apartment. The narrative voice is committed to mechanically filling out each set of possibilities.

If *Murphy*'s sentences move with the beautiful indifference of a shuttle, that movement is also abrasive and meant to be abrasive. Ostentatiously patterned language conveys authority, as any bridge player knows, once he has been told that a card laid is a card played. And, in the case of *Murphy*'s style, the reader is likely to find himself resenting that authority, if only slightly — resisting it without knowing quite where to direct his resistance. The narrator observes a world in which every movement is known well before it occurs. Already weary of his wisdom, Beckett still seems less of a sage here than a wise guy, perhaps because his epigrams are always directed at unfortunates:

> But its last occupant had been a harlot, long past her best, which had been scarlet. The telephone that she found useful in her prime, in her decline she found indispensable. (P. 7)

At other times too, Beckett's delight in balanced structures seems overindulged, though the structures devised are nonetheless genuinely elegant:

> He was split, one part of him never left this mental chamber that pictured itself as a sphere full of light fading into dark, because there was no way out. But motion in this world [i. e., mental activity] depended on rest in the world outside. A man is in bed, wanting to sleep. A rat is behind the wall at his head, wanting to move. The man hears the rat fidget and cannot sleep, the rat hears the man fidget and dares not move. They are both unhappy, one fidgeting and the other waiting, or both happy, the rat moving and the man sleeping. (P. 110)

The purpose of these remarks lies in the example they contain, not what that analogy exemplifies; one credits the cleverness here, but finds it a bit self-indulgent and gratuitous too. These formal structures seem to work best when directly connected with large, philosophical statements. In the following circular list Beckett suggests a world system in which all works out perfectly for the worst; the structure here seems to both stimulate and shape his verbal energy:

> Of such was Neary's love for Miss Dwyer, who loved a Flight-Lieutenant Elliman, who loved a Miss Farren of Ringaskiddy, who loved a Father Fitt of Ballinclashet, who in all sincerity was bound to acknowledge a certain vocation for a Mrs. West of Passage, who loved Neary. (P. 5)

This is admirable because we assent to it; it seems true or at least plausible. But at the other extreme, the style also becomes interesting when it approaches nonsense, which happens in several ways. Sometimes Beckett exposes the vacancy of a cliché by slightly altering its content or extending its logic:

> Murphy, unable to believe his ears, opened his eyes. (P. 29)

> But the garret that he now saw was . . . twice as good, because half as large. (P. 162)

Sometimes his lists set up a momentum that is symmetry gone wild; obliged to perpetuate a form, the narrative voice fills out the spaces the structure dictates with nonsensical extensions.

> Artists of every kind, writers, underwriters, devils, ghosts, columnists, musicians, lyricists, organists, painters and decorators, sculptors and statuaries, critics and reviewers, major and minor, drunk and sober, laughing and crying, in schools and single, passed up and down. (Pp. 14–15)

While this is not meaningless, form is beginning to control content ("writers, underwriters . . . "), a development that is greatly accentuated in *Watt*. These irrational perpetuations of formal mechanisms are, of course, very funny:

> and perhaps because what we know partakes in no small measure of the nature of what has so happily been called the unutterable or

ineffable, so that any attempt to utter or *eff* it is doomed to fail . . . (p. 62, italics mine)

Mr Knott, having once known a man who was bitten by a dog, in the leg, and having once known another man who was scratched by a cat, in the nose, and having once known a fine healthy woman who was butted by a goat, in the loins, and having once known another man who was *disembowelled* by a bull, *in the bowels* . . . (p. 90, italics mine)

The exigencies of these forms lead Beckett into wonderful rhetorical variations; successfully meeting the challenge again and again produces true tours de force. Here he finds five euphemisms for death:

and that a younger famished dog should in the same way be pro-cured and held in readiness, against the day when the first famished dog should *die,* and that then again another famished dog should in the same way be procured and held in readiness, against the *inevitable hour* when the *second* famished dog should *pay nature's debt* . . . there being thus two famished dogs and two needy local men for ever available, the first needy local man to own and exploit the two famished dogs in the manner described as long *as he lived, and* the other then, *as long as he drew breath,* to do the same, and so on indefinitely; and that lest, as might very well hap-pen, one of the two famished dogs, or both the famished dogs, *should fail to survive their master, and follow him at once to the grave,* a third, a fourth, a fifth, and even a sixth famished dog should be acquired and suitably maintained at Mr. Knott's expense in some convenient place in a famished condition, or that better still there should be at Mr. Knott's expense on some favorable site es-tablished a kennel or colony of famished dogs from which at any time a well-bred, well-trained famished dog could be withdrawn and set to work, in the manner described; and that on the off chance of the second poor young local man's *passing over, into the beyond* . . . (Pp. 98–99, italics mine)

This is a perfectly comprehensible game, and entertains so long as the structures prod Beckett into variations. Towards the end of the book, however, similar structures cease to stimulate invention and merely repeat without variation. In everyone's opinion, *Watt* collapses into series extended *ad nauseam,* and Beckett no doubt knew this too. Why, then, did he pursue this course? For the same reason that Murphy con-

sulted a horoscope to determine his profession; because he
was indifferent to the varieties of occupation, Murphy let the
predictive structures of astrology determine his choice. Mr.
Hackett offered a parallel interpretation of Watt's behavior:

> too fearful to assume the onus of a decision, said Mr. Hackett, he
> refers it to the frigid machinery of a time-space relation. (P. 21)

The frigid machinery of Beckett's rhetorical structures likewise relieves him of decisions. Thus *Watt*'s compulsive formalism expresses, with astonishing commitment and thoroughness,
the themes that figure so prominently throughout Beckett's
works: the "ablation of desire" and "going on" when there is
no particular inducement to do so. It is the sage's ideals of indifference and passivity that dictate Watt's progressively
mechanical formalism, though in its most extreme manifestations this formalism throws all values into confusion. That is the
point of Arsene's monologue, and the point is reinforced by the
monologue's stylistic mechanisms. Similarly, when Murphy
speculates upon "the freedom of indifference, the indifference
of freedom" (p. 105), the narrator's automatic reversal of terms
implies what Molloy would put more directly: that it's all the
same and it doesn't matter. Still, that is saying something, and
the levelling of values can sustain interest as long as distinct
values are being levelled—that is, as long as some normally
interesting consideration, such as a speaker's sex life, is described (as in *Molloy*) with devaluing indifference. In *Watt*,
however, clearly trivial actions are detailed with a monotony
that is extended to the point where it becomes interesting, and
then long past that point, making tedium irremediable. Such
scenes in *Watt* as the academic examination can only be com-
prehended as attempts to construct an aesthetic correlative to
pure philosophical indifference; but what they show is that
boredom gives birth to self-punishment and cruelty.

Beckett's writing does not suggest the seductive inner freedom of the sage until the time of his first-person narrations.
And among his characters, Molloy is the most assertively
apathetic. He tells us he has "neither taste nor humour" (p. 30)
and his indistinct descriptions (e. g., "they looked alike, but no
more than others do"—p. 9) result from the indifference that
lies in the eye of their beholder. His recollections of misad-

venture all insist upon his passivity. When his protectress tried to drug him with "insipid potions," he did not refuse, for "even sipid it would have made no difference" (p. 46). He is not sure if he enjoyed "true love," or if his sexual partner put him in her rectum: "A matter of complete indifference to me, I needn't tell you" (p. 56). Then he admits "the indifference with which I learned of her death" (p. 58) and moves on to the sea, feeling "no worse there than anywhere else" (p. 67).

The problem of the sucking stones, the most protracted piece of continuous writing in *Molloy*, may seem an exception to this pattern of indifference. Molloy undoubtedly reveals an interest there, although about a matter pointedly trivial. But the resolution of the problem produces a situation of "two incompatible bodily needs at loggerheads" (p. 74) and, like Buridan's ass, Molloy is unable to choose between them. Therefore his apathy resurges:

> But deep down I didn't give a tinker's curse about being off my balance . . . And deep down it was all the same to me whether I sucked a different stone. . . . Deep down I didn't give a fiddler's curse about being without [a supply of stones]. (P. 74)

At last the narrative concludes with Molloy longing to go back into the forest; but once again his resignation reasserts itself. As his last words remind us, "Molloy could stay where he happened to be" (p. 91).

But Molloy cannot be characterized as wholly apathetic, for he usually feels a need to "go on," sometimes specifically towards his mother, more often without definite direction. Furthermore, his assertions of indifference are intrinsically paradoxical, suggesting spite as much as resignation. And as he admits, he does not always savor tranquillity:

> I was in peace for as long as I could endure peace. (P. 67)

In fact, Molloy is not wholly contented or at ease; he even attempts suicide. But, having failed, the consoling mood of indifference comes readily to comfort him:

> I wasn't particularly disappointed, in my heart of hearts I had not hoped for anything better. (P. 66)

This strange remark is typical Beckett; if Molloy is not wholly resigned, we will surely find the degree of his resignation remarkable, given his circumstances. As Germaine Brée observed,

> Beckett's characters discuss their miserable and repugnant situation very calmly; they find it not only tolerable but, on the whole, fairly good and, primarily concerned over the possibility of eviction, accept its inevitable deterioration in good spirit. When it comes to describing this situation, enumerating its advantages, discussing its resources, effecting certain improvements, hanging on, they could hardly be excelled. Inventing "begging boards" adapted to the almsgivers' psychology; fixing up a rowboat so that it is waterproof on top with a hole in the bottom . . . Beckett's characters undertake these little diversions with happy zeal . . .[122]

The phrase "happy zeal" may go a little too far, but Brée's remark is approximately right and, oddly enough, a point not often made. The prevailing mood of Beckett's outcasts, unlike Dostoevsky's or Céline's, is serenity—or perhaps an insane calm. This is less true of the Unnamable, who has lost some of his poise, than of any of the others; but on the whole, the stage direction for Beckett's *Play* might describe the tone of all his later prose:

> Faces impassive throughout. Voices toneless except where an expression is indicated.[123]

And in turn, this suppression of emotion secures Beckett's many comic effects.

Molloy's apathy is comically extreme; but it is also clear that Beckett is drawn to this condition, takes it seriously and makes it strangely appealing. His treatment of philosophical indifference suggests the glorified apathy that is a Stoic ideal, but also the depression that is more often its awful reality. Indifference, after all, is not bliss; it is merely indifference. Yet in subjecting the ideal of apathy to comic deflation, Beckett is not just criticizing a temperament; he is also satisfying the need to give it expression as well. As Molloy explains the verbal abuse of his mother,

> I called her Mag because for me, without my knowing why, the letter g abolished the syllable Ma, and as it were spat on it, better

than any other letter would have done. And at the same time I satisfied a deep and doubtless unacknowledged need, the need to have a Ma, that is a mother, and to proclaim it, audibly. (P. 17)

The same analysis can be applied to Beckett's treatment of the sage mentality. The attempt to be wise, especially to appear wise, has been utterly discredited; that seems to be the premise of his art. And yet, with what ideal can he replace contemplative tranquillity? Surely not the life of action or religion. Molloy concedes that philosophical pursuits are worthless, but also that he cannot avoid them:

And if I speak of principles, when there are none, I can't help it, there must be some somewhere. And if always doing the same thing as it were is not the same as observing the same principle, I can't help it either. And then how can you know whether you are observing it or not? And how can you want to know? No, all this is not worthwhile bothering about, and yet you do bother about it, your sense of values gone. (P. 46)

So Beckett's books can only keep asking whether the life of the mind is equal to the problem of existence and answering in the negative; but apparently the question remains worth asking, and everytime it is raised some hope is implicitly manifested. For Beckett, the sage ideal has always beckoned, though all he can conceive are failed sages.

They fail for a number of reasons, but perhaps most obviously because "the ablation of desire" is often a false economy. Those who are satisfied with little still seem to get less than what satisfies them. What Carlyle called "lowering the denominator" of need turns out, in psychic life, to entail lowering the numerator of available interests as well. The practice of looking for the least possible sustenance not only proceeds from but reinforces a negative view of life, as indicated by Molloy's witty remark:

I was limply poking about in the garbage saying probably, for at that age I must still have been capable of general ideas, This is life. (P. 57)

And while it is not true that the attainment of apathy is always a benefit, real indifference is impossible to maintain precisely when it is necessary to do so. Let us suppose, as Moran does, that we are in the position of Sisyphus or Zeno's Achilles—anyone compelled to perform an endless task. Hope, as Moran says, will indeed be hellish, leading to successive disappointments. Sooner or later, we will realize that the goal always recedes; and we will feel that this is tolerable. That is truly a great moment, a mastering of one's fate. But as we take the next few steps, compelled to go on, what thoughts will then occur? That is the question Beckett's later works —most explicitly, *The Unnamable* and *Not I*—attempt to answer. Hope is hellish, but so is hopelessness. Beckett reports a sage's consciousness, not as it precipitates into static maxims but as it actually functions, to its misery, in the flow of time.

Truth, consolation, and apathy are unattainable because consciousness is chained to time; this makes all sages failures. That contemplation has a historical development is, in itself, its own repudiation, for the goal of contemplatives, as Beckett insists in *Proust*, is always a timeless state. This, of course, is unavailable, as the Unnamable asserts:

> For others the time abolishing joys of impersonal and disinterested speculation, I only think, if that is the name of this vertiginous panic . . . (p. 350).

One of Beckett's greatest achievements is his distinctive treatment of thought as it is weighed down by time. He makes the reader feel the effect of prior reflections, as his heroes recall them among their present thoughts, and this interpenetration deflates the whole process. Great realizations, moments of conversion, revelation, or rebirth, resolutions to do better, all are moods whose claim to significance lies in their claim to permanence; they lose their meaning, not only if they are renounced, but also if they have to keep on being repeated. Or rather, they take on another meaning. The tenth conversion, if it is known to be the tenth, discredits not only the first nine but also itself and its successors. So one merely keeps going on.

This vision is nowhere more elegantly realized than in *Krapp's Last Tape*, Beckett's most perfect work and the epitome of his thought. There are several levels of time suggested in the play, arranged to convey an infinite regress. Krapp, an old man, listens to a tape of reflections made perhaps thirty years before; but that tape comments on another one made by the younger Krapp, which no doubt contained such commentary too. After listening, Krapp makes yet another tape. As the play concludes, he is once again listening to the tape heard earlier.

The bulk of the play's text is the tape made in early middle-age, when Krapp is "intellectually at the crest of the wave" (p. 14; by permission of Grove Press, New York, 1957) and "can't believe he was ever that young whelp" (p. 16), that is, the Krapp of a prior recording. Like all diarists, Krapp is attempting to orient himself favorably in the flow of time, finding the present moment the best of all possible situations. He looks down on the past and future from a sort of summit, "at the crest of the wave," as he says. Maintaining this control or illusion of control requires two operations: renouncing the past and making resolutions about the future. Thus Krapp is always disparaging his former self and circumstances. Of an earlier love affair, he remarks, "well out of that" (p. 16). And, since he can't have the past back, he might just as well renounce it. The comedy and pathos of a sour-grapes attitude are evident here:

> Perhaps my best years are gone. When there was a chance of happiness. But I wouldn't want them back. Not with the fire in me now. No, I wouldn't want them back. (P. 28)

The purpose of Krapp's constant self-disparagement is to affirm his present self at the expense of his former self. But the voice that called his younger self a "young whelp" is in turn found to be

> that stupid bastard I took myself for thirty years ago, hard to believe I was ever as bad as that. (P. 24)

As these criticisms supersede one another, the whole process comes to seem inauthentic. Similarly, Krapp's tapes are filled with futile resolutions. The tape made in middle age is entitled "Farewell to Love," but even at this time Krapp was scoffing at his juvenile "plans for a less engrossing sexual life" (p. 16), that is, at still earlier resolutions to the same effect. And the old man at present upon the stage persists in whoring—not to mention drinking and eating bananas, vices renounced in previous tapes.

Clearly, the play is about futility and, more particularly, the futility of thought. Krapp's tapes are worthless to him if he cannot understand them, and this is now becoming the case; he is utterly baffled by much of the language and interests familiar to his former self (e. g., "viduity," "Black ball," "memorable equinox"—p. 13). And age destroys not only his mental powers but also his ideals. An earlier tape describes a love scene in rather lyrical language:

> We drifted in among the flags and stuck. The way they went down, sighing, before the stem! (*pause*) I lay down across her with my face in her breasts and my hand on her. We lay there without moving. But under us all moved, and moved us, gently, up and down, and from side to side. (P. 27)

To this Beckett juxtaposes the romantic language of the older man:

> Fanny came in a couple of times. Bony old ghost of a whore. Couldn't do much, but I suppose better than a kick in the crutch. (P. 25)

Still, Krapp's failure is not merely due to aging, for even at the crest of the wave he was enmeshed in futility. The tender love scene itself is an instance of this, though here he accepts futility gracefully enough:

> *I said again I thought it was hopeless and no good going on, and she agreed,* without opening her eyes. (*Pause*) I asked her to look at me and after a few moments—(*Pause*)—after a few moments she did, but the eyes just slits, because of the glare. I bent over her to get them in the shadow and they opened. (*Pause. Low.*) Let me in. (P. 22, italics mine)

Understandably, it is to this section of tape that the old man keeps returning. But more significant still is what he avoids —the record of what once seemed a deathless revelation:

> Spiritually a year of profound gloom and indigence until that memorable night in March, at the end of the jetty, in the howling wind, never to be forgotten, when *suddenly I saw the whole thing.* The vision at last. This I fancy *is what I have chiefly to record* this

evening, against the day when my work will be done and perhaps
no place left in my memory, warm or cold, for the miracle . . .
(hesitates) . . . for the fire that set it alight. What I suddenly saw
then was this, that *the belief I had been going on all my life, namely*
—(Krapp switches off impatiently, winds tape forward, switches
on again)—great granite rocks the foam flying up in the light of the
lighthouse and the wind-gauge spinning like a propeller, *clear to
me at last that the dark I have always struggled to keep under is
in reality my most*—(Krapp curses, switches off, winds tape forward, switches on again) . . . (pp. 20–21, italics mine).

Thus the vision that was never to be forgotten is still being
kept under. Perhaps it remains unbearable; perhaps it was
merely insignificant, making the hope it once inspired an unbearable memory now. In any case, it was not the answer to
Krapp's spiritual problems, as he formerly thought. And what
compounds the irony is that this great moment was apparently
another version of the sage's typical maneuver—a revaluation
of failure ("the dark I have always struggled to keep under is
in reality my most"). Such reflections do not bring peace and
are not a release; they are merely one more strand of obsession
in the endless, insipid delirium of life.

At the play's conclusion Krapp is "motionless staring before
him. The tape runs on in silence" (p. 28). Perhaps he is pon-
dering the same "unanswerable question" considered by Mrs.
Lambert in *Malone Dies*—what's the use?" (p. 208). For each
tape disowns its predecessor, and yet he goes on making them.
It is this futile repetition that the play dramatizes, and in the
concluding moments of silence the play's emotional intensity
attains a new plane; what had seemed comic and pathetic
—Krapp's life of meaningless routine—now seems an awesome mystery as well. The audience will agree with poor
Krapp in finding the language of his earlier days overblown
and excessive, but they will absolve him by concurring with
Moran that "all language is an excess of language (p. 116). The
only fit response to the spectacle of Krapp's situation is silence
and astonishment.

In *Krapp's Last Tape*, Beckett has no need of philosophical
allusions, for the tapes provide the same effects his allusions
normally supply. Krapp is a failed sage; his tapes form his own
sage tradition and the repetition of his concerns both dis-

credits and amplifies them. Similarly, but on a larger plane, Beckett's allusions to philosophers comment on the failure of philosophical tradition, the futile repetition of philosophical activity. This commentary authorizes his own pessimism; but at the same time, the evocation of the sage tradition lends dignity and weight to the preoccupations of Beckett's heroes—thoughts usually fleeting and trivial in themselves. All of his writing can be regarded as successive versions of Lucky's speech in *Waiting for Godot,* a testament to the futility of philosophical labors; but while this testament is pathetic and nearly incoherent, it does not lower Lucky in the audience's estimation. There is something awesome in the persistence of his consciousness.

At least since Aristotle, man has been defined as a creature of consciousness, as opposed to instinct, instinctive behavior consisting of purposive action without consciousness of purpose.[124] It has always been recognized that man could suffer from excessive consciousness, and be "sicklied o'er with the pale cast of thought," but Beckett's critique of consciousness goes much further than this and questions whether awareness of purpose ever has any value. Moran studies his bees' dance, wondering what its purpose is and whether bees "are capable of such notions" as conscious intention (p. 169). But the implication here is that their dance would be in no way enhanced by such awareness. Lichtenberg, the German aphorist, once remarked that

> Perhaps a dog, shortly before it falls asleep, or a drunken elephant has ideas which would not be unworthy of a master of philosophy. But these are of no use to them.[125]

According to Beckett, they are of no use to the master of philosophy either. Consequently, his speakers all disclaim having any good reason for expressing themselves, and Beckett's writing exhausts the standard poses of excuse: ignorance, insanity, and "obligation."

Such an approach can be termed neither tragic or comic; it is tragicomic. The narrative structures of Beckett's works, rather than leaving the reader with a definitive sense of completion, suggest a situation infinitely perpetuated. If comedies end well and tragedies unhappily (though with a consoling sense

of order reaffirmed), the characteristic conclusion of tragicomedy is endlessness. Beckett calls *Waiting for Godot* a
"tragicomedy in two acts" because the second act substantially repeats the first, leaving the audience with no anticipation other than that of the tramps "going on."

To the same end, the most continuous principle of Beckett's
style is indecorum, an astonishing juxtaposition of attitudes
that effects a sustained emotional paradox. "Tears and laughter," Molloy says, "they are so much Gaelic to me" (p. 37). And
one simply does not know how to respond to this passage from
Watt:

> Birds of every kind abounded, and these it was our delight to
> pursue, with stones and clods of earth. Robins, in particular, thanks
> to their confidingness, we destroyed in great numbers. And larks'
> nests, laden with eggs still warm from the mother's breast, we
> ground into fragments, under our feet, with peculiar satisfaction, at
> the appropriate season of the year.
>
> But our particular friends were the rats, that dwelt by the stream.
> They were long and black. We brought them such tidbits from our
> ordinary as rinds of cheese and morsels of gristle and we brought
> them also birds' eggs and frogs and fledglings. Sensible of these
> attentions, they would come flocking round us at our approach,
> with every sign of confidence and affection, and glide up our
> trouser legs and hang upon our breasts. And then we would sit
> down in the midst of them and give them to eat, out of our hands,
> of a nice fat frog, or a baby thrush. Or seizing suddenly a plump
> young rat, resting in our bosom after its repast, we would feed it
> to its mother, or its father, or its brother, or its sister, or to some
> less fortunate relative.
>
> It was on these occasions, we agreed, after an exchange of views,
> that we came nearest to God. (Pp. 155–56)

This offensive raillery that cannot be taken seriously because
it is so laughable, but which cannot be dismissed because it is
so disturbing, is the essence of the tragicomic voice. What is
typical here is the blend of archaic, literary language ("sensible of these attentions") with the unexpected violence it describes. Random and excessive violence abounds in Beckett's
works, as in Shakespeare's tragicomedies (e. g., *Measure for
Measure*); this is characteristic of the genre. The same is true

of *Candide*, where unmerited violence expresses an antiop-
timistic, anti-idealistic meaning, and also *Don Quixote* (aptly
described in a phrase of Beckett's as a "tragicomedy of the
solipsism that will not capitulate").[126] The point is not that
Don Quixote or Candide deserve their lumps (any more than
Beckett's victims do); indeed, life is bad. And it is natural to
laugh, not in spite of this vision but because of it.

Part Two: Beckett's Thought in *Proust*

Chapter 1

Approach to *Proust:* Nihilism, Spite, and Misanthropy

He took a curious attitude of hostility toward final causes,
optimism, free will and, in short, against all those philo-
sophic opinions which tend to raise the dignity of man.
— *Madame de Staël (on Voltaire)*

This division of the study differs primarily from the forego-
ing by focussing on Beckett's ideas in a single work, *Proust.*
The difference, however, is not merely one of focus but also
one of attitude. Until now I have been arguing against the
view that Beckett's writing is absolutely meaningless, im-
penetrable, unique, or unserious; I have been trying to show
that Beckett's ideas constitute a pessimistic and skeptical
meaning that is not only definite, but highly traditional. Now I
shall try to show how unique and extreme his mentality is too.
Proust is the most convenient text for this purpose, because it
presents Beckett in the act of interpreting an author concerned
with the same philosophical problems as himself, but one who
observed those problems with different emotions and responded to them with different solutions.

Proust is also a useful focal point because Beckett's chief
concerns are either already expressed in it or most readily
understood when considered as answers to the problems
raised by that youthful book. The distinctive mentality expressed in Beckett's major works—his later heroes' endorsements of futility and ignorance and their virtually complete
indifference to moral concerns—seems puzzling and absurd

because the value of these attitudes is not immediately seen. But these attitudes are the logical solutions to the problems which constitute *Proust*'s pessimistic description of life. If man can never be free from compulsion or satisfy his desires or attain certain knowledge, then it is only reasonable to "work with impotence [and] ignorance,"[1] as Beckett has done. Without such a resolve, the mood of resentment and nihilistic misanthropy, which is the governing tone of *Proust,* will predominate and remain predominant. It is because Beckett has chosen to investigate these odd revaluations that his thought is not entirely nihilistic. But a close consideration of the arguments set forth in *Proust* suggests that Beckett has offered the logical solutions to unnecessary problems, problems derived from an analytical understanding of consciousness which is highly open to question itself.

In any case, *Proust* is a remarkable book, if not for its ideas (though these merit attention), then for the extremity and militance of its tone. Conceptually, *Proust*'s description of the human condition offers nothing other than a perennial philosophy, almost pretentiously derivative: what Beckett calls "the wisdom of all the sages, from Brahma to Leopardi."[2] This appeal to ancient wisdom is characteristic of modern pessimists; Schopenhauer and Leopardi defended themselves in the same manner, and it is easy to see why they felt themselves driven to that defense. It is true that pessimists are generally obsessed with logic, strict logic, and make a considerable show of it, for as A. O. Lovejoy pointed out, "logical necessities are eternal, and the evils which arise from them must be perpetual."[3] And yet, however perfect his proofs may seem, a pessimist's conclusions remain abnormal. He will always be told that his views are pathological projections or, more simply, "sick" — in any case, temperamental in origin rather than the inescapable deductions they claim to be. Thus, dismissed as an eccentric in spite of his irrefutable reasoning, the pessimist must appeal to some prestigious norm, so he cloaks himself with "the wisdom of all the sages." Furthermore, by acknowledging his ancient forerunners, the pessimist exemplifies the futile repetition he laments; there is nothing new under the sun, and the very antiquity of the idea confirms it.

Still, Beckett's critics have generally dismissed the traditional pessimism so essential to *Proust*, focussing instead on the book's more peripheral concerns. Richard Coe attributes Beckett's interest in Proust to the latter's doctrine of the timeless inner self;[4] Hugh Kenner thinks Beckett must have found Proust's concept of involuntary memory especially appealing.[5] However, each of these views derives from the needless and probably false assumption that Beckett was interested in Proust's unique ideas or something especially Proustian. In fact, the pattern of emphasis in *Proust* indicates that Beckett found his subject chiefly useful as a source of pessimistic commonplaces; clearly, he used the study of Proust as an occasion for voicing these commonplaces, though attributing them to Proust sometimes required distortion.

Despite its pessimistic bias, Beckett's first book remains, as its critics allow, a penetrating study of Proust. Nonetheless, both the style and content of *Proust* have come in for sharp attack, the former for various excesses, the latter for triteness. Clearly, these qualities derive from Beckett's earnest and intense didacticism, and, viewed from that perspective, perhaps his first book seems more interesting than faulty. No one escapes Beckett's blame; *Proust* is the manifesto of an ostentatiously alienated sensibility, obsessed with neglected truths and crying them out in the wilderness.

This is already apparent in the foreword to *Proust*, where, in place of the conventional tone of acknowledgement, Beckett's voice bristles with self-assertion, eager to disclaim apparent indebtedness and randomly railing against any available object:

> There is no allusion in this book to the legendary life and death of Marcel Proust, nor to the garrulous old dowager of the Letters, nor to the poet, nor to the author of the Essays, nor to the Eau de Selzian correlative of Carlyle's "beautiful bottle of soda-water." I have preferred to retain the titles in French. The translations of the text are my own. The references are to the abominable edition of the *Nouvelle Revue Francaise*, in sixteen volumes.[6]

The abrupt discontinuity of these remarks places Proust's style at a polar remove from Beckett's later writing, particularly the trilogy. *Proust*'s manner is one of brash and unexplained announcement; in the trilogy, Beckett's style is welded by defensiveness; it is hesitant, heavily qualified, even full of

contradictions. Molloy's sentences look back upon their predecessors, apologizing with paranoid scrupulousness for possible sources of offense in them:

> But another who might have been my mother, and even I think my
> grandmother, if chance had not willed otherwise. Listen to him
> now talking about chance. (P. 56; by permission of Grove Press,
> New York, 1965)

Here Molloy anticipates, so as to ward off, objections that no
audience would make. And, furthering the course of this development, the Unnamable admits that all of his thoughts are
objectionable, often more or less successfully contradicting
himself; abandoning the sentence form, he lacks, as it were,
the courage to make an unqualified declaration. Thus the tone
of Beckett's later works is predominantly apologetic and, in
comparison, *Proust* seems a strikingly naked assertion of hostility. Indeed, the young Beckett's attacks against random
targets seem to derive from a fundamental and indiscriminate
malice, an unqualified misanthropy.

Proust himself was no stranger to that sentiment:

> I concluded all the same from this first evening that his [Morel's]
> must be a vile nature, that he would not, at a pinch, shrink from any
> act of meanness, was incapable of gratitude. In which he resem-
> bled the majority of mankind.[7]

But more often Proust revealed a tolerant, even affectionate
regard for man's faults, together with the sort of worldly
sophistication that precludes such sweeping ethical judgments. Beckett's misanthropy exceeds and does not derive
from Proust's. Rather, it results from his own hopeless but still
retained idealism—a set of demands whose impossible strict-
ness guarantees disillusionment. *Proust* shows the cruelty of
these ideals.

While all of Beckett's works conceive life as futile, in *Proust*
that concept seems connected with resentment and exasperation, because Beckett is requiring something more; Moran, on
the other hand, can imagine a Sisyphus "filled with satisfaction" (p. 133). The latter attitude is most readily understood in
relation to the former; Beckett's distinctive tone develops in
the direction of bizarre tolerance as a cultivated alternative to

the bitterness of *Proust* and his other early writings. His skepticism is a corresponding development. Whereas *Proust* describes the limitations of human experience in a tone of outlandish assurance, Beckett's later writing voices a continual confession of ignorance. Consequently, Beckett's youthful misanthropy has gradually become more moderated and controlled, for a helpless humanity, ignorant of its impotence, need not be scorned if ignorance and impotence can be valued or at least accepted.

Proust purposes to separate humanity into those who face reality—the author—and those who do not—virtually the rest of mankind. In Beckett's subsequent books, that distinction becomes successively blurred, then altogether abandoned. *Murphy* deals with a group of intellectuals who voice more or less the same ideas as those advanced in *Proust*, yet Beckett's narrative voice derides them too and in a somewhat smug, authoritative tone. In *Watt* the scope of authority is further reduced. Both hero and nominal narrator are "mad," and the book's sole voice of wisdom (Arsene's) admits that his is a "useless knowledge, dearly won."[8] The plot of *Molloy* recapitulates Beckett's preceding development: a knower and blamer (Moran) converts to attitudes of ignorance and indifference (Molloy). In *Malone Dies*, there are no knowers and thus neither objects nor voices to blame; faced with death, the hero consoles himself with fantasy, then loses his sense of what is fictional and real. Those very categories seem irrelevant to *The Unnamable*, which is built on a rhetoric of successive contradiction. And the narrator of *How It Is* admits his whole tale is a lie.

This apparently negative development must have reduced some psychic tensions, for Beckett's heroes in time acquire what his works have always recommended—tranquillity. The youthful author of *Proust*, in evident perplexity and contradiction, could only advocate serenity in anger; but the heroes of Beckett's later works, finding a certain measure of peace in incuriosity, exhibit an entrancing emotional detachment. So it seems that Beckett's major works, to use his own term, have acted as "Calmatives"—proposing solutions, both explicitly and in their stylistic rhythms, to the problems a spiteful misanthropy (his original attitude) presented. Of course Beckett's later heroes are very strange and wholly removed from normal society, but they no longer rationalize their removal with righteous indignation. Indeed, they go to the other extreme and never make moral or intellectual judgments.

In *Proust*, on the other hand, Beckett's contentiousness is so vehement and promiscuous as to seem wholly without basis. Here he derides a baffling array of literary figures: Gide, Nietzsche, Constant, Curtius, Leibniz, Cocteau, Chateaubriand, and Amiel are each briefly but violently attacked. And this gallery of knaves is so diverse, their particular offenses so minimally (at times, misleadingly) indicated, that it seems impossible to find an inclusive and consistent basis for Beckett's wrath. No formulation, it appears, can contain this hate; there is simply a surplus of malice here, released for its own sake. In fact, however, the contentious tone of *Proust* is not always present; it is absent when Beckett discusses Proust's affirmations (e. g., the ideal basis of art and involuntary memory) and present only in support of Proust's rejections, that is, when Beckett defends Proust's pessimism. Although Beckett says that Proust "makes a demonstration of damnation and salvation" and dutifully reports the demonstration of the latter, all his energies are devoted to attacking views less negative than Proust's—never views less positive (p. 1). Beckett knows, then, what he does not want, if only that; he does not want what he considers sentimental cant. He naturally opposes critical attempts to minimize Proust's pessimism (Curtius); philosophical optimism, of course (Leibniz); but also more threatening and complicated stances, which admit the "problem of existence" but find some consolation, whether in langourous melancholy (Constant, Chateaubriand, Amiel) or strenuous self-affirmation (Gide, Nietzsche).

Granting his rancor this degree of consistency, the reader will find that the scope and tone of Beckett's hostility remain remarkable and full of problematical implications. His lengthiest diatribe, this scathing attack upon Gide and his followers, leads to some interesting difficulties:

> At this point, and with a heavy heart and for the satisfaction or disgruntlement of Gideans, semi and integral, I am inspired to concede a brief parenthesis to all the analogivorous, who are capable of interpreting the "Live dangerously," that victorious hiccough in vacuo, as the national anthem of the true ego exiled in habit. The Gideans advocate a habit of living—and look for an epithet. . . .

They imply a hierarchy of habits, as though it were valid to speak
of good habits and bad habits. An automatic adjustment of the human
organism to the conditions of its existence has as little moral significance as the casting of a clout when May is or is not out; and the
exhortation to cultivate a habit as little sense as the exhortation to
cultivate a coryza. (Pp. 8–9)

The relatively maladroit verbal play in Beckett's early writing
usually marks, as here, some intense and localized controversy. I do not say that rage in itself must always be a bad
thing; but Beckett's most hostile writing, even later, as in
Happy Days, is usually unappealing, infelicitous. Here he responds to Gide with a graceless display of learning
("analogivorous," "cast a clout," "coryza"); the resultant tone
seems to make a contrived and unconvincing claim to authority. But the eccentricity of this language is no mere mannerism; it corresponds, in its privacy, to Beckett's isolated
moral viewpoint. After all, who does not think it "valid to
speak of good habits and bad habits?" Surely common sense
and social life require such distinctions. But Beckett is determined to maintain, above all else, that the human condition is
inevitably constant, making the cultivation of moral or
spiritual attitudes or even behavioral patterns absurdly pointless, since these regimens are supposed to make a difference
and nothing really does. In this case, with an altogether
characteristic mental gesture, Beckett points out that a regular
impulsiveness is really just another habit, the apparent exception (as always) proving the rule. In short, man is trapped,
hopelessly doomed to perpetual motions of futility. And time
has only confirmed this view; in Beckett's recent *The Lost
Ones* life is specifically envisioned as a futile attempt to escape from a futile condition.

"When the great thinker scorns man," according to
Nietzsche, "he is actually scorning [man's] inertia";[9] that is
what Beckett seems to be doing here and throughout *Proust*.
In fact, Beckett's criticism of Gide, focusing upon the valuelessness of habit because it is an "automatic adjustment," is
strikingly similar to Nietzsche's fulmination against the English moralists, who look

for the effective motive forces of human development in the very
last place we would wish to have it found, e. g., in the inertia of
habit, in forgetfulness, in the blind and fortuitous association of

ideas: always in something that is purely passive, *automatic,* reflexive, molecular, and moreover, profoundly stupid.[10] (Italics mine)

But since Beckett finds inertia inescapable, it seems pointless to blame those who suffer it. Perhaps for that reason, Beckett directs his rage more specifically against those who delude themselves about this (e. g., Gide) into thinking spontaneity available. Still, why blame even them—especially if the matter is of no "moral significance?" The philosophical perspective of *Proust* makes any morality an irrelevant consideration; and Beckett explicitly draws the amoralistic conclusion himself. At the time of *Proust,* he was a prophet without a platform, railing at mankind but convinced that human nature could not be redeemed. And that is a position at least very close to nihilism—defined by Nietzsche as "the radical repudiation of [all] value, meaning, desirability."[11]

Nietzsche's sympathetic critique of nihilism is worth looking into because it helps explain Beckett's position in *Proust;* and since Nietzsche is also mentioned by name in that book he seems to have actually influenced Beckett at this point. The latter's most frequent term of abuse at this time was "vulgar," and his rage against the "mob, plebs, rabble, canaille" suggests Nietzsche's similar invective against the "herd"[12] Some of the arguments Beckett advances in support of an extreme skeptical relativism may also have been derived from Nietzsche's thought. At the time of *Proust,* however, it appears that Beckett was breaking away from Nietzsche's influence, since he attacks the philosopher rather gratuitously. As is evident elsewhere in *Proust,* he would really like to attack some of Nietzsche's basic attitudes, but Beckett's animus expresses itself in an unfair and trivial manner. While reporting and seconding Proust's dim view of friendship, Beckett attributes the alternative view (the praise of friendship) to Nietzsche (p. 47); but Proust's novel does not make that attribution, nor is Nietzsche's view of friendship at all a central (or particularly characteristic) point of his thought.[13] Beckett does the same sort of thing, by the way, with Leibniz; the notorious optimist is derided, in passing, not for his optimism but for his view of music. This sort of misdirection exemplifies what I meant by Beckett's rage being out of control; and this is just what Nietzsche talks about in his own critique of nihilism.

Nietzsche's analysis, perhaps surprisingly, articulates the plainest common sense. On the one hand, recognizing the scope and independence of the nihilist's vision, he commends it as a spiritual achievement—"a sign of increased power of the spirit."[14] On the other hand, at the same time, like almost everyone, he finds nihilism excessive and "sick":

The nihilist's eye idealizes in the direction of ugliness . . .[15]

Nihilism represents a *pathological* transitional stage (what is pathological is the *tremendous generalization,* the inference that there is no meaning at all . . .)[16] (Italics mine)

Nietzsche's fuller explanation of the nihilistic mentality captures the spirit of *Proust* exactly:

the nihilistic consequence (the belief in valuelessness) as a consequence of moral valuation: everything egoistic has come to disgust us (even though we recognize the impossibility of the unegoistic); what is necessary has come to disgust us (even though we recognize the impossibility of any *liberum arbitrium* [free will] or intelligible freedom). We see that we cannot reach the sphere in which we have placed our values; but this does not by any means confer any value on that other sphere in which we live: on the contrary, we are weary because we have lost the main stimulus. "In vain so far."[17]

As Nietzsche's analysis suggests, Beckett's nihilism originates in disappointed (because inappropriate) moral expectations. For example, he requires a life without habit. And having discovered the impossibility of the demand does not prompt him to reconsider it; however unavoidable, habit seems nonetheless disgusting. The result is a mood of impotent frustration: "In vain so far." What, more precisely, is in vain? The nihilist's knowledge. Having intuited the inescapable misery of human life, the nihilist knows he is nonetheless subject to that misery. Like the author of Ecclesiastes, Beckett's rage is specifically that of a disappointed intellectual; he resents most keenly the fact that the wise man fares no better than the fool. The Preacher formulated the classic statement of this particular nihilistic inference:

For there is no remembrance of the wise man more than the fool for
ever; seeing that which now is in the days to come shall all be
forgotten. And how dieth the wise man? as the fool. (2: 16)

Therefore I hated life. (2: 17, italics mine)

But note that in spite of this realization, both Beckett and the
Preacher retain the need to assert their knowledge, to edify as
well as condemn. As Nietzsche said, "nihilism . . . is full of
morality that is not overcome."[18] An active state of disillusionment, such as Beckett's petulant resentment, requires that
some ideals and values still be felt behind it; though regarded
as illusions, they still to some extent retain their force.
Nihilism can then be regarded as a moralistic manner without
moral content, the need to condemn having survived the conscious discreditation of judgmental standards. And this would
have been granted by the author of *Proust* himself. The youthful Beckett was quite conscious of his futile resentment as
such; the title of his first novel, a reworking of the biblical
phrase "kicking against the pricks," clearly indicates that
realization.

Then what prompted Beckett's attack upon Nietzsche? Not
the latter's critique of nihilism, but rather the positive side of
Nietzsche's thought. Nietzsche asserted the wish to transcend
ethics, or good and evil, but he was never without values, or,
in his own terms, a sense of good and bad. Among these values, which he thought of as instincts, he most especially recommended direct expressions of will, discharges of power.
But the youthful Beckett, taking part here with Nietzsche's
rejected mentor Schopenhauer, deplored that above all else.
And thus the embodiment of large-minded energy Nietzsche
invoked is alluded to derisively in *More Pricks than Kicks* (p.
135). This superior being, an immoralist, sees life as structures
of power perpetually breaking down and building up again—
and is content that this and nothing more significant should be
the case. The trouble with that philosophy, to Beckett's way of
thinking, lies in the insufficient extremity of its nihilism.
Finding fault with prevalent values, showing the groundless-
ness of value systems generally, Nietzsche still clung to some
ideals, particularly the value of power. It was as the
philosopher for self-assertion, by the way, that Nietzsche
served as a source and model for Gide's *Immoralist*. And both

Gide and Nietzsche suggested that, on their basis at least, life might actually be worth living. That is what really rankles Beckett, who finds Gide's Nietzschean exhortation to "live dangerously," despite its satanic style, too fundamentally affirmative, in fact just one more instance of "our smug will to live, our pernicious and incurable optimisim.[19]

In general, the targets of Beckett's hostility in *Proust* are proponents of such an ameliorated pessimism. This is the source of his dispute with Ernst Curtius, the philologist and a rival critic of Proust:

> Curtius speaks of Proust's perspectivism and "positive relativism" as opposed to the negative relativism of the late nineteenth century, the skepticism of Renan and France. I think the phrase "positive relativism" is an oxymoron, I am almost sure that it does not apply to Proust, and I know that it came out of the Heidelberg laboratory. We have seen how in the case of Albertine (and Proust extends his experience to all human relations) the multiple aspects (read Blinckpundt for that miserable word) did not bind themselves into any positive synthesis. The object evolves, and by the time the conclusion is reached, it is already out of date. In a sense Proust is a positivist, but his positivism has nothing to do with his relativism, which is as pessimistic as that of France . . . (p. 65)

Here Beckett is rejecting an attempt to tone down Proust's negativism. This particular attack on Curtius, while perhaps justified in itself, reveals Beckett's habitual intolerance of qualification, his refusal to think in terms of degree. Throughout *Proust*, this intolerance is rationalized by Beckett's assault on the very concept of continuity or extension. Like Zeno of Elea, one of the philosophers Beckett most frequently cites, he simply will not allow that a continuum (such as Gide's "hierarchy of good habits and bad habits") is intelligible. And this sort of philosophical speculation is not, as some critics have suggested, merely toying with thought; it relates directly to Beckett's deep-rooted temperamental ambivalence and extremity.[27] Correlative with his philosophical rejection of the continuum, each of his critical judgments must be an all-or-nothing matter. Unfortunately, that tendency leads to some needlessly extreme assertions: Constant's classic *Adolphe*, for example, is compared to Proust's study of love and found "a petulant dribbling, the mock-epic of salivary hypersecretion" (p. 38).

Beckett generally champions Proust with intense fervor, but there are some confusing exceptions. I am not referring to his objections to Proust's political interests and personal sociability (e. g., on p. 49); these are coherent enough, following consistently from Beckett's more purely pessimistic and alienated temperament. But some of the sarcasm simply resists that (or any) explanation. Why the derisive reference to Proust's style, which Beckett elsewhere energetically defends, as a "treasury of nutshell phrases" (p. 17)? It is also difficult to account for the following reference, vaguely deprecatory in tone, to Proust's concept of involuntary memory. Beckett calls it

> the pearl that may give the lie to our carapace of paste and pewter. May—when we escape into the spacious annexes of mental alienation, in sleep of the rare dispensation of waking madness. From this deep source Proust hoisted his world. His work is not an accident, but its salvage is an accident. The conditions of that accident will be revealed at the peak of this prevision. A second-hand climax is better than none. But no purpose can be served by witholding the name of the diver. Proust calls him "Involuntary Memory."
> (P. 19)

Perhaps this is the proper way to cast such a "pearl" before a swinish audience. But Beckett's antipathy does not seem to be limited to his audience. The cleverly extended metaphor ("hoisted . . . salvage . . . diver") also seems to present the concept of involuntary memory and its author, Proust, with withering contempt. But why? This is not made clear; Beckett makes no explicit objection to involuntary memory's efficacy. It might be concluded that his sarcasm here is simply inexplicable and thus an instance of that intermittent lack of good taste which marks all of Beckett's early writing. But there is a basis for this lack of discrimination, a reason why Beckett felt he must attack his favorites too. He would have liked, I think, to make entirely unqualified assertions of taste; but he knew that value judgments (such as would be involved in praising Proust) can never be grounded in absolute certainty, only in partial and relative considerations. Kierkegaard has perfectly expressed this realization and its consequent reaction. Because impossibly extreme demands secure perpetual dissatisfaction, one chooses to will that dissatisfaction:

Content—entirely and absolutely and in every way content—one never becomes, and to be tolerably content is not worth the trouble, so it is better to be entirely discontented.[20]

I am saying that *Proust* is governed by one vexatious obsession: that all human actions imply their own unending futility. And at the time of *Proust*, this obsession was centering on certain exasperating antinomies. Like Schopenhauer, Beckett wanted to abolish willfulness, but he knew that this required a willful effort; like Nietzsche, he wanted to transcend ethics, but he knew that this implied an ethic. Yet more significant than these particular problems is the bent of mind underlying them. The point is that in every case, in every thought, Beckett sees a meaningless assertion, contradicting itself by virtue of its apprehension of itself—an endless, tangled spiral. Such a vision can eventuate in a mad, wild sort of wit or in a resigned aestheticism or in what T. E. Hulme called the "religious attitude" (meaning self-denial and fideism) or in what Adler termed the inferiority complex.[21] In Beckett's case, at the time he was writing *Proust*, it led chiefly to a mood of childish spite, a misanthropic nihilism so inclusive that it led him to attack (in lieu of himself) his dearest values and his favorite works of art.

Chapter 2

Beckett, Proust, and Schopenhauer

Reason is the philosophy which is in vogue at the moment.

—Schopenhauér

Proust provides an excellent opportunity to describe the tone and range of Beckett's pessimism, by comparing the latter's interpretations with Proust's actual thought. Consistently, and not always fairly, Beckett strives to make the many-sided Proust seem little more than a pessimistic sage, an extreme, thoroughgoing expounder of a rigorous intellectual system that "damns the life of the body on earth as a pensum and reveals the meaning of the word: 'defunctus' " (p. 1; by permission of Grove Press, New York, 1960). Of course Proust's own pessimism is extensive and not merely a matter of mood; the events of his novel are shaped to a significant extent by a pessimistic vision, and Proust takes care to support that vision with a full set of philosophical formulations, amounting almost to a system. Nonetheless, Beckett ignores another side of Proust, a number of related factors that counterbalance his pessimism.

Does Proust's book really damn the life of the body on earth? And reveal the meaning of the word *defunctus*—that is, emphasize the fact of death? On the contrary, Proust's novel is explicitly dedicated to rescuing experience from oblivion.[1] Thus Proust asserts, as a general principle in support of that end,

the philosophy . . . according to which everything is destined to oblivion, is less true than a contrary philosophy which would predict the conservation of everything.[2]

137

And what sort of experience does Proust think worth conserving? The visions that emerge from his narrator's fateful teacup consist of

> flowers or houses or people, permanent and recognizable, and the flowers in [his] garden and in Mr. Swann's park, and the water-lilies on the Vivonne and the good folk of the village and their little dwellings and the parish church and the whole of Combray and of its surroundings . . .[3]

In other words, Proust's hero records a whole welter of natural and social phenomena, "the life," one might say, of the "body on earth," and in a tone which affectionately distances and diminishes this world rather than damns it. It is in Beckett's books, of course, that the beauties of nature are made to seem irrelevant, social life becomes an infernal pecking order generally not worth noticing, and physical life a succession of agonies. This is not to condemn Beckett's works but to point out that their predominantly grotesque sensibility emphasizes pain, whereas the dominant emphasis in Proust's writing is on pleasurable sensations. This cannot be ignored while drawing conclusions about Proust's view of life, because the pessimism formulated in Proust's philosophical prose is qualified by his descriptive writing.

Even if Beckett is allowed the liberty of focussing on Proust's philosophy and literary theory, his account of these formulations is itself one-sided. There are, to be sure, many pessimistic statements in Proust's novel; these are important and Beckett elucidates them brilliantly. However, he ignores Proust's various criticisms of pessimism. First of all, Proust points out that pessimism, like optimism, is a generalized rationalization of specific and intense emotions; it is these emotions, he thinks, that are more "real" and important than such philosophical attitudes. Here he distinguishes pessimism from grief:

> grief is in no way a pessimistic conclusion drawn freely from a number of lamentable circumstances, but it is the intermittent and involuntary revival of a specific impression, come to us from without and not chosen by us.[4]

The point is that pessimism is merely a cultivated and second-hand reflection of experience, not experience itself, which is the artist's main concern. Worse still, Proust found that pessimism, skepticism, and related other-worldly attitudes are often insincere social poses. In the manner of La Rochefoucauld, he portrays Swann as one who shows "that contempt for the things of the world that some men of the world like to affect."[5] And he ironically observes of another character that

> the less she believed in the reality of the external world, the more desperately she sought to establish herself, before she died, in a good position in it.[6]

On the other hand, Proust sometimes depicts characters drawing pessimistic conclusions that really are painfully sincere but intellectually contemptible. When Swann goes off to visit Odette:

> On his way to the house, as always when he knew they were to meet, he formed a picture of her in his mind; and the necessity, if he was ever to find any beauty in her face, of fixing his eyes on the fresh and rosy protruberances of her cheekbones, and of shutting out all the rest of those cheeks which were so often langourous and sallow, except when they were punctuated with little fiery spots, plunged him into acute depression, as *proving* that one's ideal is always unattainable, and one's actual happiness mediocre.[7] (Italics mine)

The point being made here is that Swann's situation hardly counts as proof of pessimism.

To cite a more specific point of difference, Beckett misrepresents Proust's and his narrator's relation to society and to social concerns. Beckett is especially hostile to Proust's occasional interest in politics and treats this as an inexplicable lapse from Proust's usually more general and philosophical focus (p. 46). But in making that point, Beckett fails to observe the care Proust takes to integrate his political material with more philosophical themes, such as his treatment of time and change. The Duc de Guermantes' reluctant conversion to the Dreyfusard position, in fact Proust's treatment of this character's development in general, gives important testimony to the dignity man can achieve, not only through revelatory experience (as an artist) but also through more ordinary but persistent efforts.

Again, Beckett would have Proust and his narrator reconciled to a heroic solitude after realizing their artistic vocation.
That view is not groundless. Proust, at one point, calls society
"the realm of nullity."[8] He also observes once that art, particularly art based on ideal revelation, requires solitude:

> Ideas are goddesses who deign at times to make themselves visible
> to a solitary mortal . . . But as soon as a companion joins him they
> vanish, in the society of his fellows no man has ever beheld them.[9]

Such remarks, however, do not represent Proust's only or final
view of the subject. The tone of Beckett's analysis reflects his
own bias toward solitude. The refracting effect of his antisocial temperament on Proust's material is clearly marked in this
passage from *Proust:*

> The artistic tendency is not expansive, but a contraction. And art is
> the apotheosis of solitude. . . . surely the scorn of half a dozen—or
> half a million—sincere imbeciles for a man of genius ought to cure
> us of our absurd puntiglio and our capacity for being affected by
> that abridged libel we call an insult. (P. 47)

The tone of spiteful assertiveness here ("I can take it") is
never to be found in Proust, but is peculiar to Beckett's early
writing. For that matter, the theme of indifference to insult
runs throughout Beckett's fiction, and no wonder; this is the
constant note, almost in itself the distinguishing mark, of a
detached sage's approach to life. Antisthenes the Cynic,
among many such figures, advised that "when men are slan-
dered they should endure it more courageously than if they
were pelted with stones."[10] But as it happens, Proust's narrator
resolves, for reasons of social convenience, not to tolerate
insults.[11] And at the book's conclusion, he is reconciled to society, not determined to avoid it. The series of beatific involuntary memories, which inspire him at last to artistic dedication,
occur at the moment of his return to social life. This does not
mean that his revelations were caused by that return, but it
does suggest, at least, that solitude is no artistic necessity.
Proust makes that point quite explicitly:

> But I was not at all disturbed in the line of reasoning I had just
> started by the fact that it was a social gathering, my return to society

life, that had furnished the starting point for a new life which *I had not been able to find in solitude.* There was nothing remarkable about this, since an impression which might reawaken in me the eternal human being was *no more necessarily linked to solitude than to society*—as I had formerly believed.[12] (Italics mine)

And the same conclusion is once again emphatically repeated:

there was no reason why I should not receive stimuli of that sort [involuntary memories] when among my fellow beings, quite as well as in . . . solitude . . . [13]

As further evidence of Proust's indifference to social concerns, Beckett asserts that his subject is "completely detached from all moral considerations"(p. 49). The statement has some basis. "As soon as one is unhappy," Proust sarcastically observed, "one becomes moral."[14] Other remarks of Proust's associate talent with a lack of moral qualities,[15] dissociate habits from moral significance,[16] and confess a personal "want of moral sense."[17] Beckett hammers this point home. Twice he says that for Proust "there is no question of right and wrong" (p. 49). And more particularly, he adds that "homosexuality is never called a vice" (p. 49). Once again, Beckett is trying to make Proust fit the mold of a cynical sage—Diogenes asserted that "everything is permitted."[18]

But in fact, Proust calls homosexuality "the vice," to which he adds, parenthetically ("we use the word for convenience only").[19] Indeed, Proust is relatively free (but not "completely detached") from moral considerations; by adopting, if only "for convenience," a normal moral vocabulary, he lets moral implications into his great work. And that is the very least that can be said about his moralism. On the whole, the novel is informed by a specific and quite conventional moral structure: it tells of a writer, unable to write, who at last finds the will to "consecrate himself to his vocation."[20] Has the value of uncovering difficult truths ever been moralized about more earnestly?

Ten times over I must essay the task, must lean down over the abyss. And each time the natural laziness which deters us from every difficult enterprise, every work of importance, has urged me to leave the thing alone, to drink my tea and to think merely of the

worries of to-day and of my hopes for to-morrow, which let themselves be pondered over without effort or distress of mind.[21]

Nor is Proust's sense of value engaged only in connection
with artistic creativity and what will further it. Several of his
characters are shown going into moral decline and suffering a
social fall. Proust's tone in discussing such stories, tolerant but
clear-sighted, is that of ironical moral literature. He refers
once to a compulsion

> which urges young women of the Faubourg Saint Germain to live
> in a scandalous fashion, to set every convention at defiance, to scoff
> at the entreaties of their relatives, until the day when they set
> themselves with perseverance but without success to reascend the
> slope down which they had found it so amusing, *or rather had not
> been able to stop themselves,* from gliding.[22] (Italics mine)

The ambiguity of moral judgment here is typical of Proust; he
wants to condemn, but the italicized phrase interjected above
suggests a suspension of moral judgment. In fact, Proust wants
to sustain both responses and achieves a characteristic complexity. He wants to pity the women being blamed and to let
the reader experience a liberation from having to condemn
them, but he also wants to establish the order, meaning, and
aesthetic structure that can be supplied only by a conventional
moral focus on flamboyant unconventionality. Furthermore,
the passage suggests that those who wrongly blame compul-
sives ought to be blamed themselves; but this entails an
infinite regression if the latter are themselves compulsive
blamers. In short, the passage suggests a thorough critique of
moral judgment, but, at the same time, it does not stop making
moral judgments.

The same sort of complexity can be discerned in Proust's
discussion of Mlle Vinteuil, a sadistic lesbian who deliberately and systematically dishonors her father's memory. Here
the element of conscious and regularized evil—present by
definition in the "sadist"—is undeniable. And yet Proust's narrator offers this exoneration:

> I have since reflected that if M. Vinteuil had been able to be pres-
> ent at this scene, he might still, and in spite of everything, have
> continued to believe in his daughter's soundness of heart, and that

he might even, in so doing, have been not altogether wrong. .... A "sadist" of her kind is an artist in evil, which a wholly wicked person could not be, for in that case the evil would not have been external, it would have seemed quite natural to her, and would not even have been distinguishable from herself; and as for virtue, respect for the dead, filial obedience, since she would never have practiced the cult of these things, she would take no impious delight in their profanation. "Sadists" of Mlle Vinteuil's sort are creatures so purely sentimental, so virtuous by nature, that even sensual pleasure appears to them as something bad, a privilege reserved for the wicked. .... It was not evil that gave her the idea of pleasure that seemed to her attractive; it was pleasure, rather that seemed evil.[23]

In other words, Proust's strategy is to place the maker of moral judgments on the horns of a dilemma. Either the wrongdoer does not know that her action is wrong, in which case blame is inappropriate; or the wrongdoer does know that the action is wrong, in which case (as above) we have a touching proof of her real inner goodness. But just because the act of placing blame entails some contradictions doesn't mean—as Beckett apparently concluded—that it must be avoided. Proust finishes his analysis of Mlle Vinteuil by attributing her "sadism" (a term never abandoned) to her obtuseness in self-scrutiny. The tone of moral condemnation emerges clearly at the conclusion, not only because cruelty must be denounced, but because the "sadist" lacks the narrator's heroic self-knowledge:

Perhaps she would not have thought of wickedness as a state so rare, so abnormal, so exotic, one which it was so refreshing to visit, had she been able to distinguish in herself, *as in all her fellow men and women*, that indifference to the sufferings which they cause which, whatever names else be given it, is the one true, terrible and lasting form of cruelty.[24] (Italics mine)

The reason Proust never abandons the moral capacity, never stops blaming and praising, is because he finds that a certain freedom and dignity (which at the least are necessary fictions) cannot be maintained without it. He dramatizes the discovery of this realization by a childhood recollection:

And thus for the first time my unhappiness was regarded no longer as a fault for which I must be punished, but as an involuntary evil which had been officially recognized, a nervous condition for which I was in no way responsible. . . . I ought then to have been happy; I was not.[25]

Similarly, in speaking of Charlus' exemplary homosexual fall (out of the closet and into hell), the narrator moralizes quite conventionally, for in casting blame the capacity to have resisted evil is affirmed:

> But one vice or another—and that greatest vice of all, *lack of will power*, which makes it impossible to resist any of the others—brought them [the debauchees] together there [a brothel] . . . habit always brought them back to their common rendezvous of vice.[26] (Italics mine)

Clearly, then, Beckett's presentation of Proust as a consistent amoralist is severely oversimplified, and, similarly, he has Proust simply preaching asceticism, though there is a considerable difference in tone between their statements on this point. Beckett's phrase, "ablation of desire," is itself somewhat ambiguous, since the unusual term "ablation" can indicate either total and violent removal (the preferred definition is "surgical removal") or a gradual and passive decline (as in geological erosion).[27] Proust's language about desire is characteristically worldly, proposing a moderate and deliberate self-control:

> If happiness or at least freedom from suffering can be found, it is not the satisfaction, but the gradual reduction, the eventual extinction of our desire that we must seek.[28]

And in another discussion of the topic, Proust reveals a good deal of qualification and ambivalence:

> As for the girl, I never came across her again any more. . . . Seeing and losing them all thus increased the state of agitation in which I was living, and I found a certain wisdom in the philosophers who recommend us to set a limit to our desires. . . . At the same time I was inclined to regard this *wisdom as incomplete*, for I said to myself that these encounters made me find even more beautiful a world which thus caused to grow all along the country roads flowers at once rare and common, fleeting treasures of the day, windfalls of the drive, of which the contingent circumstances that

would never, perhaps, recur had alone prevented me from taking advantage, and which gave a new zest to life.[29] (Italics mine)

"Fleeting treasures" and frustrated anticipation giving "zest to life"? Yes, Proust makes several statements of that sort (once the narrator even speaks of his "eager desire to live"),[30] but Beckett's commitment to pessimism won't allow him to admit this. To his credit, perhaps, Proust's pessimism was somewhat inconsistent, and he took the trouble to rationalize this inconsistency:

There is no idea which does not carry in itself a possible refutation, no word that does not imply its opposite.[31]

Beckett's analysis does not deal justly with this emotional and intellectual complexity; but perhaps, as Proust himself observed, a sense of justice is incompatible with genius. In any case, Beckett required a more simplified intelligibility of the world than Proust did and thus drew different conclusions— despairing and exasperated—about its perplexities.

Since Proust's thought, in fact, provided insufficient basis for the rigorous pessimism formulated by Beckett, the latter required some other authority; in this function, Schopenhauer served him perfectly. That modern sage is mentioned four times in Beckett's brief text; in comparison, Descartes and Dostoevsky, also linked to Proust as predecessors, are named only twice. At that, Beckett fails to indicate the extent to which he relies on Schopenhauer, translating Proust consistently into that philosopher's terms. In consequence, it has not been noticed that Beckett's analysis depends not only on Schopenhauer's main ideas, but also on details of that philosopher's thought, even on his literary allusions and examples. (For example, the lines from Calderón cited in *Proust*—"Pues el delito mayor / Del hombre es haber nacido"—are cited twice in *The World as Will and Idea*.)[32] Nor are Schopenhauer's ideas and learning the only elements of interest here; the tone of his writing suggests a sensibility midway between Beckett's rage and Proust's tolerant resignation. Accordingly, the philosopher can be thought of as the link between Proust and Beckett; he seems to help make the one accessible to the other.

No doubt Beckett's reliance on Schopenhauer was well warranted, since Proust himself acknowledged the philosopher, who explained hypochondria as a form of overwillfulness, to be an early favorite. There is in fact a core of interests common to all three authors, Schopenhauer, Proust, and Beckett. Each condemns the human condition, deriving his pessimism not from life's physical oppressions and limitations but rather from a thoroughly rationalized psychological fatalism. That is, each finds that insatiable need is inherent in man's nature, a doctrine at least as old as Ecclesiastes:

The eye is not filled with seeing, nor the ear with hearing. (1:8)

Consequently, each is concerned to point out what must be the commonest human error: supposing that satisfaction lies in the enjoyment of some particular object. Such an object, according to Schopenhauer, is really a manifestation of the will and, like a mirage, a set of perceptions organized in the interests of bodily desires. As Proust puts it,

We try to discover in things, endeared to us on that account, the spiritual glamour which we ourselves have cast upon them . . .[33]

Thus when Swann, at the end of his long love, wonders that he has "wasted years . . . for a woman that did not please [him], was not in [his] style,"[34] Proust terms this reflection an "intermittent fatuity." It is fatuous because Swann is still inclined to look for satisfaction or account for its frustration in the qualities of some particular object he has been pursuing.

This sequence of ideas—that volition determines perception and guarantees frustration—is treated by Beckett in language closer to Schopenhauer's than Proust's but more opaque than either's. On the first page, for example, Beckett says that Proust disdained realism but still found it "necessary to interrupt (disfigure) the luminous projection of subject desire with the comic relief of features." This remark, which assumes the reader's acquaintance with Schopenhauer's philosophy means that Proust disdained realism (attention to superficial particularities) because he found it insufficiently real; reality lies in the will and its projections ("subject desire"), making such objects as Odette only desire's arbitrary "concretions."

Because they find all efforts aiming at gratification inevitably futile, Beckett, Proust, and Schopenhauer concur on another ancient and virtually universal doctrine: that life may be viewed as a punishment. Nonetheless, their differences of tone in making this point are worthy of notice, and through comparison the particular mood of Beckett's early pessimism can be assessed. He puts the situation thus:

> we are rather in the position of Tantalus, with this difference, that we allow ourselves to be tantalized. And possibly the perpetuum mobile of our disillusions is subject to more variety. (P. 3)

Beckett's statement is characterized—and this is altogether typical—by its attempt to find grounds for a righteous denunciation of the condemned. They "allow themselves to be tantalized," which implies that therefore they deserve it. Also characteristic is the insistence with which Beckett emphasizes the analogy to Tantalus. Any difference, he assures his readers, between us and that unfortunate is merely one of degree; furthermore, his flashy, somewhat sarcastic manner ("possibly ... perpetuum mobile") suggests that the difference in degree is itself insignificant. But it should be noted too that Beckett's use of the first-person plural ("we ... ourselves") indicates a self-criticism. There seems to be no exception, no escape, then, from this generalized disgust.

Schopenhauer also found the plight of Tantalus an apt description of the human condition. More specifically, he said (and the precedent for Beckett's language is to be found here) that

> the *subject of willing* is thus ... the everlonging Tantalus.[35] (Italics mine)

But a fuller passage from Schopenhauer reveals some interesting qualifications through tone, chiefly attempts to distance and dissociate himself from what he also designates the common human plight. We might call his tone aristocratic: he speaks as if from above the spectacle described and addresses a like-minded happy few. In contrast, Beckett's approach could be called cynical: he addresses the crowd, with authority but derision, speaking, as it were, from below. If Beckett seems entirely unconsoled, the philosopher takes consolation in cultivating a standoffish tolerance:

> Amongst the evils of a penal colony is the society of those who form it; and, if the reader is worthy of better company, he will need no words from me to remind him of what he has to put up with at present. If he has a soul above the common, or if he is a man of genius, he will occasionally feel like some noble man of state, condemned to work in the galleys with common criminals; and he will follow his example and try to isolate himself.
>
> In general, however, it should be said that this view of life will enable us to contemplate the so-called imperfections of the great majority of men . . . without any surprise, to say nothing of indignation.[36]

Indignation, on the other hand, is precisely Beckett's attitude. Ultimately, Schopenhauer derives an ethic of compassion from this *noblesse oblige,* and there Beckett does not follow him; his use of Schopenhauer is quite selective, however close at times; he omits, for the most part, Schopenhauer's consolations.

Proust's description of life as punishment, though again derived from his conviction of the will's insatiability, is still different in tone, still further from Beckett's spiteful rancor, which shows the wide range of reactions available to a pessimistic vision. Proust likens the victim's plight to the oscillations of a water lily,

> always in the same helpless state, suggesting victims of neurasthenia . . . who present without modification, year after year, the spectacle of their odd and unaccountable habits, which they always imagine themselves to be on the point of shaking off, but which they always retain to the end; caught in the treadmill of their own maladies and eccentricities, their futile endeavors to escape serve only to actuate its mechanism, to keep in motion the clockwork of their strange, ineluctable, fatal daily round. Such as these was the water lily, and also like one of those wretches whose torments, repeated infinitely throughout eternity, aroused the curiosity of Dante . . .[37]

At times in *Proust,* Beckett identifies Proust's vision with Dantesque torture; here is the explicit textual basis for that comparison. However, Proust also calls his victims neurasthenics, which has a moderating, distancing effect: they seem an exceptional and pathological type. Yet as the novel develops, we learn that the narrator and virtually everyone else are neurasthenic too. Proust's judgment, then, suggests neither Beckett's moral indignation nor Schopenhauer's social pride; it is not at all misanthropic but reflects a perfectly characteristic harmony of attitudes: doleful lament, wistful humor, and clinical curiosity. Proust's tone securely attains the note of distance that Schopenhauer found necessary to assert and which Beckett, railing in spite, found neither available nor appropriate.

In some respects, it should be stressed, Beckett's pessimistic view is remarkably like Schopenhauer's. This difficult passage from *Proust*, couched in abstract terminology almost certainly derived from Schopenhauer, explains life as the eternal separation of subject and object, which an insatiable willfulness struggles vainly to bridge:

> The aspirations of yesterday were valid for yesterday's ego, not for today's. We are disappointed at the nullity of what we are pleased to call attainment? But what is attainment? The identification of the subject with the object of his desire. The subject has died—and perhaps many times—on the way. For subject B to be disappointed by the banality of an object chosen by subject A is as illogical as to expect one's hunger to be disappointed by the spectacle of uncle eating his dinner. Even suppose that by one of those rare miracles of coincidence, when the calendar of facts runs parallel to the calendar of feelings, realization takes place, that the object of desire (in the strictest sense of that malady) is achieved by the subject, then the congruence is so perfect, the time-sense of attainment eliminates so accurately the time-state of aspiration, that the actual seems the inevitable, and, all conscious intellectual effort to reconstitute the invisible and unthinking being fruitless, we are incapable of appreciating our joy by comparing it with our sorrow. (Pp. 3–4)

This demonstration of the necessary and frustrated dependence of subject and object is continued with characteristic relentlessness. As if the fragmentation of the subject, discussed above, were not enough, Beckett goes on to demonstrate the infection of the object with the subject's perspective mobility and finally the intrinsic mutability of the object. While this analysis accurately and incisively conveys one side of Proust's thought, it takes a distinctly different tone, offering, as Beckett later admits, a "too abstract and arbitrary statement of Proust's pessimism" (p. 8). Beckett's philosophical terms and air of demonstration are quite foreign to Proust, who never refers to the subject-object dichotomy *per se*. On the other hand, that is Schopenhauer's constant theme:

> No attained *object* of desire can give lasting satisfaction. . . . The *subject* of willing is thus . . . the ever-longing Tantalus.[38] (Italics mine)

And Beckett prefers the more general, thus more damning, language of Schopenhauer. Furthermore, the clever twist at the conclusion of Beckett's argument cited above, proving even momentary satisfaction unavailable, has its apparent source in Schopenhauer. Gratification, Beckett postulates, requires a simultaneous consciousness of want; otherwise there would be nothing to be satisfied; but "attainment," he says, "eliminates so accurately the time-state of aspiration that . . . we are incapable of appreciating our joy by comparing it with our sorrow." This is how Schopenhauer puts it:

> The wish, i. e., some want, is the condition which precedes every pleasure. But with the satisfaction the wish and therefore the pleasure cease. . . . The satisfaction and the pleasure we can only know indirectly through the remembrance of the preceding suffering and want, which cease with its appearance.[39]

It ought to be noted that this whole line of argument is quite objectionable. First, every pleasure does not require some wish or want as condition or precondition. If that were so, there would be no such thing as a wholly unexpected pleasure; but such experiences do occur. The cliché itself testifies to this, and Beckett uses the phrase too, in *Molloy* (p. 150). Furthermore, unexpected pleasures are essential in determining Proust's outlook. In a vague and inexact way, they are the "fleeting treasures," giving "zest to life" which lend his prose its dense and subtle texture; more precisely, the involuntary memories which lead to Proust's narrator's salvation are the purest, most emphatic kind of unexpected pleasure.

Unconscious wishes may underlie unexpected pleasures in

some cases, but to suppose that this is always the case (as Schopenhauer did, in conceptualizing his "Will") requires a considerable act of faith. What motivates that act of faith, in both Beckett and Schopenhauer, is the need to prove any satisfaction impossible, even the most instantaneous gratification, because to admit exceptions in describing man's misery might legitimate the abhorrent round of worldly pursuits. And their pessimistic arguments seem plausible because their terms are so precise, but that precision is also their flaw. Both Beckett and Schopenhauer, that is, assume (without stating it) that psychic states are aptly represented by rather simplified physical models. Desires are containers to be filled; but they never reach fulfillment, so the containers must be bottomless. Because bodies cannot be in the same place at the same time, neither can psychic states (e. g., longing and attainment) be simultaneous. But there is no reason to think that these models, or metaphors, are apt, especially in view of the evident fact that we are, at times, if not satisfied, quite glad.

Whatever their merit, however, Beckett has maintained an interest in Schopenhauer's pessimistic arguments throughout his career. The passage from Schopenhauer upon which Beckett's reasoning in *Proust* is based, continues with a reflection later reaffirmed by the *Unnamable:*

> Hence it arises that we are not properly conscious of the blessings and advantages we actually possess, nor do we prize them, but think of them merely as a matter of course, for they gratify us only negatively by restraining suffering. Only when we have lost them do we become sensible to their value . . .[40]

This is cause for complaint and not, as may first appear, a consolation; the Unnamable's more sardonic tone makes it clear that blessings are valueless if we cannot be conscious of them, but counting our blessings is bound to cause anxiety, not assurance. Whatever its truth, this observation is witty, and that is its justification:

> It is true that one does not know one's riches until they are lost and I probably have others still that only await the thief to bring them to my notice. (P. 314; by permission of Grove Press, New York, 1965)

Because we can only be conscious of suffering, not of attainment, Schopenhauer found that "life swings a pendulum backward and forward between pain and ennui."[41] The same formulation recurs in Beckett's analysis of Proust:

> The pendulum oscillates between these two terms: Suffering . . . and boredom. (P. 16)

Clockwork is perhaps Schopenhauer's favorite image:

> men are like clockwork, which is wound up, and goes it knows not why; and every time a man is begotten and born, the clock of human life is wound up anew, to resume the same old piece it has played innumerable times before, passage after passage, measure after measure, with insignificant variations.[42]

And it is true that Proust also mentions "clockwork" mechanism in describing neurasthenia.[43] Furthermore, he often refers to the alternation of boredom and suffering:

> The anaesthetic effect of custom being destroyed, I would begin to think and feel melancholy things.[44]

But I cannot find in Proust the pendulum image used in this exact connection, nor can I find the law, that is, a bald statement asserting man's inevitable oscillation between suffering and boredom in his writing. The sentence cited above, though moving along the lines of Schopenhauer's thought, is characteristically moderated; the narrator feels "melancholy" (not the same as "suffering") in alternation with dullness. However, my point is not only that Schopenhauer is more pessimistic than Proust but that Beckett is still more pessimistic than Schopenhauer, who modified his system in various ways not followed by Beckett. Schopenhauer felt obliged to explain "happiness" in his own terms (as if it existed!):

> happiness and well-being consist simply in the quick transition from wish to satisfaction to new wish.[45]

By means of this quick transition the dread specter of ennui is avoided. But here Schopenhauer admits, it seems, that satisfaction (however partial or fleeting) is attainable; yet by his own system, satisfaction is inexplicable and unintelligible. Beckett, even more rigorously logical than the philosopher, makes no such admission.

Chapter 3

Relativism

The whole universe is but an array of signs and images to which the imagination gives a relative place and value.
—*Baudelaire*

The fact of Beckett's admiring acquaintance with Schopenhauer's writing is, in itself, perhaps, of little interest; what is significant, however, is the seriousness of Beckett's philosophical preoccupations, a seriousness which also manifests itself in his need to disparage other philosophers, like Leibniz, whose views most contemporary artists simply ignore. And underlying this erudition is an intensely philosophical spirit, an intellectual and theoretical tendency which, in one form or another, permeates all of Beckett's art. It is possible to detect the influence of abstact philosophical concepts as structural models in the simplicity and elegance of his later works, where philosophical allusions are usually less explicit; *Film*, however, is a case in which this influence is made clear. In any case, Beckett's thought is thoroughly dominated by an abstract and logical tendency, a demand for conceptual simplification, which finds that it cannot understand its own experience except as a series of irresolvable problems and perpetual paradoxes. Therefore, in *Proust* life is condemned as intrinsically tragic, worse than nonexistence, and Beckett's later works, in different ways, address themselves to the same problematic situation.

It is this determined attitude which Beckett found valuable in Schopenhauer—pessimistic relativism, cogently demonstrated. The philosopher proved that satisfaction is unintelligible, given the inevitable conceptual framework of subject-object dichotomy. (Beckett is also inclined to demand intelligibility; only those who do so find the world absurd.) However, the subject-object dichotomy and the problems it entails are by no means a preoccupation limited to Schopenhauer, Proust, and Beckett; as the latter points out in *Proust*, pessimistic relativism is nothing less than "the wisdom of all the sages." And Schopenhauer himself credited several predecessors for his relativistic vision of "this whole world [as] only object in relation to subject, perception of a perceiver."[1] He refers with special gratitude to Indian philosophy, also to the "skeptical reflections from which Descartes started," and to Berkeley, "the first who distinctly enunciated the principle."[2] Characteristically, Schopenhauer slighted the relevant contributions of those German (therefore rival) philosophers, such as Leibniz, whose thought, in some basic respects, Shopenhauer simply inverted, and Kant, whose philosophy surely influenced such of Schopenhauer's statements as this:

> We must not disguise the fact that what the sciences consider in things is also in reality nothing more than this: their relations, the connections of time and space, the causes of natural changes, the resemblance of forms, the motives of actions—thus merely relations [and not things in themselves].[3]

The problems entailed by relativism, distinguished rather arbitrarily, are: (1) that there are no absolutes or privileged points of reference, including God, though humankind is held to have need of such absolutes; (2) that all thought is self-contradictory; thus the curse of consciousness separates the subject from his own experience and even denies the experience at the moment he becomes aware of it; (3) all experience, but especially the most authentic, is atomized; and (4) no self-integration, sincerity, or real responsibility is possible. In consequence of these realizations of failure, it follows that meaning, satisfaction, and consistent systems of value are all, strictly speaking, impossibilities too. Of somewhat greater interest, perhaps, in the works of creative artists, are the emotional pathologies often concomitant with these reflections: (1) an exasperated and resentful sense of having always to react instead of act or a consciously futile desire, as Sartre puts it, to be one's "own basis;" (2) the suspicion that life is a dream —being the object of some other subject—with attendant feelings of alienation, paranoia, and apathy; and (3) the fear of being stuck in a moment, unable to progress in one's being. This last condition, which can be termed continuation anxiety, was apparently suffered by Proust.

If, as Proust sometimes felt, it is impossible to move from mental point A to B because that movement is inexplicable and if thought is envisioned as a spiral—a coil that can only progress by turning in upon itself—then (as Beckett says in *Proust*) "the only possible spiritual development is in the sense of depth" (p. 47; by permission of Grove Press, New York, 1960). But profundity is a development; a total unwillingness to dwell on irresolvable problems or to accord them some legitimacy invites the charge of shallowness, and that is a charge which is never brought against Beckett. A continued fascination with irresolvable problems lies at the core of his creativity. Still, the obsessions generated by relativism form a Gordian knot of overcomplication which almost everyone, including Beckett, sooner or later determines to break. Never to transcend that tangle is to remain in a wholly nonfunctional madness.

Basically, there are only two ways of dealing with an irresolvable dilemma. One, without denying the conditions that constitute the problem, is to deny them their problematical interpretation, either by finding some associated benefits, or else by exaggerating the problem to the point where one simply must become resigned to it. The other basic alternative is to transcend the dilemma by a simple assertion of faith, claiming that in some other realm or by some means not immediately apparent the problem is actually solved. The different variations upon these strategies philosophers and artists develop often become the means used to distinguish them.

The inevitable separation of subject and object is the problem to which East Indian religion addresses itself. The consequence of insatiable craving and the related doctrine of Karma (another version of life as punishment) has been connected with Beckett's writing by the critics Richard Coe and Northrop Frye.[4] Confronting the problem of separation and longing as intrinsic to consciousness, the ancient Hindu texts respond by denying its ultimate reality. Instead, they posit an essential reality, not apparent, in which all is one; thus they find that "pain, body, multiplicity, and the subject-object dichotomy are illusions."⁵ This is religion's most normal and fundamental gambit, and, in Greek philosophy, Parmenides and Plato make the same sort of postulation—that of an ideal being as the realm of undifferentiated wholeness. Parmenides' claim was defended by Zeno's paradoxes, which demonstrate (in models that have haunted Beckett's works) the unbridgeable gaps and perpetual futility which result when reality is held to consist of separate and related bodies moving in time. Similarly, what fuels the Platonic dialogue is the realization that endless contradiction is always possible, that an additional negation can always be found, and it is just this realization that also necessitates Plato's leap to the concept of being. The Christian doctrine of the Trinity—"the one being of God as Father, Son, and Holy Spirit"⁶—is another such leap, as asserted resolution of apparent contradiction (and the comic version of Oedipal conflict). Proust too, as will be seen, resolved the difficulties inherent in his conceptual system by a kind of leap.

That is not Beckett's way of doing things; his tactics are paralleled, however, in Buddhist thought, particularly in the Madhyamika school, which developed a version of relativism, sometimes called nihilism, that is known to have interested Nietzsche, while its chief spokesman, Nagarjuna (*c.* 200 A. D.), has also been called a forerunner of Sartre.⁷

All Buddhist thought, including Nagarjuna's, is addressed to the problem of suffering:

His [the Buddha's] Four Noble Truths are that there is suffering, that it has a cause, that it can be suppressed, and that there is a way to accomplish this. All things pass away, dreams, hopes, fears and desires. None can resist the universal supremacy of death.⁸

These are the problems in *Proust:* suffering, mutability, and death; and Nagarjuna, like the author of *Proust,* finds that craving underlies the whole conceptual framework (Beckett uses Schopenhauer's term, "Will").

Now this, O monks, is the novel truth of the cause of pain: that craving which leads to rebirth, combined with pleasure and lust, finding pleasures here and there, namely the craving for passion . . .⁹ (Italics mine)

This craving is insatiable, because

> The Buddha postulates that life is a stream of becoming. There is
> nothing permanent in the empirical self.[10]

Beckett too finds that objects are in flux and that the self is
unsubstantial—"dies many times," he says, "on the way" to its
object of desire.[11] In consequence, the self who wins the prize,
estranged from the former self who wanted it, finds the object
useless, even a burden, boring. And never satisfied, it is
nonetheless necessary to "go on."

Nagarjuna does not, like a Hindu or a Platonist, "affirm a
positive reality underlying the world of change."[12] On this
point, he is agnostic, and "whereof we cannot speak we must
be silent."[13] Rather, his solution lies in giving the concept of
flux its fullest and most extreme realization; paradoxically, resignation to the infinite divisiveness of reality does away with
the experience of painful separation nearly as well as a postulated wholeness. For example, as long as the Jewish wor-
shipper faces Jerusalem, he is made conscious of his separation from Jerusalem (as well as his relation to it); his reformed
brethren, who pray facing anywhere they wish, lose consciousness of this relation and its attendant longing. Nagarjuna's
world is entropic, a stabilized chaos, and thus, to sensibilities
like Beckett's, soothing.[14] And like the author of Ecclesiastes,
the Buddhist holds that there is nothing new:

> The Madhyamika-Sastra teaches relative existence, or dependent
> origination, because nothing really new is produced.[15]

Nor is there any such thing as causality (an insistent point in
Proust). By denying privilege to any point of reference, the
Buddhist envisions a blur, a whole undifferentiated to the
mind that no longer cares to make distinctions within it. The
problem of separation entailed by relation is dissolved by exaggeration; not only are other relations possible, but all relations are equally possible, and what results is

> Nirvana, *the quiescence or equalization of all plurality, because
> when it is critically realized* there is for the philosopher absolutely
> *no differentiation of existence.* Thoughts and feelings do not arise

in this *undifferentiated whole, there is no subject and no object of knowledge,* there is consequently no turmoil like birth, old age and death, there is eternal bliss . . .[16] (Italics mine)

A dominant attitude in Eastern religion, this extreme quietism surfaces in the West only as a sport. Madame Guion (whose words below were cited approvingly by Schopenhauer) is one such exception:

Everything is alike to me; I cannot will anything any more; often I know not whether I exist or not.[17]

Beckett is another: the extreme indifference exemplified in Molloy and Malone is the most characteristic attitude of his later writing. The tendency first becomes explicit in *Murphy,* when the hero is derided for eating a number of biscuits in order of preference; were he to make "no differentiation of existence" (as Nagarjuna says), then, Beckett assures us, "the assortment would spring to life before him, dancing the radiant measure of its total permutability" (p. 97; by permission of Grove Press, New York, 1957). The "equalization of all plurality," in other words, "is bliss." This is also the beatific vision entertained at the top chamber of Murphy's mind: a "matrix of surds" (p. 112).

Indeed, a whole complex of Buddhist ideas is reproduced by Beckett. Nagarjuna continues:

Our view is that Nirvana represents quiescence, i. e., the non-applicability of all the variety of names and non-existence of particular objects. . . . The quiescence of plurality is also a bliss because of the cessation of speech or because of the cessation of thought.[18]

The cessation of thought and speech sought by the Unnamable is suggested here. And, as Beckett reported, Proust was also struck with the "non-applicability of . . . names." Albertine's multiplicity leads him to conclude that "the Name is an example of barbarous society's primitivism."[19] In other words, suffering is minimized when regarded as withdrawal from an unknown substance; error and excessive misery lie in naming what we think we need. For *everything* is the disease it proposes to cure; the person who wants to sleep is in reality depressed, and the lecher lacks not a woman but self-control. In fact, nothing is better than something, and it is best of all not to be born.

Analogously, as Lucky's soliloquy points out, there are those who have dealt with the fear of death by spending their lives contemplating a skull.[20] There and elsewhere, Beckett counters his inclination to a sort of nihilistic Buddhism with considerable qualification. Beckett resists any doctrine, however appealing. Thus Murphy's Nirvana-like bliss is described with rather heavy sarcasm:

> It is most unfortunate, but the point of this story has been reached where a justification of the expression "Murphy's mind" has to be attempted. . . . How pleasant was the sensation of being a missile without provenance or target, caught up in a tumult of non-Newtonian motion. So pleasant that pleasant was not word. . . . This painful duty having been discharged, no further bulletins will be issued. (P. 107)

In *Watt* a similar ideal is put forth and retracted with still greater force. Mr. Knott's house is idyllic because

> Nothing changed, in Mr. Knott's establishment, because nothing remained, and nothing came or went, because all was a coming and going. (Pp. 132–33; by permission of Grove Press, New York, 1959)

Then follows the inevitable deflation:

> Watt seemed highly pleased with this tenth-rate xenia [hospitality]. Spoken as he spoke it, back to front, it had a certain air, it is true. (P. 133)

What Beckett cannot accept in Buddhism is its assurance that enlightenment will bring liberation. The Buddha's world system ("twelvefold concatenation of cause and effect") may seem bleak enough:

> On ignorance depends karma; on karma depends consciousness; on consciousness depend name and form; on name and form depend the five organs of sense; on the five organs of sense depends contact; on contact depends sensation; on sensation depends desire; on desire depends clutching; on clutching depends existence;

on existence depends birth; on birth depend old age and death, sorrow, lamentation, misery, grief and despair.[21]

But note, it all depends on ignorance; wisdom annuls the whole process of suffering. And this hope is what Beckett's *Watt* explicitly denies:

And if I could begin it all over again, knowing what I know now, the result would always be the same. (P. 46, italics mine)

Furthermore, although Beckett's later heroes are remarkably apathetic, their craving is never completely renounced; indeed, their will to "go on," though often indefinite in objective, is not only made evident but rendered sympathetically, even dignified perhaps, by Beckett's treatment. Finally, the quiescent contemplation of chaos was certainly not Beckett's sole desire at the time of *Proust*. As the language of *Proust* indicates, he also craved experience more definite and intense, if painful; no doubt Beckett hated himself for this. As for Proust, that author yearned for conviction of "the eternal in Man," as Beckett reports;[22] the afterlife settings established in some of Beckett's later works suggest the same fixation. But Nagarjuna's Buddhism does not seek to persuade the believer that he always will be — rather, it would persuade him that he never was. Birth and the ego are somehow illusions dependent upon ignorance.

Though these differences should be kept in mind, the common ground amongst relativistic thinkers is something that can also be stressed, and it is a peculiar virtue of Beckett's books to have made his readers mindful of these connections. Platonists, Hindus, Buddhists, and Christian philosophers who dwell upon the Trinity all tend to agree in valuing asceticism, probably because their chief concern is to sustain a train of thought which a passionate emotion would interrupt. And those who insist that experience is primarily a matter of relations are also apt to think schematically and problematically, to be disposed to generalize, to stress form over content, and to be attracted to mathematics, logic, music, and chess, that is, systems frankly composed of mere relations.

The German philosopher Leibniz is an important relativistic thinker to whom Beckett has alluded several times. As observed above, *Proust* concludes with a parting shot at Leibniz's view of music, a needless attack that indicates both Beckett's interest and antipathy. According to Leibniz, the world is the only one that is "compossible," that is, the only one which could have resulted from the available reciprocal or mutual possibilities being effected. He added that this world was good, thereby earning the hostility of pessimists since Voltaire. The most significant aspect of his thought, however, is the prominence he gives to considerations of relativity, thus anticipating (as Cassirer points out) Kant and Einstein.[23] Against Newton, for example, Leibniz argued that what is called space is not an actual medium but simply "the order or relation of things amongst themselves" and that without such objects it is nothing.[24]

In a remark that helps account for Beckett's interest in Leibniz, Kierkegaard observed,

> modern philosophy will teach that the whole of life is a repetition. The only modern philosopher who had an inkling of this was Leibniz.[25]

Kierkegaard is referring to Leibniz' doctrine of the monad, the constituent entity of life so programmed by its creator that "its present is pregnant with its future."[26] Monads are self-contained, "windowless," Leibniz says, and do not actually interact; their relations are ensured by a "Pre-Established Harmony" rather than causation. Beckett refers to Leibniz' monadism in making Murphy's last room a "windowless cell" (p. 181). This philosopher is certainly on Molloy's mind: he makes two explicit references to Leibniz' concept of "Pre-Established Harmony."[27] Molloy may also allude to Leibniz' analysis of virtual identity, or propositions which approach but do not achieve an actual congruence. To suggest this relation Leibniz supplied the analogy of inscribing an increasing number of many-sided polygons in a circle; the polygons come closer and closer in shape and area to the circle but never really attain congruence. Molloy also attempts to negotiate a circle, but achieves only "a great polygon"; "perfection," he notes, "is not of this world."[28]

The monad's inherent tendency to endless regeneration precludes its absolute death. Leibniz' strangely phrased doc-

trine of the essential continuity between life and death, with
"death" described as a state of indistinct perception, suggests
both the Buddhist's Nirvana and the afterlife milieu of
Beckett's *Unnamable:*

> it [the monad] cannot perish, nor on the other hand would it exist
> without some affection and affection is nothing but perception.
> When, however, there are a great number of weak perceptions
> where nothing stands out distinctively, we are stunned; as when
> one turns around and around in the same direction, a dizziness
> comes on, which makes him swoon and makes him able to distin-
> guish nothing. Among animals, death can occasion this state for
> quite a period.[29]

In the image that contains an image of itself, ad infinitum,
many thinkers other than Leibniz have found a compelling
fascination. Proust's involuntary memories are such a case; in
the paradoxical subject-object relations implied by these temporal interpenetrations, Proust's narrator detected a deeper
authenticity and invitations to heroic investigation. On the
other hand, when considering the work of art as a timeless
image of itself and perfect type, Keats's poetic spokesmen
found a terror from which they had to withdraw;[30] and in
Nietzsche's concept of eternal recurrence there seems to lie a
model of obsession and prefiguration of his madness. At the
beginning of the second act in *Waiting for Godot,* Beckett also
presents, for his own purposes, a monadic image—a self-
propelling mechanism, regenerating itself out of its own inner
relations:

Vladimir: A dog came in—
          Having begun too high he stops, clears his throat, re-
          sumes:
            A dog came in the kitchen
            And stole a crust of bread.
            Then cook up with a ladle
            And beat him till he was dead.

            Then all the dogs came running
            And dug the dog a tomb—
          He stops, broods, resumes:
            Then all the dogs came running
            And dug the dog a tomb

And wrote upon the tombstone
For the eyes of dogs to come:

A dog came in the kitchen
And stole a crust of bread
Then cook up with a ladle
And beat him till he was dead.

Then all the dogs came running
And dug the dog a tomb—
He stops, broods, resumes:
Then all the dogs came running
And dug the dog a tomb—
He stops, broods. Softly.
And dug the dog a tomb ... (Pp. 37–38;
by permission of Grove Press, New York, 1954).

The moods and values implied at this point intersect with a complexity that is characteristic of Beckett. Because the events on stage, like the events in Vladimir's recitation, also imply an endless reiteration, the recitation seems to be confirmed, that is, to be offered seriously as an image of life. And it is prolonged with surprising insistence. At the same time, to prolong this perpetuation indefinitely, to keep on reciting the chant just because it suggests an endless regeneration, would be madness itself; Vladimir stops reciting it. So the poem about dogs and cooks associates two ideas: that life is the endless perpetuation of a fundamental process and that such a perpetuation is irrational. Were this all, Beckett would be expressing a conventional Romantic anguish, not unlike de Sade's. By a very significant decision, however, Vladimir's poem is made to sound like a nursery rhyme, its tone thoroughly and pointedly trivial; thus Beckett scales down what might seem like a painful madness to something more like mere absurdity. The poem's Punch-and-Judy violence is an integral aspect of that absurdity.

In other words, Vladimir's poem expresses a dog's eye cynicism in which the element of levity is more than usually insistent—even self-conscious and apologetic. Shortly after his recitation Vladimir remarks that he feels fine, though acknowledging, significantly, that he cannot justify this:

One is not a master of one's moods. All day I've felt in great form.
(P. 38)

Likewise, Molloy and Moran associate inner peace with intuitions of endlessness achieved while contemplating aesthetic structures. But *Molloy* reports on the comic failures of these characters; that is, while they are affirming the value of activities essentially futile and, at best, impossible to value, a degenerative process ensues within them. This is also the scheme of *Krapp's Last Tape.*

Then what is the point of these humorous demonstrations? In the "Dialogues with Duthuit," Beckett claims that such statements are the artist's only real rationale and "obligation."[31] The Problem Beckett deals with in those pages is coming to terms with a "bourgeois" consciousness which (like Celia in *Murphy*) demands that apparently pointless creative activity justify itself. Beckett grants that the more authentic the creative inspiration, the more unconventional will be the order of its ideas. Random connection and sheer fixation, apparent pointlessness and failure characterize the authentic work of art. For the general experience of life, Beckett maintains, is dealing with chaotically shifting relations by repetition and thereby making a fool of oneself; value lies in realizing that this is unavoidably the case and then trying to affirm it. The heroic and political affirmation of such a situation, advanced by Camus in *The Myth of Sisyphus*, is a solution that alters the terms of the problem and is proscribed by Beckett's temperament. His chief concern is to justify mental activity, contemplative or creative, so his characters play the fool while insisting that everything else is also foolish. In this way, the image of monadic repetition reflecting the overall structure of *Waiting for Godot* is a means Beckett employs to justify thinking, while granting that the latter can often seem endless and pointless.

This attitude is not the necessary result of preoccupation with relativity. Beckett's thought is distinguished by its insistence that experience remain thoroughly problematical. On the other hand, Leibniz always sought to resolve the tensions and difficulties his ideas implied, even to the point of holding that nothing exists without "sufficient reason."[32] In another version of this principle, he said that a statement is true only if its predicate is in its subject. In *Proust*, Beckett points out that even such a perfect truth contains a tragic inner tension:

> The most ideal tautology presupposes a relation and the affirmation of equality involves only an approximate identification and by asserting unity, denies unity. (P. 52)

Still, such a temperament as Leibniz' is soothed by holding, as he did, that everything which exists does so by logical necessity. All events occur, according to Leibniz, because they are irreplacable "compossibilities"; he even maintained that a demonstration of this could be indicated, though not actually made, because it would entail an infinite number of considerations. Since he was unable to make the demonstration, Leibniz took consolation in its imperviousness to disproof, and he postulated an omniscient observer, in whose all-encompassing view the infinite regression of subject-object relations is resolved. This observer proved to be none other then "God, who is able to see, not the end of the series, since there is no end, but the nexus of terms, or the inclusion of the predicate in the subject, since he sees everything in the series."[33]

That God is a logical and emotional requirement of many philosophical systems does not, however, mean that He must exist. That is where the thought of rationalists like Leibniz must seem to Beckett most vulnerable and dated. This is not to deny that Beckett's conceptual repertoire, as Hugh Kenner observed, remarkably resembles that of a baroque philosopher; the tendency is most elaborately in evidence at the conclusion of *How It Is,* where narration turns into a kind of mathematical metaphysics. But given this similarity in conceptual tendency, Beckett's heroes (unlike a Leibniz or Descartes) keep insisting, as at the very end of *How It Is,* that their conceptions are purely hypothetical and don't matter, that they are fictions. And this was a vision already asserted in *Proust;* life consists of the tension between its reality and the possible ideas about it. No predication, even a tautology, can adequately coincide with it.

This concept of perpetual inadequacy, of always approaching and never reaching a designated limit, is another fundamental image shared by Beckett and Leibniz. Characteristically, Leibniz attempted to resolve its disturbing implications in several ways: by asserting that things indiscernibly different were identical, that important truths about probability were available, and that ultimate unions were effected at infinity in the view of God. In *Proust,* Beckett insists that the complete "identification of the subject with the object of his desire," which is impossible, is the necessary condition of happiness (p. 3). Against this position (which must lead to pessimism) Leibniz held that

> Our happiness will never consist and ought not to consist in full enjoyment, in which there could be nothing further to desire, and which would render our spirit stupid, but rather in a perpetual advance to new pleasures and perceptions.[34]

Happiness consists of partial satisfaction, together with renewed anticipation:

> it is true that desire cannot always completely attain to the whole perception at which it aims, but it always attains something of it and reaches new perceptions.[35]

If desire is susceptible of some gratification and is a pleasure in itself, then "the ablation of desire" need not always be recommended. And that, I daresay, is what most people think. Leibniz' formulations nicely point out, by contrast, the extremity of Beckett's demands and expectations, in which, because subject and object must exactly coincide for satisfaction, enjoyment is either theoretically complete or actually nil. The objection to this extreme pessimism is obvious: that it has no relation to anyone's real experience of life. And yet I think that is not quite the case either. A mind obsessed with the laws of pessimism finds its experience conditioned by the pressure of those concepts. And of course, the experience of disappointment, if sufficiently consistent, makes pessimistic interpretations available.

Berkeley, cited in *Murphy, Film,* and *Waiting for Godot,* is another relativistic thinker whose ideas have supplied Beckett with pessimistic implications. The philosopher's chief tenet is the denial that objects have independent existence. Rather, they require a perceiving subject as foundation:

> For as to what is said of the absolute existence of unthinking beings without any relation to their being perceived, that is to me per-

fectly unintelligible. Their *esse est percipi*, nor is it possible that
they should have any existence out of the minds of thinking things
which perceive them.[36]

These reflections led Berkeley with apparent cheerfulness to
God as the necessary guarantor of existence. For Beckett,
however, their consequences are negative and, in *Waiting for
Godot*, Lucky alludes to Berkeley's death as if to demonstrate
that this philosopher's thought was no real use to him (p. 29).
That one is necessarily the object of another subject is a
spooky thought. *Film* envisions the feeling of always being
observed or even hunted down that can derive from reflecting
on Berkeley's principle. And an even more likely inference,
extensively developed in *Waiting for Godot*, is that, because
one is merely the object of another subject, all of one's experience might be that subject's dream or figment. This is why
Vladimir cannot bear to hear about Estragon's "private night-
mares"; they remind him of that possibility, which Estragon,
unkindly, also articulates:

Estragon: I had a dream.
Vladimir: Don't tell me!
Estragon: I dreamt that—
Vladimir: DON'T TELL ME!
Estragon: (*gesture towards the universe*). This one is enough for
   you? . . . (p. 11)

At the play's conclusion, Vladimir conceives an endless regression of such subject-object relations, while watching the
sleeping Estragon:

Vladimir: At me too someone is looking, of me too someone is
   saying, He is sleeping, he knows nothing, let him sleep
   on. (*Pause.*) I can't go on! (*Pause.*) What have I said?
   (P. 58)

Two conclusions are being drawn here. The first (I can't go
on") is that such a vision constitutes a kind of tragic suffering,
a point Beckett was already making in *Proust* by citing
Calderón's drama, *La vida es sueño*. The next thought, however, shifts towards the realization that this judgment in itself
was suspect, since the speaker had been lost in

thought—"What have I said?" The parallel to the last lines of Keats's "Ode to a Nightingale" is evident, and Beckett, like the poet, seems to be attempting affirmation of the painful, fleeting ecstasy of thought:

> Was it a vision, or a waking dream?
> Fled is that music:—Do I wake or sleep?

The pessimism and skepticism of Vladimir's speech are, to be sure, complementary and mutually reinforcing; movement from one to the other is, logically, equally possible. But in fact, it is the movement from pessimism to skepticism that most frequently characterizes Beckett's mature writing. At least from *Watt* on, his efforts have focussed on developing a rhetoric built on repetition and non sequiturs, including a good deal of direct address and acknowledgement of artifice. The effect on the reader is the stimulation of a train of thought eventuating, like Vladimir's soliloquy, in that very realization—that one has been thinking, even lost in thought. Another realization shortly follows: that life in general is (much more than is usually recognized) a matter of sheer mental activity, chaotic and trivial as this is.

It is in this emphasis upon the role of mental activity— subjectivity, perspective, projection—that Beckett agrees with Berkeley, Schopenhauer, Proust, and relativist thinkers generally, whether optimistic or otherwise. Berkeley's "subject" is no mere passive observer. Another term for subject, he says, is spirit, the cause of our ideas, and "as it produces them, or otherwise generates about them, it is called the Will."[37] This emphasis upon active will approaches Schopenhauer, who reproduces, in main outline, the Buddhist ascetic creed: life is only mental activity, which is only willfulness, in other words, need, which is always evil.

While Beckett's discussion of subject-object relations seems to have derived mainly from Schopenhauer, his general acquaintance with German idealistic philosophy ought to be noted. He was certainly acquainted with Hegel and Kierkegaard's criticism of Hegel. The latter attempted to overcome the subject-object dichotomy by hypothesizing a "thought which is its own object, and which is therefore identical with its object, with what is thought; so that we have the one and the other and the unity of both.'[38] Kierkegaard finds this impossible and irrelevant, hence his "existentialism":

> The systematic idea is the identity of subject and object, the unity of thought and being. Existence, on the other hand, is their separation.[39]

Whereas Kierkegaard's chief concern is the nature and quality of the inner life, Hegel discusses the subject-object relationship in terms of the individual and his environment. To be "free," according to Hegel, is to like the world.[40] "Freedom," he says, is a "voluntary peace with reality";[41] similarly, "to be educated is to be free."[42] Beckett uses the term frequently, and usually with a pointed irony suggesting reference to these Hegelian rationalizations:

> Can it be we are not free? It might be worth looking into.[43]

Hegel's historical dialectic is certainly in mind at the conclusion of *Murphy*, when Mr. Kelly's kite is observed going "out, back a little, stop; out, back a little, stop. The historical process of the hardened optimists." (P. 279)

The philosophical tradition indicated by Beckett's allusions consists of writers who shared a significant amount of imagery; thus these allusions cannot always be assigned with confidence. The contrast between circle and polygon, mentioned earlier in connection with Leibniz and brought up by Molloy, also appears in Kierkegaard's *Concept of Irony* (where the polygon represents empirical determination, the circle intuition).[44] In *Watt* there is a curious statement which for a while was taken by some critics as an allusion to Wittgenstein's *Tractatus:* "Do not come down the ladder, Ifor, I haf taken it away" (p. 44). Wittgenstein does indeed use a ladder image at one point, but Beckett reported that he had not read Wittgenstein at the time of *Watt*'s composition. Kierkegaard, however, uses the image in *Repetition:*

> This indeed would be the same as telling her that she was an incomplete being, that he had outgrown her, that he no longer had need of the rung of the ladder on which he had climbed.[45]

Some of Beckett's language in *Proust* is very close to Kierkegaard's in *Either/Or*. At one point, Beckett discusses the reflexive relationship or mutual dependence of remembering
and forgetting:

> The man with a good memory does not remember anything be-
> cause he does not forget anything. (P. 17)

Kierkegaard wrote, to much the same point, that

> Forgetting is the shears with which you cut away what you cannot
> use, doing it under the supreme direction of memory. Forgetting
> and remembering are thus identical arts, and the *artistic achieve-
> ment* of this identity is the Archimedean point *from which one
> lifts the whole world.*[46] (Italics mine)

In remarks also relating artistic achievement, remembering,
and forgetting, Beckett said that "from this deep source Proust
hoisted his world." (Italics mine) Furthermore, the passage
from Kierkegaard cited above is immediately followed by a
diatribe against friendship, another theme in *Proust;* thus it
seems likely that *Either/Or* was a source for Beckett.

His debt to Nietzsche is also considerable and lasting.
Proust's demonstration of the subject's merely fictional unity
could as easily have been derived from Nietzsche as Schopenhauer.[47] Nietzsche's concept of Dionysian chaos might have
served as model for the top chamber of Murphy's mind. And
the aesthetic theory Beckett formulated in the *Dialogues
with Duthuit* closely parallels Nietzsche's remarks about the
inescapable relativity of language.[48]

More significant, however, than these particular attribu-
tions, is the deep source from which Beckett hoisted his own
world so frequently, especially in *Proust:* the German philosophical tradition in general. In that body of literature he
found a congenial conceptual confidence and intensity, a
capacity for taking thought seriously, a franker intoxication
with thought, even temperamental extremity and unbalance
—all of this that development of the philosophical type then
being called for by the Surrealist manifestos. And this intensity stems from the tradition's relativism: its insistence on
subjectivity, perspective and paradox, eventuating in the

contemplative "sense of depth."[49] This is the maddening experience which Moran, at a time when he was finding it "painful not to understand," labelled "spurious depth," but which Beckett himself as early as *Proust* was calling the "only possible development" (p. 47).

In *Proust* this commitment to intensified solitude directly follows the treatment of love as just one more form of futility, at best a "tragic" "failure to possess" (p. 46). Proust's lovers according to Beckett are "two separate and independent dynamisms related by no system of synchronization" (pp. 6–7). The impossibility of love is deduced from the inexplicable phenomenon of the continuum, a problem illustrated in the paradoxes of Zeno. Take any ostensible unit, like the racecourse in Zeno's dilemma, and regard it as a continuum of entities; an infinite regress follows when you try to relate the figures on this common ground. Proust's lovers, Beckett's "subject and object," relate like Zeno's Achilles and the tortoise; by the time the conclusion is reached, as Beckett says, it is already out of date. The being grasped for is already in the past. The lover's quest is thus shown to be a perpetual labor, and, as Proust points out, nothing can induce a desperate exasperation like this:

> There can never be any peace of mind in love, since the advantage one has secured is never anything but a starting point for new desires.[50]

Furthermore, one desires to possess a totality, the loved one of the past, present, and future, but this is impossible at any given instant. Beckett cites Proust's explanation of this failure, a selection no doubt prompted by its exact reflection of his own mentality:

> We imagine that the object of our desire is a being that can be laid down before us, enclosed within a body. Alas! it is the *extension* of that body to all the points of time and space it has occupied and will occupy. If we do not possess contact with such a place and such an hour we do not possess that being. *But we cannot* touch all these points.[51] (Italics mine)

And forgetting the loved one, by virtue of the same pessimistic logic proves to be another perpetual task. Beckett quotes part of this passage too. I have added a bit of its context:

> A great weakness, no doubt, *for a person to consist merely in a collection of moments;* a great strength also: it is dependent upon memory, and our memory of a moment is not informed of everything that has happened since; this moment which it has registered endures still, and with it the person whose form is outlined in it. And moreover, this disintegration does not only make the dead man live, it multiplies him. To find consolation, it was not one, it was innumerable Albertines I must forget. When I had reached the stage of enduring the grief of losing this Albertine, I must begin afresh with another, with a hundred others.[52] (Italics mine)

Chapter 4

Time and Habit

Time means succession, and succession, change.
—*Nabokov*, Pale Fire

Proust begins with a lengthy and difficult analysis of time, so abstruse that I have thought it better to approach the topic indirectly, looking first at its place in Beckett's pessimistic relativism and his treatment of love. But Beckett's ideas about time are absolutely central; it is generally recognized that his treatment of time in *Proust* forecasts the whole complex of problems that would occupy him throughout his career. The concern itself is by no means idiosyncratic: time is frequently a problem in the literature of solitary complaint, the tradition with which Beckett's writing seems to be most consistently connected.

When does time become a problematical concern? An uncomfortable relationship to an end that is either too near or too distant can call the measurement of that relation into question. This can occur when death is dreaded and there is not enough time, or when an end is longed for and there seems to be too much. Such extremes of spiritual experience also tend to succeed one another or even paradoxically overlap. For example, in the case of Proust, preoccupation with time frequently signifies his hero's anxious awaiting of spiritual change, something like religious conversion; but on the other hand, Proust also worried about the ego's continuance, wondering, that is, am I still myself? These are forms of intensified consciousness, heightened interest. In Sartre's *Nausea* the quality of adventure is simply defined as feeling the flow of time.[1] There is a somewhat divergent tradition, exemplified by Schopenhauer, Baudelaire, and Mallarmé, which with equal plausibility describes a mood of despairing impotence as "pure time, or boredom."[2] All of these moods and issues are reflected in Beckett's treatment of time, though boredom and aridity is stressed while melodramatic interiority is characteristically deflated; as the Unnamable observes, "when you have nothing to talk about, you talk about time" (p. 395; by permission of Grove Press, New York, 1965).

For Beckett, time is a "frigid machinery,"[3] relentless, oppressive, above all, inescapable. Watt's idyllic retreat at Mr. Knott's house approaches a timeless state, because his routine there is constant and stabilized. At the moment of his replacement, he falls back into time and decay:

> So the moment was come. Watt lifted the cork lid from his glass and drank. The milk was turning. (P. 216)

The narrator continues in this vein:

> So it is with time, that lightens what is dark, and darkens what is light. (P. 218)

Watt's first remark upon re-entering the normal world is to ask about time (p. 228); thus *Watt* appears to underline the irrevocability of time, a point made explicitly in *Waiting for Godot*, where time is slowed down and, as in Sartre's *Nausea*, "everything oozes."[4] So little happens that it seems "night will never come" (p. 46) and at one point Vladimir announces that "time has stopped" (p. 24). Pozzo makes the requisite correction:

> (*cuddling his watch to his ear*) Don't you believe it sir, don't you believe it. (*He puts his watch back in his pocket.*) Whatever you like, but not that. (P. 24)

Again, Winnie wonders in *Happy Days* if she "may still speak of time" (p. 50; by permission of Grove Press, New York, 1958). Her doubt is unwarranted: time surrounds her in the grains of sand piling all about, which she refuses to recognize. The pattern that emerges is that Beckett insists upon time but also slows it down, as if wishing to conceive of life taken instant by instant. In what emotional context does this strange wish occur? When death, darkness, and the unknown are feared, then time is slowed down so as to put off the end. But in such a mental state it seems that each instant might be the end, and then it is felt that death and fear are inescapable.

This self-perpetuating temporal and emotional climate is well grounded in Beckett's philosophizing and philosophical learning. In the excerpts from Proust's novel last examined, a discussion of love, an obsessive fragmentation was observed at work; time became a "collection of moments," precluding, at any given instant, the possession of durable phenomena. Albertine changes from moment to moment and thus can never be known. And as Leibniz, among countless philosophers, pointed out, this unknowability holds for all worldly objects:

> It is thus evident that men can never attain to better than confused knowledge regarding contingent particulars, their nature being accessible to us only in piecemeal experience.[5]

And if the loved one cannot be known, she certainly cannot be dominated. As Beckett observes, for Proust, Albertine's indomitability is a function of her temporality:

> No object prolonged in the temporal dimension tolerates possession, meaning by possession total possession, only to be achieved by the complete identification of the subject and object.[6]

In saying that an object is "prolonged" in the temporal dimension, Beckett is implying that it also has another and, in some sense, prior mode of being: that of instantaneous existence. As Richard Coe observes, this is more or less the standard metaphysical outlook, the dominant view philosophical tradition takes of time; "all reality—in any metaphysical sense—is in the present, that is, is instantaneous."[7] But that view, in turn, denies reality to future and past, in fact, to what is usually meant by "time." Indeed, the classic description of being, Parmenides', does just this:

> What is is uncreated and imperishable, for it is entire, immovable and without end. It was not in the past, nor shall it be, since it is now, all at once, continuous. . . . Nor is it divisible, since it is all alike; nor is there more here and less there, which would prevent it from cleaving together, but it is full of what it is. So it is all continuous . . .[8]

As Parmenides himself well realized, his description of being bears no relation to ordinary experience; it is assumed that reality is divisible, including time (which is also divisible by definition). And yet any divisibility entails certain problems, as Zeno's paradox of the impossible heap, alluded to in *Endgame*, points out (p. 70). If the smallest part of a heap is indivisible, it has no magnitude and cannot be; it would contribute nothing if added to the heap. And if the smallest part is divisible, then that is not its smallest part, ad infinitum; thus a whole heap cannot be moved by shifting half of it at a time because the process would be endless.

In spite of these difficulties, time is ordinarily regarded as a succession of smallest parts or instants; this is Beckett's view and one that he consistently associates with suffering. In *More Pricks than Kicks*, Bellacqua "curses the *dribble* of time," which he likens to "sanies *dripping* [that is, *not flowing*] in a bucket."[9] (Italics mine) Similarly, he found "the local publication of the *hours* was like *six of the best* on the brain every hour."[10] (Italics mine) Note that time is consistently quantified, solidified and pluralized into instants, a vision the Unnamable finds both inescapable and painful:

> the seconds pass, one after another, jerkily, no flow, they don't pass, they arrive, bang, bang, they bang into you, bounce off, fall and never move again . . . (P. 395)

The problems of time discussed in *Proust* also revolve around the hypostatization of the instant. That is, time becomes a critical concern and its experience a punishment by virtue of Proust's postulation of the atomic moment. The novel begins with the narrator's recollection of an instantaneous awakening in childhood. Until memory comes to the rescue, the hero suffers an anxious loss of identity:

> when I awoke at midnight . . . I could not be sure at first who I was; I had only the most rudimentary sense of existence, such as may lurk and flicker in the depths of an animal's consciousness; I was more destitute of human qualities than the cave-dweller . . [11]

(Molloy also observes that "you don't know who you are, immediately, when you awake"—p. 38). Proust's hero develops a

sense of himself as a set of divergent identities, barraged by
memories of countless discrete selves which fragment his experience because "our memory of a moment is not informed of
all that has happened since."[12] This disintegration becomes
most painfully acute when he remembers his grandmother,
now dead, with a sudden intensity; with this recollection he
seems momentarily to regain his own former existence. But as
Beckett points out, the dominant impression is not one of gain,
but of loss:

> he has recovered the lost reality of himself, the reality of his lost
> self. (P. 27)

This intermittent penetration of present identity with a past
self produces a new sense of time. Proust calls it a set of "different and parallel series — without *loss* of continuity."[13]
Beckett's discussion of this famous scene, *The Intermittences
of the Heart,* gives the problem a more pointed expression than
Proust's, typically phrasing the latter's emotional problem
as a philosophical dilemma:

> As though the figure of Time could be represented by an endless
> series of parallels, his life is switched over to another line and
> proceeds, *without any solution* of continuity. (P. 27, italics mine)

But Beckett is right in indicating that Proust's task, his
quest, is to discover a secure continuum of self, while the very
structure of time, a succession of instants, and consequently
a structure of successive deaths and incarnations of discrete identities, seems to preclude the possibility of personal
integration.

Once again, this preoccupation has a background which
demonstrates the coherence of Beckett's literary allusions and
intellectual influences, in this case a tradition extending from
St. Augustine to Sartre. Perhaps the first really significant
treatment of time, explicit and extensive, in which the concept
is developed as an urgent emotional problem as well as a
philosophical puzzle, occurs in the *Confessions* of St. Augustine. The saint described his life as a quest for conversion, that
is, an intense instant of awareness, a present moment, *now,* no
longer put off, in which "the burden of habit and custom" will

be thrown off, detachment from worldly desires achieved, and intuitive union with the timelessness of God effected.[14] As with Proust, it is the very achievement of this instantaneous experience, stopping the flow of time, which makes that flow such a potent philosophical problem. It is easy enough to understand eternity; the problem is to understand created existence, time, and its ethical corollary, original sin. But some of Augustine's formulations about time are quite close to Beckett's. Both are concerned to locate the present instant in relation to future and past. Beckett sees the individual's experience of the present moment as

> the seat of a constant process of decantation, decantation from the vessel containing the fluid of future time, sluggish, pale and monochrome, to the vessel containing the fluid of past time, agitated and multicolored by the phenomena of its hours.[15]

The image, characteristic of his earlier prose style, is learned, even scientific, precise, confident of its capacity to visualize adequately. Augustine's explanation takes the same form, but it is more abstract, vague, mysterious, and ridden with anxiety. It anticipates Beckett's later writing, particularly the tone of his "confessional" fiction:

> time emerges from some secret refuge when it passes from the future to the present, and goes back into hiding when it moves into the past.[16]

> But while we are measuring it [time], where is it coming from, what is it passing through, and where is it going? It can only be coming from the future, passing through the present, and going into the past. In other words, it is coming out of what does not yet exist, passing through what has no duration, and moving into what no longer exists.[17]

In grappling with the present instant's reality, Augustine finds that it consists, by definition, of a relation to what is not. Thus consciousness must always, but especially at its most acute pitch, be provisional, paradoxical, ironical, and consequently anguished.

> Of the three divisions of time, then, how can two, the past and the future, *be* when the past is no longer and the future is not yet? As

for the present, if it were always present and never moved on to become the past, it would not be time but eternity. If therefore, the present is time only by reason of the fact that it moves on to become the past, how can we say that even the present *is*, when the reason why it *is* is that it is *not to be*? In other words, we cannot rightly say that time is, except by reason of its impending state of *not being*.[18] (Italics mine)

Only God could get St. Augustine out of such a problem, and as the style of his reflections becomes increasingly confused, he increasingly resorts (like Beckett's heroes in his later writing) to a vatic posture:

> I see time, therefore, as an extension of some sort. But do I really see this, or only seem to see it? . . . I hear your voice which tells me this.[19]

At last the saint collapses into a tortured incantation, enmeshed in circularity, his speech unable to articulate what it exemplifies, that the mind is always ahead of, and behind, itself; so he confesses his ignorance. This prose nearly achieves what Leibniz hoped was impossible, an infinite regression of reflections precluding any mental progress:

> it is impossible for us always to reflect explicitly upon, i. e., be reflexively aware of, all our thought; otherwise the mind would make a reflection upon each reflection *ad infinitum* without ever being able to pass on to a new thought.[20]

The stylistic similarity of the following and other passages in *The Confessions* to Beckett's trilogy is clearly marked:

> I confess to you, Lord, that I still do not know what time is. Yet I confess too that I do know that I am saying this in time, that I have been talking about time for a long time, and that this long time would not be a long time were it not for the fact that time has been passing all the while. How can I know this, when I do not know what time is? Is it that I do know what time is, but do not know how to put what I know into words? I am in a sorry state, for I do not even know what I do not know.[21]

This is what Beckett calls letting the chaos in. The repetitions, paradoxes, admissions of impotence and of ignorance suggest the tone and temporal rhythms of *Molloy,* of which Richard Coe observes,

> the writer [is] writing about a past which can never catch up with the present moment of writing, because, even as he writes the word "now" or "it is midnight," the instant of "now" has already vanished, and "it was not midnight."[22]

In other words, the ideal of St. Augustine and Beckett is a sustained present moment, which of course is impossible; time cannot be stopped or controlled, and this dictates continuous awareness of failure. At the same time, such a confession gives testimony to the discovery of interior depths and implicitly affirms the value of that discovery.

The problematical awareness of time occasioned by an intense introspective straining after instantaneous awareness is revived in seventeenth-century French reflective literature. My reading of this period and of the temporal problem in general is much indebted to the bold and penetrating analyses of Georges Poulet's *Studies in Human Time.* As Poulet explains, the "baroque rationalists" (like Proust) are shocked by the evident discontinuity of atomic time and live in quest of a simultaneous experience. Pascal laments that "only one thought can occupy us; we are unable to think of two things at the same time."[23] Poulet describes the mood of the period as anxiety over time's succession:

> *Confined in the moment* in which it exists, the consciousness watches its *successive* modes of existence pass one after another and escape it.[24] (Italics mine)

As Beckett asserts in *Proust,* "at the best, all that is realized in time can only be possessed successively, by a series of partial annexations—and never integrally and at once. We have already noted his argument that time's succession precludes even the simplest satisfaction; for that requires a simultaneous presence of need and fulfillment, but simultaneous states are precluded if time is constructed of successive instants. In *Watt,* Beckett conceives Mr. Knott's realm as exempt from temporal limitations. His porridge can satisfy him because in this case simultaneous need and fulfillment are possible:

the tiniest spoonful *at once* opened the appetite and closed it, excited and stilled the thirst, compromised and stimulated the body's vital functions, and went pleasantly to the head. (Italics mine)

On the other hand, when Watt leaves Mr. Knott's house and re-enters the normal world, he asks "what time it *was*," not "is," because the present moment is already past.

This is St. Augustine's theme; noting the revived influence of Augustine in seventeenth-century French letters, Georges Poulet cites Boileau's lament as indicative of that influence:

The moment in which I speak is already far from me.[25]

Every hour we are swept away from ourselves.[26]

A poem of Beckett's makes this very complaint. The atomization of time, its quantification, renders life a series of successive losses.

what would I do without this world faceless incurious
where to be lasts but an instant, where every instant
spills in the void the ignorance of having been. . .[27]

The anxiety provoked by temporal discontinuity receives perhaps its most full and precise investigation by Descartes, whose debt to Augustine's conversion (as a model of instantaneous experience) is noted in Beckett's "Whoroscope."[28] This philosopher also postulates the atomization of experience, held to consist, at least as a desideratum, of ideas that are clear because they are distinct. Resolved to doubt all sensory experience, he is convinced of his being in an ecstatic moment, the *cogito ergo sum*. But "to be lasts but an instant," as Beckett says; so Descartes comes to dread the gaps between successive instants. As Malone asserts, citing Democritus, "nothing is more real than nothing"; void is a necessary consequence of any atomism, including temporal atomism. There must be something—that is, nothing—between instants, and this vision entails the discontinuity of personal being. Thus Descartes requires some basis for the threatened self:

For all the course of my life may be divided into an infinite number of parts, none of which is in any way dependent upon the other;

and thus from the fact that I was in existence a short time ago it does not follow that I must be in existence now, unless some cause at this instant, so to speak, produces me anew, that is to say, conserves me. It is as a matter of fact perfectly clear and evident to all those who consider the nature of time, that, in order to be conserved in each moment in which it endures, a substance has need of the same power and action as would be necessary to produce and create it anew, supposing it did not yet exist, so that the light of nature shows us clearly that the distinction between creation and conservation is solely a distinction of reason.[29]

So Descartes resolves St. Augustine's dilemma (between creation and conservation, being and becoming, time and eternity) by deducing a continuous creation. From there it is a short step, indeed no step at all, to the occasionalism of Malebranche and Geulincx, each referred to several times by Beckett.[30] Their doctrine maintains that God must "create us anew" at every instant of existence. The attention given to occasionalism in previous Beckett criticism has emphasized the solution's quaintness and naivete, qualities that might well appeal to Beckett's sensibility. I am trying to show that his interest lies rather in the problem itself, which he sees as authentic, and in the emotional desperation the occasionalist answer indicates. Furthermore, the atomic discontinuity of time, together with the sense of loss and insecurity this vision imposes, is far from being confined to Beckett and the occasionalists; it is the norm pervading the whole tradition of French reflective writing Beckett's works extend.

The same is true of Rousseau. An especially eloquent statement of the temporal problem is to be found in the works of this author, mentioned twice in Beckett's fiction of the *Proust* period, *More Pricks than Kicks*. Rousseau too looks for a reliable foundation on which to base the soul's tranquillity; like Beckett he urges a withdrawal of the soul from desired objects, the cessation of all emotions, and a consequent triumph over time's succession. The conclusion of this passage suggests Beckett's description of Murphy's mind.

But if there is a state where the soul finds a position sufficiently solid to repose thereon, and to gather together all its being, without having need for recalling the past, nor to climb into the future; *where time counts for nothing, where the present lasts forever, without marking* its duration in any way, and *without any trace of succession*, without any other sentiment or privation, neither of enjoyment, of pleasure nor pain, of desire nor of fear, than this alone can fill entirely; so long as this state lasts, he who finds it may be called happy, not with an imperfect happiness, poor and relative, such as that which one finds in the pleasures of life but with a sufficing happiness, perfect and full, which does not leave in the soul any void which it feels the need of filling.[31] (Italics mine)

But Rousseau finds that consciousness cannot be confined to the instant; succession prevails, and he returns, as Beckett puts it in *Proust*, "to a life all in length, a sequence of dislocations and adjustments" (p. 50). In consequence, Rousseau concludes pessimistically that

Happiness is a permanent state which does not seem to be made for men here below; everything upon earth is in a continual flux which does not permit anything to take on a fixed form. *Everything* changes about us, we change ourselves, *and no one can be certain that he will love tomorrow what he loves today;* thus all our plans of felicity in this life are illusions.[32] (Italics mine)

Note the exact resemblance of this pessimistic rationale to Beckett's explanation of unhappiness in *Proust;* the only difference lies in the latter's use of Schopenhauer's terminology: the subject changes, the object changes, and, as a result, "what we are pleased to call attainment" is necessarily a nullity.

Schopenhauer's treatment of time seems to have influenced Beckett in other respects as well. Each represents life as a prolonged dying or series of successive deaths. Schopenhauer draws the morbid inference from a traditional temporal image first noted in Augustine:

[Man's] real existence is only in the present, whose unchecked flight into the past is a constant transition into death . . .[33]

However, the potential horror of this thought is artfully toned down by Schopenhauer's humor; the comic imagery of inefficient mechanism anticipates the style of Beckett's comic pessimism:

as our walking is admittedly only a constantly prevented falling, the life of our body is only a constantly prevented dying . . .[34]

A closer verbal parallel can be found in Beckett's assertion, "the mortal microcosm cannot forgive the relative immortality of the macrocosm" (p. 10). Schopenhauer's man

> finds himself as finite in infinite space and time, and consequently as a vanishing quantity compared with them. He is projected into them, and, on account of their unlimited nature, he has always merely relative . . . existence.[35]

Previous philosophers answered the problems implied by temporality by referring to a timeless state of being, an intellectual and emotional necessity most often called God; and in invoking this solution, Augustine, Descartes, and Rousseau accorded their yearnings an honest legitimacy. On the whole, Schopenhauer is content to make quips about a hopeless situation—constituting a different tone altogether; he is reconciled to the tragic relativity of existence, the subject's consciousness of its relative finitude, by taking a posture that is decadent in its easy admission of failure and aristocratic in its emotional distance. This defeatism anticipates Baudelaire, also given prominence in Beckett's study of Proust. Beckett notes that Proust "understood Baudelaire's definition of reality as the adequate union of subject and object, the world exterior and the artist himself," a formulation Schopenhauer might have made (p. 57).

Baudelaire also complains of time's succession, linked in his mind with original sin, as the soul's movement away from the contemplation of God and toward the pursuit of worldly desires.[36] Furthermore, like everyone else examined in this chapter, Baudelaire counsels the ablation of desire. But what is new in Baudelaire and later affirmed by Beckett is his ambivalence toward this apathy—an ambivalence that is stressed:

> To know nothing, to teach nothing, to will nothing, to sleep, and only to sleep, that today is my vow. An infamous and disgusting vow, but sincere.[37]

While Proust's narrator admits his passivity, often in a tone of regret, that voice never assumed such self-hating sarcasm—a link between Baudelaire and Beckett. And a more specific and suggestive connection can be found in the way Baudelaire relates several of Beckett's most characteristic themes:

> Nothing equals in length the limping days
> When under the heavy flakes of snowy years
> Boredom, fruit of dull incuriousness,
> Assumes the proportions of immortality.[38]

The tempo here is often invoked by Beckett, one not previously noted among his earlier predecessors; both he and Baudelaire slow down time. Baudelaire calls this condition boredom ("ennui"), but with characteristic ambivalence connects the pejorative term with a desideratum: immortality. And linking the two is a term crucial to Beckett's thought, "incuriousness." Why does Molloy, an incurious seeker, find peace in that condition? Baudelaire's lines suggest that incuriousness allays the fear of death; boredom "assumes the proportions of immortality," an unhappy condition, but with this advantage—it precludes anxiety about dying or about other more particular and limited terminations. Already in *Proust* Beckett was calling "boredom . . . the most tolerable of human evils" (p. 16).

Again like Beckett and especially like Rousseau, Baudelaire associates time's passage with the uncontrollable and humiliating oscillation of emotions. What is the objective difference between what he praises as "indolence" and laments as "boredom?" None, apparently; but from one moment to the next the same circumstances provoke entirely different subjective reactions. This oppressive power of time is dramatized in "The Double Room." The narrator, like Descartes and Molloy, is alone in a room, "taking a bath of indolence, scented with all the aromatic perfumes of desire and regret."[39] If desire and regret are negative notes, the dominant emphasis here is nonetheless pleasurable, and the pleasure soon becomes wholly unqualified:

> To what good demon am I indebted for this encompassing atmosphere of mystery, silence, perfume and peace? O bliss! What we are wont to call life, even in its happiest moments of expansion, has nothing in common with this supreme life which I am now experiencing, and which I relish minute by minute, second by second.[40]

The haunted touch is typical of this reflective mode, and the "good demon" will soon be replaced by a "spectre" more like Descartes' demon and the Unnamable's tormentors. But meantime Baudelaire's bliss becomes complete when he senses that time is abolished; specifically, there are

> no more *minutes*, no more *seconds!* Time has disappeared; it is Eternity that reigns, an eternity of bliss![41] (Italics mine)

As always, it is the quantified and pluralized aspect of time that is associated with suffering. Bliss ends when this time returns:

> Then a Spectre enters. . . . Horror! I remember! Yes, I remember! this filthy hole, this abode of eternal *boredom* is truly mine.[42] (Italics mine)

Indolence becomes boredom because

> Time has reappeared; Time is sovereign ruler now, and with that hideous old man the entire retinue of Memories, Regrets, Spasms, Fears, Agonies, Nightmares, Nerves and Rages have returned.
>
> I can assure you that the seconds are now strongly accented, and rush out of the clock crying: "I am Life, unbearable and implacable Life."
>
> There is only one second in human life whose mission it is to bring good news, *the good news* that causes everyone such inexplicable terror.
>
> Yes, time reigns; he has resumed his brutal tyranny. And he pokes me with his double goad as if I were an ox. "Then hoi, donkey! Sweat, slave! Man, be damned and live!"[43] (Italics in text)

With a stunning force that derives from concision, Baudelaire at once connects the tradition's chief topics. Time brings a succession of moods, catalogued to suggest their meaninglessness (as Beckett says repeatedly in *Proust,* "the mood is of no significance"); again, time is a matter of "seconds," pluralized, discrete, produced by a clockwork mechanism; death comes to mind as both blessing and terror; but time is above all a punishment. The reader might be reminded of Schopenhauer but a Schopenhauer who takes no trouble to conceal, who even flaunts, a frenzied despair. Beckett is also anticipated, except that the language is not "weak enough"; Beckett's interior monologues describe a similar sequence of emotions, but their amplitude is flattened. To place Beckett in a more contemporary French context, John Fletcher observes that he

> faces the same situation that Sartre faces in *La Nausée* and Robbe-Grillet in *Dans le labyrinthe:* that we appear a series of consecutive phenomena in time, fragile and unstable, threatened in every instant by submersion in an all-pervading nothingness.[44]

This is not, of course, a sensibility Sartre wants to endorse, thought he grants its fascination. He finds the same time-sense in Camus' *L'Etranger*—"the succession of present moments before an ever conscious spirit"—and calls it an ideal, but it is "the ideal of the absurd man."[45] The trouble with this mode of temporal experience lies in its ethical implication: "one experience is as good as another," and "everything is permissible." [46] (Hence the theme of the unmotivated crime in *L'Etranger,* recurrent in Beckett's trilogy and also Baudelaire's *Paris Spleen.*)

However dangerous the cultivation of this time-sense might be, Sartre also finds that its ideal, a continuous present moment, is impossible; in this respect his examination of temporality in *Being and Nothingness* yields a thorough pessimism similar to Beckett's in *Proust.* The mind struggles to possess, to coincide with itself, and simply to be itself or, in Sartre's terms, "its own basis."[47] But prolongation in time makes this impossible:

> I can be happy only in the past. . . . By definition the for-itself* exists with the *obligation* of assuming its being. . . . It can assume its being only by a recovery of that being. By the very affirmation that I am in the mode of the in-itself, I escape that affirmation, for in its very affirmation it applies a negation.[48] (Italics mine)

---

*Sartre's terminology requires some clarification. One can consider the "for-itself" a subject striving to perceive itself as object; the "in-itself" may be understood as a pure, static subject. All mental process is a frustrated relation of these two conditions.

Sartre's language at the conclusion of this remark comes very close to Beckett's similar assertion in *Proust* that coincidence is an impossibility:

> The most ideal tautology presupposes a relation and the affirmation of equality involves only an approximate identification, and by asserting unity, denies unity. (P. 52)

Each of these observations concerns language; what is impossible is an *"affirmation* of equality" and why? Because all experience is relative (takes the form of a subject-object relation); this relativity entails time; and "time means succession, and succession change."[49] I cannot say, in truth, "I am myself," because the instants that expression entails carry me well past the "self" with whom identity is being affirmed. According to Richard Coe, this is the dominant idea in *Proust* and throughout Beckett's writing:

> Essentially, what Beckett discovered in Proust, and later developed in his own writing, was an attempt to resolve the conflict between "awareness," which is instantaneous, and the linear extension in time of that same awareness when translated into language. Because words "take time," they are fundamentally ill-adapted to the task of defining any aspect of absolute reality, since all "reality"—in any metaphysical sense—is in the present, that is, is instantaneous.[50]

This is quite right, but only a small part of Beckett's pessimism, because his concerns are not so narrowly literary; significantly, the *Dialogues with Duthuit* is about painting. Nor are his concerns confined to artistic expression, whatever the art. Rather, the basis of his writing is the assumption that any expression, achievement, or satisfaction is impossible, because it requires something the nature of time (in other words, consciousness) precludes: the prolongation of the instant or the simultaneous experience of instants. As Sartre says, "I can be happy only in the past";[51] but of course he cannot *be* in the past. Thus any satisfaction is precluded, even when the precise terms of the wish are met, by the absence of the former need which required a future fulfillment. Here is Sartre's version of the argument already observed in Schopenhauer and Beckett:

> Even if my present is strictly identical in its content with the future toward which I projected myself beyond being, it is not *this* present toward which I was projecting myself; for I was projecting myself toward the future qua future.[52]

Now everyone will agree that neither the past nor the future can be directly experienced or attained; but Sartre also debars the experience of the simple present, for the reason that it does not exist. Descartes' *cogito* is re-examined and shown to prove only that if "I think, therefore I was"[53] (a criticism made in the seventeenth century by Daniel Huet).[54] This denial of the present as ordinarily understood is a necessary consequence of relativism. Einstein, for example, said that "there is no such thing as simultaneity, there is no such thing as 'now,' independent of a system of reference."[55] No one can experience perfect communication at the instant of communication, because one subject's "now" is not its respective object's "now"; face to face, they stand apart in time, removed at least by distances that light and neural messages must traverse, and that entails duration. Nor can the simple present be experienced in solitude, because reflective contemplation consists of two related systems of reference: a self or faculty that thinks and a self or faculty that knows it is thinking; and they do not coincide. Sartre phrases his exclusion of instantaneous awareness geometrically:

> As for the instantaneous present, everyone knows that this does not exist at all, but is the limit of an infinite division, like a point without dimension.[56]

With Proust's involuntary memories in mind, Sartre denies that there are "perfect moments," because there are no moments of any sort. And thus barred from a retrospective, projective, or immediate integration of self, Sartre concludes that we must be irreparably unhappy:

> The being of human reality is suffering because it rises in being as perpetually haunted by a totality which it is without being able to be it, precisely because it would not attain the in-itself [pure subject] without losing itself as for-itself [subject in need of objectification]. Human reality is by nature an unhappy consciousness with no possibility of surpassing its unhappy state.[57]

Sartre's denial of the atomic instant's existence leaves man as unhappy as its postulation, for we remain nonetheless "haunted," he says, by the possibility of instantaneous self-integration. He agrees with Bergson that the instant is an illusion but rejects that philosopher's easy accommodation to time's flow. For consciousness is "structured"; that is, we are "obliged," as Beckett would say, "to assume our being," which involves a quest for stasis doomed to futility.[58]

Let us summarize, then, the main lines of the tradition underlying the explanation Beckett offers of Proust's time-sense. The tradition is cumulative; each figure incorporates the ideas first introduced or emphasized by his predecessors. Zeno of Elea demonstrates that time involves irresolvable intellectual paradoxes. Because St. Augustine cannot solve these paradoxes or describe the present moment, he is driven to confessions of ignorance and impotence. The Cartesian atomization of time entails morbidity and insecurity about the self's continuity. Rousseau draws the pessimistic conclusion that time must make man unhappy and, more particularly, a prey to oscillating moods. Schopenhauer underlines the generality by stating the temporal problem in the terms of relativism. For these thinkers, time is generally too fast. For Baudelaire, it is too slow, a guarantee of boredom, fear, and self-loathing, and also defeat, since it is not slow enough: it cannot be altogether stopped. Sartre applies these pessimistic conclusions to language: affirmations about the present, simultaneous experiences, and continuous entities like the self are false or meaningless or at best very loose. And he denies not only that instantaneous awareness can be sustained but even that it can be experienced at all. The same point was made by Kierkegaard[59] and is generally maintained by the Existentialists. In this Beckett follows them. There are no revelations or ecstacies in his works; Krapp once thought he saw "the whole thing" (p. 21) but the point of the play is that this was a delusion or, if a genuine revelation, useless. Nor are there Proustian involuntary memories in Beckett's works, though critics have detected some of these, on no evidence whatsoever;[60] these are merely cases of ordinary memory.

There are several emotional and ethical implications to this temporal outlook and obsession besides the morbid anxiety and unhappiness, and the sense of perpetual crisis already noted above. Each of these thinkers shows a rare capacity for visualizing and feeling something (time) that is invisible and impalpable; the narrator of Beckett's *Texts for Nothing* remarks, at one point, that "time has become space" (p. 112). This capacity can be observed in other forms: extreme religiousness in Augustine and Pascal, a haunted feeling in Rousseau and perhaps Descartes, certainly Baudelaire, a sort of animism in Sartre's Roquentin. But at the same time, their ordinary experience is fleeting, thin, and tenuous since, as Boileau says, "the moment in which I speak is already far from me."[61] Thus Malone wonders, in a mood characteristic of Beckett's heroes, whether he will "die before [he] has lived" (p. 234). Sartre has analyzed Zeno's paradoxes of moving bodies, one of the literary origins of all these problems, and concluded as his solution that the thing (e. g., arrow, Achilles) at once "is and is not there."[62] As Nietzsche remarked of Schopenhauer, the latter

> considered the ability to view at certain times all men and things as mere phantoms or dream images to be the true mark of philosophic talent.[63]

The members of this tradition insist upon asserting their critical capacity for distancing reality, their power to reformulate and doubt it, while also insisting upon its intractable element. This tense dualism is intrinsically paradoxical.

To note another consequence, the atomization of time or experience leads to a certain amoralism and irresponsibility. No one feels responsible for the acts of a former discontinuous self, one which, in Boileau's terms, is "swept away from [itself] . . . at every hour," a self which cannot even, in truth, make statements about itself in the present; in that sense, I am not writing this and you are not reading it. Of course this postulated discontinuity is extreme, theoretical, exaggerated. Malone says, "I have been nothing but a series of local phenomena all my life," and the reader smiles because, as Beckett knows, this is an odd and particularly learned way of looking at things (p. 234). But it is not without relation to experience, at least a certain kind of experience: the life of contemplation. And most of the writers in the tradition just examined are philosophers or write in the reflective mode.

Most of them are also French, which provides an occasion to offer another speculation about Beckett's choice of literary language. He has attributed the change from English to a need "to make myself noticed" and also remarked upon the desired "weakening effect" of French, a language more abstract than English. But in the course of this review, it has become apparent that the attitude toward time and related preoccupations John Fletcher rightly finds in Beckett, Sartre, and Robbe-Grillet ("that we appear a series of consecutive phenomena in time, fragile and unstable, threatened in every instant by submersion in an all-pervading nothingness") is an attitude typically and traditionally French, by no means limited to moderns or "absurdists." French prose is then the most developed medium for the treatment of this theme, a theme the traditionality of which Beckett is at pains to emphasize; for that underlines and authorizes his pessimism.

And the authorization of pessimism is what *Proust,* Beckett's first book, is about. In other words, Beckett used Proust to accord legitimacy to his own literary strategy of describing life in the terms and images of insoluble problems. More particularly, Beckett found in Proust a focal point of that long literary tradition which, because it values introspection and precise conceptualization, conceives of consciousness as a series of distinct events, and time as a series of distinct instants and consequently cannot account for enduring satisfaction or any personal continuity. As William James pointed out (here citing James Mill) it is the manner of conceptualization that entails these difficulties:

> If the constitution of consciousness were that of a string of bead-like sensations and images, all separate, "we never could have any knowledge except that of the present instant. The moment each of our sensations ceased it would be gone forever; and we should be as if we had never been. . . . We should be wholly incapable of acquiring experience. . . . Even if our ideas were associated in trains . . . we should still be without the capacity of acquiring knowledge. One idea, upon this supposition, would follow another. But that would be all. Each of our successive states of consciousness, the moment it ceased, would be gone forever. Each of these momentary states would be our whole being. . . ."[64]

Of course, no one really thinks his experience of life is as jerky and fragmented as this. Those wishing to hold to such primitive and confident abstractions as the atomic instant have generally had to invoke the individual's relation to God or some other timeless state of being as a solution to the problem of personal discontinuity. For those of a less religious mentality, the concept of habit has served the same function. "Such is the force of Habit" — a phrase from Proust's novel repeated in *Molloy* — that the individual's multifarious selves can be normally glued together in a tolerable continuum.[65] But since Beckett insists that life be regarded pessimistically, in terms of insoluble problems, this tolerable continuum must also be invalidated. Accordingly, along with Proust, he holds that habit is only a spurious affirmation of personal identity, an individuality affirmed at the loss of experiencing reality.

In *Proust,* Beckett passes directly from his analysis of atomic, disintegrated time to a consideration of habit as "the guarantee of a dull inviolability" (p. 8). The same transition is made in Hume's philosophy, and it seems likely that Beckett had Hume in mind here. The connection is made especially likely by a number of remarks in *Proust* about causality, the topic of Hume's most famous discussion. And, actually, Proust himself seems to have alluded to Hume's analysis of causation as a questionable idea acquired through habit:

> as a habit gives the mere association of ideas between two phenomena, *according to a certain school of philosophy,* an illusion of the force, the necessity of a law of causation.[66] (Italics mine)

But for Proust this is a passing interest, whereas it is persistent in Beckett's analysis. According to Beckett, Proust would like to "detach effect from cause" (p. 1); again, and more particularly, "from the sanity of a cause" (p. 11); and in *More Pricks than Kicks,* his fiction of the *Proust* period, Beckett refers sarcastically to the "benevolence of a first cause (p. 32). To Beckett, naming a cause is an illegitimate way of easing pain, since it shifts attention from rigorous subjective instability towards something objective and external. To grasp the rationale of this odd and characteristic animus, it will be helpful to look at its basis in Hume's epistemology.

For Hume, as for most rigorous introspectors, the self is

experienced as a succession of states without fundamental basis:

> Whatever is distinct, is distinguishable; and whatever is distinguishable is separable by the thought or imagination. All perceptions are distinct. . . . It is the composition of these which forms the self.[67]

As was seen above, Descartes was driven to the "benevolence of a first cause"—holding that God creates us anew at each moment—to correlate these distinct perceptions. For Hume such a God was out of the question. Furthermore, he held that not only a first cause but the principle of causality itself may be doubted. Causation as a relation or connection between perceptions is not itself perceptible:

> all our distinct perceptions are distinct existences, and mind never perceives any real connection among distinct existences.[68]

Still, there must be some joining force between distinct experiences, and Hume settles on habit:

> Suppose a person, though endowed with the strongest faculties of reason and reflection, to be brought on a sudden into this world; he would, indeed, immediately observe a continual succession of objects and one event following another, but he would not be able to discover anything further. He would not, at first, by reasoning, be able to reach the idea of cause and effect. . . . There is some other principle which determines him to form such a conclusion . . .
>
> This principle is custom or habit. . . . Custom, then is the great guide of life.[69]

While acquiescing in the logical necessity of Hume's Tory epistemology, both Proust and Beckett view habit as a baneful necessity, at best. Fortunately for comic literature but not for habit's victims, this force affects a ludicrous regularity. Employing this vision in his novel, Proust did not disdain to theorize about it as well:

> Here we may perhaps remark that the regularity of a habit is generally in proportion to its absurdity. The sensational things, we do as a rule only by fits and starts. But the senseless life, in which the

maniac deprives himself of all pleasures and inflicts upon himself
the greatest discomforts, is the type that alters least. Every ten
years, if we had the curiosity to inquire, we should find the poor
wretch still awake at the hours when there is nothing to do but let
oneself be murdered in the streets, sipping iced drinks when he is
hot, still trying desperately to cure a cold.[70]

The character who draws these themes together for Proust is
the narrator's aunt Léonie. Like her nephew, this neurasthenic invalid suffers from perpetual anxiety about the continuity of the ego; like one of Beckett's later heroes, she has
also "formed the habit of thinking aloud."[71] Keeping track of
her complaints and confirming her identity are for this compulsive babbler the same activity. The narrator recalls,

> I would often hear her saying to herself: "I must not forget that I
> never slept a wink"—for "never sleeping a wink" was her great
> claim to distinction, and one admitted and respected in our
> household vocabulary; in the morning Françoise would not "call"
> her, but would simply "come to" her; during the day, when my
> aunt wished to take a nap, we used to say just that she wished to
> "be quiet" or to "rest"; and when in conversation she so far forgot
> herself as to say "what made me wake up," or "I dreamed that," she
> would flush and at once correct herself.[72]

Thus the comical creature of habit affirms a distinct and continuous identity at the expense of authenticity. What is worse,
the cessation of a gratifying custom can occasion tragic suffering:

> I was so much in the Habit of seeing Albertine in the room, that I
> saw all of a sudden a fresh aspect of Habit. Hitherto I had regarded
> it chiefly as an annihilating force which suppresses the originality
> and even our consciousness of our perceptions; now I beheld it as a
> dread deity, so riveted to ourselves, its meaninglessness aspect so
> encrusted in our heart, that if it detaches itself, if it turns away from
> us, this deity which we can barely distinguish inflicts upon us
> suffering more terrible than any other and is as cruel as death
> itself.[73]

Although habit imposes a comic uniformity penetrated with
tragic deprivations on all mankind, it is the artist who suffers
most acutely from its limitations. For the artist's obligation is

to know reality or, in Beckett's terms, following Schopenhauer, the "object exempt from causality (Time and Space taken together)" (p. 69). And Proust longed for such a direct ecstatic perception of reality but found that "stupefying Habit, during the whole course of our life, conceals from us almost the whole universe."[74] As Beckett explains:

Unfortunately, Habit has laid its veto on this form of perception, its action being precisely to hide the essence—the Idea—of the object in the haze of conception—preconception. (P. 11)

Thus the subject is barred, says Beckett, from "the enchantments of Reality," a paradoxical phrase taken from Proust himself:

For if Habit is a second nature, it prevents us from knowing our original nature, whose cruelties it lacks and also its enchantments.[75]

Therefore the artist must resign himself to suffering, indeed he must seek it. For it is only when habit ceases, Beckett says,

when it is opposed by a phenomenon that it cannot reduce to the condition of a comfortable concept, when, in a word, it betrays its trust as a screen to spare its victim the spectacle of reality, it disappears, and the victim, now an ex-victim, for a moment, free, is exposed to that reality . . . (p. 10)

This is to say that the perception of reality is always painful. And that is Beckett's position in *Proust,* although it is clearly not the view of Proust himself. Beckett consistently associates optimism with vague perception; thus he speaks of "the haze of our smug will to live" (p. 5). And similarly,

Whatever opinion we may have on the subject of death, we may be sure that it is meaningless and valueless. . . . The possibility is indistinct and abstract . . . (p. 6)

On the other hand, when habit ceases to function "the suffering of being [or] provisional lucidity" becomes available (p. 9). Reality is connected with precision and pain:

His eye functions with the cruel precision of a camera; it photographs the reality of his grandmother. (P. 15)

And because "suffering opens a window on the real," it is "the main condition of the artistic experience" (p. 16).

There is a statement peculiarly Beckett's. It is not Schopenhauer's, and, as we shall see, Proust's involuntary memories, particularly the concluding cluster which set him to work, are anything but painful. The novelist does indeed endorse suffering but not in Beckett's sense. He associates suffering with necessary labor. Pain is part of an elaborate system of goads and consolations, leading both to performance and resignation:

> Happy years are wasted years; we wait for suffering before setting to work. The idea of suffering as an ineluctable prerequisite has become associated in our minds with the idea of work; we dread each new undertaking because of the suffering we know we must first go through to formulate it in our imagination. And when we understand that suffering is the best thing we can encounter in life, we contemplate death without dismay as a sort of emancipation.[76]

Beckett cannot resist treating Proust's work-ethic with some sarcasm:

> He [Proust] is a Romantic in his anxiety to accomplish his mission, to be a good and faithful servant. (P. 61)

Perhaps Proust's endorsement of work, of regular application, comes too close to an endorsement of habit to suit Beckett. But Proust's critique of habit is much gentler than Beckett's and much less consistent. According to Proust, it is possible to derive some real pleasure from custom's ministrations:

> For my judgement was now aware that Habit—Habit which was even now setting to work to make me like this unfamiliar setting, to change the position of the mirror, the shade of the curtains, to stop the clock—undertakes as well to make dear to us the companions we at first disliked, to give another appearance to their faces, to make attractive the sound of their voices . . .[77]

This is surely better than boredom, which, according to Beckett, is always the effect of habit. Proust even asserts, paradoxically, that it is possible to acquire the "habit of finding life interesting."[78] This certainly does not accord with Proust's view of habit as the force of stupefaction. But the ideas set forth in Proust's novel are less systematic, less philosophically rigorous, than Beckett's analysis would suggest. Proust's philosophy is only one aspect of a novel that in general expresses an accommodation with the world of physical and social experience. Beckett is much more completely committed to the terrifying inexorability of logical relations.

Chapter 5

Problems and Solutions

To reason well is to submit.
—Pope

As Proust acknowledged, he was by nature a complainer and even a crybaby. His earliest memories, loaded with shame and guilt, consisted chiefly of interminable, anxious nights, nights he spent demanding his mother's attention by asserting childish needs; and in his maturity he authenticated his laments by generalizing them. Still further simplified and exaggerated by Beckett, these complaints describe mankind as perpetually struggling to establish adequate relations with a reality that cannot be securely known or controlled. This description of the human situation as reiterative futility is also the core of a pessimistic literary tradition each author inherited; their differences lie in how they responded to its strictures. Without doubt, Proust sought to resolve the difficulties classic pessimism describes, and to explain through the avenue of consolations—exceptional but valid ecstatic moments—how the whole of human existence could be more satisfactorily reconceived. These "involuntary memories" and the conclusions Proust drew from them are neither implausible nor abnormal nor are they necessarily convincing in the way that Proust regarded them; but solutions to the problems of pessimism will be found by those who really want to find them. Because he did not wish to be consoled, Beckett treated Proust's conclusions with evident disinterest and some distortion, adding a few words of explicit disapproval.

Since Proust held that time, defined as the succession of present instants, precludes the stable relation of subject and object, destroying them both, it is only natural that he turned to memory as the mode of consciousness most likely to bring inner peace. However, he found that ordinarily the past could not be recollected in tranquillity. First, it does not seem sufficiently real to be satisfying:

> the images selected by memory are as arbitrary, as narrow, as intangible as those which imagination has formed and reality has destroyed.[1]

Furthermore, Proust's critique of memory connects that faculty with the same kind of futile craving it was his object to transcend:

> there is always less egoism in pure imagination than in recollection.[2]

As Beckett explains, memory is an inadequate means of contact with reality, because, like all intellectual faculties, it is conditioned by will; "the more interested our interest, the more indelible must be its record of impressions" (p. 18). Hence the "impurity" of what is remembered. Voluntary memory produces a "blurred and uniform projection once removed of our anxiety and opportunism—that is to say, nothing" (p. 20). As usual, Beckett is somewhat overstating the case. Proust found the connection between memory and volition in the philosophy of Bergson, who did not go so far as to equate practicality with nullity:

> The cerebral mechanism is arranged just so as to drive back into the unconscious almost the whole of this part, and to admit beyond the threshold only that which can cast light on the present situation or further the action now being prepared—in short, only that which can give useful work.[3]

Thus Bergson describes the development of an unconscious self which, unlike Freud's, is not a repository of only too interesting, taboo desires; on the contrary, it is a record of everything that was perceived without interest and immediately forgotten because it was never needed. According to Bergson, it is only the survival of a few exceptional, logically superfluous memories from the depths of this unconscious realm that suggests the self's real profundity. This is a liberating discovery because it makes available a layer of self more authentic than the social personality—a series of defensive tics, nervous mannerisms, and irrational habits designed to supply the threatened individual with a tolerable sense of continuity. And it is just such memories, fortuitous and involuntary, which serve as Proust's consolation. A succession of sensations unlock his forgotten past, "whose integral purity," Beckett explains, "has been retained because it has been forgotten" (p. 54) and was forgotten because it was apparently so trivial. The chance reduplication in the present of these trivial impressions makes them available, if only accidentally, to recollection. And Beckett demonstrates that this interpenetration of past and present seems to resolve the problematical aspect of life by bridging the gap between what are normally felt to be its mutually exclusive but equally necessary alternatives.

> The identification of immediate with past experience, the recurrence of a past action or reaction in the present, amounts to a participation between the ideal and the real, imagination and direct apprehension, symbol and substance. Such participation frees the essential reality that is denied to the contemplative as to the active life. What is common to present and past is more essential than either taken separately. . . . Thanks to this reduplication, the experience is at once imaginative and empirical, at once an evocation and a direct perception, real without being merely actual, ideal without being merely abstract, the ideal real, the essential, the extratemporal. (Pp. 55–56)

This rather tricky settling of accounts is rattled off in a manner suspiciously rapid and mechanical, because Beckett was not very interested in Proust's solution; what stirred his imagination was chiefly Proust's complaint. But Beckett was also considerably intrigued by what, to Proust, seemed at most a means to an end. Proust held that only what is incuriously perceived can pass into the fund of impressions potentially available to involuntary memory; he did not think that incuriosity was a valuable sensibility in itself. Beckett detected the promise of a more imminent access to salvation in "the *mysterious* element of inattention that colors our most commonplace experiences" (p. 19, italics mine). He favorably contrasts this inattention with curiosity in a way that foreshadows the characteristic and somewhat puzzling recommendations of incurious search later voiced in *Molloy:*

> Curiosity is the hair of our habit tending to stand on end. It rarely happens that our attention is not stained in greater or lesser degree by this animal element. (P. 18)

The implication of this disparagement, which took Beckett many years and many works to fully explore, is that if man were wholly indifferent to the world, it would always seem new and wonderful to him—which is an evident contradiciton in terms. Beckett went about exploring this interesting dichotomy by constructing a prose which deflects attention away from the habitual grooves of interest, expectations dictated by a selfish and socially sensitive curiosity. Thus instead of following the careers of personalities, replete with moral and political implications, his fictions guide the reader toward the aesthetic contemplation of things, the recognition of an imperative and irrational formal element in thought, and an awareness of the groundless philosophical assumptions that lie hidden in the clichés of literature. In other words, all that retards the utilitarian and practical mentality, while stimulating the disinterested play of thought, Beckett brings into focus. Not that this different sort of attention brings real peace or satisfaction; Beckett's heroes confess residual exasperation to retain the tension of authenticity, for Beckett cannot conceive an existence that does not remain fundamentally problematical.

Accordingly, Beckett took exception to Proust's conclusion, with an "impertinent" self-assertion:

> But if this mystical experience communicates an extratemporal essence, it follows that the communicant is for the moment an extratemporal being. Consequently the Proustian solution consists, in so far as it has been examined, in the negation of Time and Death, the negation of Death because the negation of Time. . . . (At this point a brief impertinence, which consists in considering *Le Temps retrouvé* almost as inappropriate a description of the Proustian solution as *Crime and Punishment* of a masterpiece that contains no allusion to either crime or punishment. Time is not recovered, it is obliterated. Time is recovered, and Death with it, when he leaves the library and joins the guests, perched in precarious

decrepitude. . . . If the title is a good title the scene in the library is
an anti-climax.) (P. 66)

As usual, Beckett allows no blurring of harsh and logical
realities; there is no middle ground between the temporal and
extratemporal; we must have one or the other. The same
fidelity to logical precision leads him in *Molloy* to parody the
rather artificial distinctions underlying the explanation of involuntary memory.

> By the time she [my mother] came to the fourth knock she imagined
> she was only at the second, the first two having been erased from
> her memory as completely as if they had never been felt, though I
> don't quite see how something never felt can be erased from the
> memory, and yet it is a common occurrence. (P. 18)

What Beckett always refused to see about involuntary memories was how these exceptional moments could effect a
reconciliation to a painful norm and even cause that norm to
be revaluated. He could grant the miracle, the hiatus, but
found no good reason, that is, no sound intellectual explanation, for the supposed consoling effect of time's momentary
obliteration. After all, it doesn't last; Proust leaves the library
and rejoins the guests. And yet, the moments in the library cast
a new light on both his subsequent and retrospective experience. The placement of the library scene (the cluster of inspir-
ing involuntary memories) seems anticlimatic to Beckett because it is in that scene that reality is most directly and ecstati-
cally perceived, yet the book does not end there. For Proust's
is also a social novel and he needs to affirm the temporality of
social experience. Beckett neglects the positive side of this
aspect of time; it is not, as he suggests, a morbid fall from bliss.
For Proust, peace of mind could only be sustained through an
inner conviction of social integration.

Back among the guests, Proust recalls the tinkling of a bell
which in his childhood had signalled his mother's departure
and his own ensuing desolation:

> To endeavor to listen to it from nearby, I had to descend again into
> my own consciousness. It must be then, that this tinkling was still
> there and also, between it and the present moment, all the
> infinitely unrolling past which I had unconsciously been carrying

within me. When that bell tinkled, I was already in existence and, since that night, for me to have been able to hear that sound again, there must have been *no break in continuity, not a moment of rest for me, no cessation of existence, of thought, of myself,* since this distant moment still clung to me . . .[4] (Italics mine)

Here Proust is solving the Cartesian problem of personal identity: the evidence of involuntary memory indicates that there has been no break in self, which always thinks, if subconsciously, and no "cessation of existence."

> It was this conception of time as incarnate, of *past years as still held close within us,* which I was now determined to bring out into such bold relief in my book.[5] (Italics mine)

Taking care to apply his experience to others, to generalize it, Proust rejoices in a common humanity, based on common temporality:

> Moreover, everyone realizes that we occupy a steadily growing place in Time, and this universality could not fail to rejoice me, since it was truth, the truth vaguely sensed by each, which I must seek to make clear to all.[6]

Proust's eagerness to communicate this truth should be borne in mind, since Beckett wrongly asserts as an idea of Proust's that "art is the apotheosis of solitude. There is no communication because there are no vehicles of communication" (p. 47). This sentiment is clearly not shared by Proust, whose vision of a common fate, of man enduring and gaining stature through time, enabled him to conclude on a note of ambition, hope, and generosity:

> If, at least, there were granted me Time enough to complete my work, I would not fail to stamp it with the seal of that Time the understanding of which was this day so forcibly impressing itself upom me, and I would describe men—even should that give them the semblance of monstrous creatures—as occupying in Time a place far more considerable than the one so restricted allotted them in space, a place, on the contrary, extending boundlessly, since giant-like, reaching far back into the years, they touch *simultaneously* epochs of their lives—with countless intervening days between them—so widely separated from one another in Time.[7] (Italics mine)

Clearly, Proust is celebrating the discovery he had thought logically impossible, the simultaneity of existence, a revelation which gives him, paradoxically, a new appetite for time. But Beckett, in quoting this passage at the beginning of his study, curiously misinterprets it, quite distorting Proust's elevated, emotional tone. According to Beckett, the passage means that

> Proust's creatures, then, are victims of this predominating condition and circumstance—Time; victims as lower organisms, conscious only of two dimensions and suddenly confronted with the mystery of height: *victims* and *prisoners*. (P. 2, italics mine)

Indeed, throughout his criticism, Beckett misinterprets the tone of the novel, substituting his own bitterness about life's futility and loss for Proust's absolutely essential acceptance of the temporal process. Specifically, Proust's moment of extratemporal vision led not only to authorship but to an attitude of social reconciliation. Though this shift in mood is not logical, that is, not easy to explain, it is not very hard to understand either, since it conforms to a fairly common type of experience. Kierkegaard's *Journal* recounts another mystical moment, with a similar sequence of emotional consequences:

> it was as though I were out of the body . . . and I turned back with a heavy heart to mix in the busy world, yet without forgetting such blessed moments. . . . I did not as so frequently happens to me lose myself in the moment, but saw everything as a whole and was strengthened to understand things differently, to admit how often I had blundered, and to forgive others.[8]

What is going on in such cases is something like religious conversion, more specifically, the soothing acknowledgement of a merciful grace. If these moments were just tacked on at the conclusion of Proust's novel, Beckett might well have complained of their inconsistency with the author's pessimism; but life's power to produce soothing exceptions is noted throughout the book. That established beliefs remain oddly impervious to damaging evidence—the governing principle of Proust's social and intellectual comedy—suggests that different laws really do apply to different levels of experience.[9] Other exceptions, surprises, and conversions abound: only the village knave can produce, at Aunt Léonie's death, the requisite religious emotion, and the reader also learns, long after the folly of putting trust in doctors has been established, that it is even more foolish not to trust them.[10] Typically, Proust's exceptions are noted in the service of tolerance, common sense, and kindness, if not for the sake of these virtues themselves, then—as I said—because he felt that peace of mind could be achieved only through a sense of accommodation with the world.

Beckett, the champion of solitude, would not allow Proust any sentiments of this sort, or, for that matter, any emotional responses whatever. He praises the novelist for writing "without sentiment," and "with pathological power and sobriety"; he distinguishes Proust from Amiel and Chateaubriand on the basis of the "melancholy" of the latter writers (p. 62). This severity with regard to all emotion is paralleled in *More Pricks than Kicks*, where the reader is directly advised not to indulge his moods, in themselves of no significance:

> Bellacqua had passed an excellent night, as he always did when he condescended to assign precise value to the content of his mind, whether that were joy or sorrow. (P. 136)

But of course Proust's writing is emotionally toned (not "pathologically sober") and, what is more, colored by something rather close to the "melancholy" Beckett derides in his subject's predecessors. Proust's philosophical reflections about time are suffused with a distanced sadness:

> the arithmetical divisions of time assumed a *dolorous and poetic* aspect.[11] (Italics mine)

And like melancholy, Proust's sorrow is mixed with a certain self-esteem. Generalized, this pride in suffering becomes the basis of his social sentiment:

> the mysteries of life, of love, of death, in which children imagine in their optimism that they have no share, are not set apart, but *we* perceive with a *dolorous pride* that they have embodied themselves in the long course of our life.[12] (Italics mine)

If Proust is sympathetic to man, Beckett seems rather to be snarling with the gods; that is, he seems actually to appreciate the force of time, which renders his study a "science of affliction" (p. 4). Such homilies in *Proust* as "death will cure many of the desire for immortality" (p. 14) generally have the excuse of a religious context, and urge the reader to prepare for judgment; in Beckett's case, nothing seems to underlie them but misanthropy. His cruelty attempts to defend itself in connection with a mania for "precise value," but the following rationale implausibly locates all truth and dignity in those who inflict, never those who receive, pain:

> The insistent memory of cruelties to one who is dead is a flagellation. . . . And pity for what has been suffered is a more *cruel and precise* expression for what has been suffered than the conscious estimate of the sufferer, who is at least spared one despair—the despair of the spectator. (Italics mine)

These lines suggest the disciplinarian's disclaimer, a cliché but unbelievable: "this hurts me more than you." And Beckett's implicit pride in the ability to estimate suffering precisely is especially unconvincing in view of his consistent exaggeration of the painful element in Proust's hero's experiences. For example, Beckett paraphrases a moment of involuntary memory as follows:

> Drabness is obliterated in an *intolerable* brightness. (P. 52, italics mine)

Proust's description of the same moment, though establishing intensity, suggests nothing "intolerable":

> A deep azure blue intoxicated my sight, impressions of coolness and dazzling light hovered near me.[13]

While intense impressions of pain and sorrow and considerable humor are certainly not lacking in Proust's writing, these emotions are harmonized into a dominant and continuous mood, a blend without tension or conflict.

That is not Beckett's way. Almost all of his writing establishes a sensibility whose response to pain is oddly plastic and inconsistent, producing tensions and discords Beckett has chosen to retain and exploit. Suffering is both exaggerated and minimized, so that it is experienced twice, both in its presence

and by its absence, and thus problematically. As early as
Proust, Beckett's love of giving lessons, his violent examples
(e. g., "the tortured body of La Balue in his cage" —p. 12) and
his contempt for all emotion suggest a sadistic relish of man's
suffering. The hostility to feeling in general is particularly
suggestive of de Sade himself, whose philosophy amounts to
this recommendation:

> The delights of *apathy* are worth more than you get of your sensi-
> bility; the latter can only touch the heart in one sense, the other
> titillates and overwhelms all of one's being.[14] (Italics mine)

The titillation de Sade describes is otherwise known as laughter, and Beckett's most stunning humor derives from his descriptions of torturous relationships and a style that deliberately witholds pity. To discover Moran, as well as the more
genial Molloy, he had to look no farther than within.

I am not suggesting that Beckett is insensitive. On the contrary, I think that he discovered within himself an inclination
to what most people, including himself, regard as oversen-
sitivity. He seems to have felt, if not guilt, some sort of impotent and anxious relation to all the world's suffering, which is
regarded as both inevitable and gratuitous; thus he needs to
witness not only the suffering of mankind but also of the animals man slaughters, even boils alive and gelds. In "Dante
and the Lobster," Beckett's first hero is presented as simply
the outer face of these tense relations. Bellacqua's sickish tendency is shown to be foolish, since he always eats the boiled
lobster anyway; but when he tries to resolve his anxiety by
denying the creature's suffering, the reader is directly told that
this is wrong.[15] Apparently, both realizations are necessary
—that the creature does suffer, and that the reaction of humans
(at least certain intellectuals) is apt to be oversensitive. Suffering must be acknowledged, faced, but in a relatively composed manner; in other words, what is needed is pessimism.

Yet Beckett's heroes confess an inability to compose such a
response. What is adequate emotional stability in a world of
sublime and meaningless violence, where life only feeds off
life? From the tension of this unconsoled pessimism there
reverberates a prose profuse, precise, inventive, strangely
poetic, disturbing, and—at least to many readers—wildly

funny. The catalogue of the Lynch family's ailments in *Watt* is a frequently cited instance of this grotesque comic style. The following lines from *Mercier and Camier* are to much the same effect:

> The only branches in which I may boast of having, if not excelled, at least succeeded, were the slaughter of little lambs, calves, kids and porklings and the emasculation of little bullocks, rams, billy goats and piglets, on condition of course they were still unspoiled, all innocence and trustingness. It was therefore to these specialties I confined myself, from the age of fifteen. I have still at home some charming little—well, comparatively little—ram's testes dating from that happy time. In the fowlyard too I was a terror of accuracy and elegance. I had a way of smothering geese that was the admiration and envy of all. Oh I know you are listening with only half an ear, and that half unwilling, but that is nothing to me. . . .
>
> Butcher's boy, said the old man, poulterer's boy, knacker's boy, undertaker's man, sexton, one corpse on top of another, there's my life for you. (Pp. 37–38)

Rarely has the didactic function of such material been more explicit. Beckett is simply insisting that the reader witness this, that is, a world of violence strangely without pain, consequently comical and absurd, but still sufficiently shocking to remain cruel. A trace of squeamish guilt is the price to be paid for relishing this kind of absurdity. To some extent, accordingly, this prose is also conceived as a barrier to sentimentalists. The readers that remain are raked over the coals of violent absurdity to make fools of them, an effective prelude to any message, but chiefly to the value of peace. For it is Beckett's peace of mind, his calm indifference, that requires spectacles of violence in order to test and demonstrate itself, so that it can feel itself; gratuitous violence is its necessary obverse, its reciprocal entailment. It also puts impotent old people in an especially touching light to learn that this sort of "gab" is their "salvation" (p. 39).

This sort of gab would nonetheless seem cheap and forced, too categorical in its cruelty, were it not, as jumping point to a plane of poetic bafflement, part of a larger literary system whose fascinating difficulties tend to resolve themselves without, however, doing so completely. Beckett's art is characteristically a tragicomedy in which the dominant mood always seems to be at the point of tipping over into something else, especially an ecstatic skepticism. He developed this volatile but oddly suspended form of tragicomedy by retaining the materials of the pessimistic tradition that he first claimed in *Proust*, but refocussing them so as to somewhat relax painful and unproductive tensions. And he clearly was in need of such relaxation. The reader of *Proust* will find Beckett strangely overengaged by Proust's prose, fighting something that doesn't really call for such a response:

> One is exhausted and angry after an hour, submerged, dominated by the crest and break of metaphor after metaphor: but never stupified. (p. 68)

Apparently Beckett is overcomplicating, that is, demanding, for the sake of mental stimulation, more clarity and logical consistency than Proust's material either offers or chooses to make an issue of. And Beckett's contemporaneous hero, Bellacqua (the one who is tortured by the sight of boiling a lobster) responds to a difficult passage in Dante with a correlative intellectual sado-masochism:

> Still he [Bellacqua] pored over the enigma, he would not concede himself conquered, he would understand at least the meanings of the words. . . . He was still running his brain against the impenetrable passage.[16]

This is clearly the portrait of someone who is taking something too seriously and not in the appropriate aesthetic spirit. Reacting against this tendency in himself, Beckett, who called life tragic because it is futile (in *Proust*) developed his distinctive tragicomic focus by accepting futility, endorsing ignorance, deciding that thought is more like compulsive masturbation than an ennobling need, and taking a more relaxed and flexible attitude towards logical contradiction. He came to see the contradiction as a relation at least as legitimate as any other and even, as the Unnamable admits, his normal *modus operandi:* "affirmations or negations invalidated as uttered, or sooner or later? Generally speaking" (p. 291.)

The logical development pertains most particularly to the contradiction that Beckett couldn't accept in Proust, which led

Schopenhauer to invoke the void: the contradiction between exceptional moments and the futile systems that make them seem emotionally necessary. As has been seen, extratemporal moments reconciled Proust to temporality, but they could not do so for Schopenhauer. And Beckett, typically, understood Proust's involuntary memories in terms of Schopenhauer's aesthetics:

> And we are reminded of Schopenhauer's definition of the artistic procedure as "the contemplation of the world independently of the principle of sufficient reason." (P. 66)

The problem to which Schopenhauer addressed his aesthetics is that man craves effective contact with essential reality, while all that can be known is shifting relations, objects transient in time and space, effects of causes perceived according to his needs. What cannot be known is the thing in itself, which Schopenhauer likened to the Platonic idea. Then the philosopher indicated an escape route through art. What is required, according to Schopenhauer, is that one forget

> even his individuality, his will, and only continues to exist as the pure subject, the clear mirror of the object, so that it is as if the object alone were there, without anyone to perceive it, and he can no longer separate the perceiver from the perception, because both have become one, because the whole consciousness is filled and occupied with one single sensuous picture; if thus the object has to such an extent *passed out of all relation* to something outside it *and the subject out of all relation to the will,* then that which is so known is no longer the particular thing as such; but it is the Idea, the eternal form.[17] (Italics mine)

And what is the effect of this disinterested contemplation?

> We answer, *Art,* the work of genius. It repeats or reproduces the eternal Ideas grasped through pure contemplation, the essential and abiding in all the phenomena of the world... Its one source is the knowledge of Ideas; its one aim the communication of this knowledge.... *It plucks the object of its contemplation out of the stream of the world's course,* and has it isolated before it. And this particular thing, which in that stream was a small perishing part, becomes to art the representative of the whole, and equivalent of

the endless multitude in space and time. It therefore pauses at this particular thing; the course of time stops; the *relations vanish* for it; only the essential, the Idea, is its object. We may therefore define it as the *way of viewing things independent of the principle of sufficient reason.*[18] (Italics mine)

I am quoting Schopenhauer's reasoning at length because Beckett's own aesthetics retain the same conceptual system, while responding somewhat differently to the problems it implies. His heroes also look to the contemplation of objects, absurdly detached from the normal worldly relations that "explain" them, as a means of bringing peace. That is the function of Molloy's silver object, Moran's bees' dance, and Watt's broken circle, and it is only sensible to suppose that focussing attention on the formal elements of such things can calm the will by correlating its diverse and contradictory impulses. However, Schopenhauer's demands and explanations go further. The subject of aesthetic contemplation, unable to separate its object from itself, no longer strives to possess it (or anything) at all. For once adequately objectified, the subject (as will) perceives itself, while recognizing that the whole world is its will and its idea. Thus the aesthetic contemplation of an object is soothing because it is really an apperception (e. g., self-perception, a term Beckett employs straightforwardly in *Proust,* with irony in *Murphy*).[19] It is only through complete and adequate knowledge of itself that the will can be sufficiently calmed. Unfortunately, when more strictly considered, such knowledge is inconsistent with the most basic assumptions of pessimistic ideology; unintelligible, it must remain ineligible.

As Schopenhauer was obliged to admit,

even that inward experience which we have of our own will by no means afford us an exhaustive and adequate knowledge of the thing in itself.[20]

What should reappear but the inevitable subject-object relation and time:

This would be the case if it were entirely an immediate experience; but it is effected in this way: . . . it is bound to the form of the idea, it is apprehension, and as such falls asunder into subject and object.[21]

The following could serve as a cogent preface to Beckett's *Film:*

> For even in self-consciousness the I is not absolutely simple, but consists of a knower, the intellect, and a known, the will. The former is not known, and the latter does not know, though both unite in the consciousness of an I. But just on that account that I is not thoroughly intimate with itself, as it were transparent, but is opaque *and therefore remains a riddle to itself,* thus even in inner knowledge there also exists a difference between the true being of its object and the apprehension of it in a knowing subject.[22] (Italics mine)

Thus the individual returns, as Beckett says in *Proust,* "to a life all in length, a sequence of dislocations and adjustments" (p. 50), that is, to time:

> Yet inner knowledge is free from two forms which belong to outer knowledge, the form of space and the form of causality, which is the means of effecting all sense-perception. On the other hand, there still remains the form of time, and that of being known and knowing in general. Accordingly in this inner knowledge the thing in itself has indeed in great measure thrown off its veil, but still does not appear quite naked. In consequence of the form of time which still adheres to it, everyone knows his will only in its successive acts, and not as a whole, in and for itself: therefore no one knows his character *a priori,* but only learns it through experience and always incompletely.[23]

These remarks, which anticipate the substance of Sartre's existentialism, are perhaps the basis of a dispute cited above between Murphy and Celia:

> "I am what I do," said Celia.
> "No," said Murphy. "You do what you are, you do a fraction of what you are, you suffer a dreary ooze of your being into doing." (P. 37)

If the self is a will that can only be known through its acts, and thus incompletely, it can never be thoroughly known; and if peace of mind depends upon such knowledge, it will never be attained. So Schopenhauer concludes his work by calling forth the final and most desperate consolation. Perception is based upon the will to live. In actuality,

Before us there is certainly only nothingness. . . . Yet this is the only consideration which can afford us *lasting consolation*, when, on the one hand, we have recognized incurable suffering and endless misery as essential to the manifestations of will, the world, and, on the other hand, see the world pass away with the abolition of will, and retain before us only empty nothingness. Thus . . . we must banish the dark impression of that nothingness which we discern behind all virtue and holiness as their final goal, and which we fear as children fear the dark; we must not even evade it like the Indians, through myths and meaningless words, such as reabsorption in Brahma or the Nirvana of the Buddhists. Rather do we freely acknowledge that what remains after the entire abolition of will is for all those who are still full of will certainly nothing; but, conversely, to those in whom the will has turned and has denied itself, this our world, which is so real, with all its suns and milky ways—is nothing.[24]

The only fit response here is a pause.

§   §   §

As a number of critics have observed, the ideal of nothing and silence (its literary equivalent) have certainly played an important part in Beckett's art. And as R. M. Adams' admirable study *Nil* demonstrates, the experience of nothingness can indeed be suggested by aesthetic structures; but it is always a relative nothingness, a shockingly vacant reply to carefully provoked anticipations, as in Henry James's perhaps somewhat crude "The Beast in the Jungle." In this relative sense, it can be said that a palpable "nothing" is a part of experiencing Beckett, for the reader meets with meaninglessness, hopelessness, and bitterness where he has been trained to expect meaning, hope, and consolation. That a great deal of suffering is literally based upon nothing, in that it is inexplicable, unjustifiable, and thus absurd, is surely a realization Beckett wants his readers to deal with. Still, this is far from the absolute nothing that Schopenhauer invokes above, nor could such an experience ever be triggered by art; indeed, it is Schopenhauer's ironical point that this nothing cannot be experienced at all, since it requires the absence of a subject. In *Murphy* and *Watt*, as I argued above, Beckett does experiment with the notion of Nirvana (dismissed by Schopenhauer as evasive). Theoretically, an equalization of plurality, a blissful blur, ought to be produced by Beckett's automatic, indiscriminate, and exhaustive permutations. Far from wishing to relax all tensions, Beckett resists this outcome by making sure that the mannerism is felt to be abrasive. Similarly, the nothingness discussed in *The Unnamable* and the *Texts for Nothing* is far from "the final goal" "behind all virtue and holiness" Schopenhauer desires; rather, it is closer to the good old-fashioned terrifying void "we fear as children fear the dark." In the "Three Dialogues" with Georges Duthuit, Beckett seems forthrightly to reject the void as an æsthetic alternative, because it always is an alternative to something else and therefore not a real void:

> The void [Masson] speaks of is perhaps simply the obliteration of an unbearable presence, unbearable because neither to be wooed nor to be stormed. If this anguish of helplessness is never stated as such, on its own merits and for its own sake, though perhaps very occasionally admitted as spice to the "exploit" it jeopardized, the reason is doubtless, among others, that it seems to contain in itself the impossibility of statement. Again an exquisitely logical attitude. In any case, it is hardly to be confused with the void.[25]

What remains in need is some means of going on, and to find the theoretical groundwork of Beckett's most rich and sustained accomplishment (I would say particularly the first two books of the trilogy), it is generally agreed that the place to look is Beckett's discussion of Bram Van Velde, his artistic surrogate. Here Beckett responds to the traditional obligation to articulate his motives for writing and to rationalize his artistic activity by defining its value. His response is, first, to reject the traditional rationalizations, recognizing them as rationalizations of an essentially obsessive and pointless activity. Nonetheless, the reactive craving for nothing which Schopenhauer thought the only "lasting consolation" is not to be found here either; nor does Beckett speak of art as knowledge, Schopenhauer's more affirmative idea. Rather, art is discussed in the same terms that Schopenhauer and Beckett, in *Proust*, used to describe life; art is unending futility. And Beckett concludes that the artist must accept his art's futility. This determination to work wholly within the pessimistic tradition is of notable interest in itself.

The artist fails because, in Schopenhauer's terms, he must have access to "Ideas" or perceive things in themselves at certain exceptional moments. If this is granted, as Beckett says in *Proust*, "the artist has acquired his text: the artisan translates it" (p. 64). And Beckett goes on to quote Proust: "The duty and task of a writer (not an artist, a writer) are those of a translator" (p. 64). What the writer is translating is the ineffable. In the act of writing no one is an artist because words bind the writer to time, succession, a mode of experience that is extensive and never whole at once; the artist, as Schopenhauer showed, can be only in the moment, particularly the moment of will-less apperception. This realization is shattering to anyone trying to write of the moment at that moment —the continuous present sense which is the goal of all contemplatives. And in any case, upon reflection, Schopenhauer conceded that such moments are impossible, *qua* moments, let alone impossible to extend. Consequently, Beckett's argument in the dialogues with Duthuit parallels the proof of suffering's inevitability in *Proust*. What were "subject" and "object" are now called "artist" and "occasion"; again, their relation dooms them to eternal separation; that is, the artist's expression of his occasion is never adequate. Here Beckett sets the terms of the discussion:

> The analysis of the relation between the artist and his occasion . . . does not seem to have been very productive. . . . It is obvious that for the artist obsessed with his expressive vocation, anything and everything is doomed to become occasion, including. . .the pursuit of occasion.[26]

As in *Proust*, Beckett emphasizes in the *Dialogues* the difficulties of relation by pointing out that both subject and object (here artist and occasion) are themselves in constant flux:

> But if the occasion appears as an unstable term of relation, the artist, who is the other term, is hardly less so, thanks to his warren of modes and attitudes.[27]

A fuller description suggests a situation characteristically associated with doom, terror, and punishment.:

> The objections to this dualist view are unconvincing. . . . All that should concern us is the *acute and increasing anxiety* of the rela-

tion itself as though *shadowed more and more darkly* by a sense of invalidity, of inadequacy. . . . The history of painting [literature, any art] . . . is the history of its attempts to *escape from this sense of failure,* by means of more authentic, more ample, less exclusive relations between representer and representee . . .[28] (Italics mine)

Like Schopenhauer, Beckett has no doubt of art's function: to bring peace, escape from anxiety. But the problems entailed by the subject-object relation are inescapable, and the solution to this situation is to admit its insolubility:

My case . . . is that Van Velde [i. e., Beckett] is the first to . . . submit wholly to the incoercible absence of relation, in the absence of terms, or, if you like, in the presence of unavailable terms, the first to admit that to be an artist is to fail . . .[29]

In spite of such realizations, the artist must "go on" because he is "obliged" to do so. Beckett seems to accept a condition of ceaseless striving under impossible circumstances. Because he says Van Velde is the "first to accept a certain situation and consent to a certain act,"[30] such an act becomes an affirmative statement in the context of self-imposed and needless difficulty: a situation with humorous, touching, heroic, and horrifying implications. But on the whole, it suggests a relaxation of tensions, because by no longer aiming at an adequate art (an expression of timeless ideas), Van Velde is no longer prey to anxiety and resentment; he can find some peace in an art "unresentful of its insuperable indigence."[31]

That is not all, however. Lest this acknowledgement of failure seem too blithe to be authentic, it is followed by successive contradictions, implying neither affirmation, nor negation, nor indifference, but an unstable and ongoing oscillation among these attitudes: a tragicomedy that reverberates perpetually. At the very beginning of the explanation Beckett announced that, as at the end of *Molloy* and in the preface to *Film,* there would come a retraction. Reminded of this promise by his interlocutor, he ultimately concludes "(*Remembering warmly*) Yes, yes, I am mistaken, I am mistaken."[32] Again, the contradiction is not meant to qualify the strategic acceptance of failure, but to so tightly wind its paradoxical quality that it will be reinforced to a pitch of lyric intensity.

It is in this vein that he reminds the reader not to confuse acceptance of failure with a kind of success; Beckett confesses that he really is unable "to make of this submission, this admission, this fidelity to failure . . . a new occasion, a new term of relation."[33] Then how can Van Velde's art be explained at all? It cannot, and that is why it can provoke an ecstacy of bafflement:

> For what is this coloured plane, that was not there before. I don't know what it is, having never seen anything like it before. It seems to have nothing to do with art, in any case, if my memories of art are correct.[34]

Thus, after all, the admission of failure becomes concomitant with its apparent contradiction: the mystic's reward, a truly exceptional moment. Beckett sees Van Velde's art as wholly new because it establishes no relation to anything else; typically, Van Velde's image is sustained against the background of nothingness and impossibility by a fascinating because wholly inexplicable buoyancy. Like one of Schopenhauer's aesthetic images, Beckett has "plucked the object of contemplation out of the stream of the world's course," but unlike Schopenhauer's object it remains unknown, mysterious. According to Beckett, accepting this uncanny, gratuitous quality of objects is the only soothing alternative to making sense of them. And incurious ignorance is a necessary alternative if no object can be related to its subject through means sufficiently ample and authentic. The history of art, "shadowed more and more darkly by a sense of invalidity," re-enforces this pessimism. But the soothing thing about a wholly confusing and eminently profound image is that it promises to reverberate through all eternity, invincible in its unknowability. Such treasured objects as Molloy's little piece of silver are repositories into which Beckett's heroes can project their need to consider themselves in extratemporal terms.

Paradoxical intersections of most and least meaning, these images are perhaps the most adequate emblems of life for those who hold the problematical response most valid. Living, when conceived as growing old and dying, is a situation that demands both acceptance and rejection, a poised ambivalence. But as Beckett's career has continued to develop, the dominant tendency has been less to describe the context that

occasions and legitimizes such images (that is, the tragicomic
world of Moran and Molloy) than to simply concentrate upon
such images themselves. This results in an art that tends (to
my taste) to be somewhat too abstruse, both overcharged and
bland, devoid of tragicomic tensions sufficiently defined to
produce that unexpected order and disorder which invites the
reader of *Watt* or *Malone Dies* to rediscover the world. In *The
Unnamable* and *How It Is, Come and Go, Ping, Imagination
Dead Imagine,* and *The Lost Ones,* Beckett offers quasi-holy
images of people caught in utterly strange situations, literally
trapped, repeating futile gestures, and engaging in meaningless rituals. The reader is encouraged to contemplate inexplicable mysteries which, not unlike the Trinity or God's son suffering on the cross, can only serve to justify suffering and give
a means of encouragement to the sort of essentially harmless,
passive souls who claim their chief interest is inner peace. Of
course there is some of this in everyone.

Beckett's writing is most humane, interesting, and consistently entertaining when it is also most in touch with literary
tradition. And in suggesting a long line of predecessors, solitary, introspective pessimists from Heraclitus to Proust, Beckett also suggests the context of alternatives in which it is most
appropriate to judge him. In itself, the pessimistic tradition
imposes, more or less as the *donnée* whose repetition affirms
its continuity, somewhat unrealistically simplified models of
consciousness (so as to produce proofs of misery's inevitability); it also imposes a rather arbitrary limitation of moods. And
in a world in which most humans are either substantially sick
or substantially well, it deals with something more like hypochondria, a condition which seems to invite intolerance. But
even within the pessimistic tradition, as the comparison of
Proust to Beckett should indicate, there is much in the latter's
point of view that seems forced, needlessly extreme.

On the other hand, perhaps no one has succeeded so well as
Beckett in sustaining, within the structures of literature, the
seductive rhythms of genuine contemplation. In this respect,
his heroes' repeated admissions that they have been babbling
nonsense can be read as proud assertions. Flattering themselves in their imperviousness to insult and lack of venality,
they remain infantile and resentful in paying back with indifference a world that once did not return their now diminished

interest. These ironies are infinitely exploitable, and it has been through Beckett's inclination to see everything in the mode of implicit self-contradiction that he has indicated how alienation from the world can help sustain a train of thought and frame of mind. The likely benefits are aesthetic raptures including laughter, while the price is likely to include some madness, impotence, bitterness, guilt, and plain depression. In thus putting the spiritual program of solitary contemplation to the test and finding it largely a futile mania, Beckett's heroes perform a useful as well as an intriguing service. And having realized this, it is necessary to go on, at last, to something else. But what.

Notes

Part One, Chapter One
1. Samuel Beckett, "Dante . . . Bruno. Vico . . . Joyce" in *Our Exagmination round his Factification for Incamination of Work in Progress*, by Samuel Beckett, Eugene Jolas, *et al.* (London: Faber and Faber, 1929), p. 13.
2. Ibid., p. 14.
3. Alan Schneider, "Waiting for Beckett," *Chelsea Review*, No. 2 (Autumn 1958), rpt. in B. Gail Chevigny, ed., *Twentieth Century Interpretations of Endgame* (Englewood Cliffs, N. J.: Prentice-Hall, 1965), p. 17.
4. Ibid.
5. See Hugh Kenner, *Samuel Beckett: A Critical Study* (New York: Grove Press, 1961), Chap. 4.
6. Samuel Beckett and Georges Duthuit, "Three Dialogues," *Transition 49*, rpt. in Martin Esslin, ed., *Samuel Beckett: A Collection of Critical Essays*, Twentieth Century Views (Englewood Cliffs, N. J.: Prentice-Hall, 1965), p. 19.
7. Israel Shenker, "Moody Man of Letters," *New York Times*, 6 May 1956, sec. 2, p. 1.
8. Samuel Beckett, *Proust* (New York: Grove Press, 1960), p. 68.
9. Beckett and Duthuit, "Three Dialogues," p. 21.
10. Friedrich Nietzsche, *The Will to Power*, ed. and trans. Walter Kaufmann (New York: Vintage, 1958), p. 423.
11. David Hayman, "Molloy or the Quest for Meaninglessness: A Global Interpretation," rpt. in Melvin Friedmann, ed., *Samuel Beckett Now* (Chicago: University of Chicago Press, 1970).
12. Samuel Beckett, *Watt* (New York: Grove Press, 1959), p. 44.
13. Soren Kierkegaard, *The Concept of Irony*, ed. and trans. Lee M. Capel (Bloomington: Indiana University Press, 1965), p. 107.
14. Jean Paul Sartre, *Nausea*, trans. Lloyd Alexander (New York: New Directions, 1964), p. 172.
15. Ibid., p. 177.
16. Samuel Beckett, *Molloy, Malone Dies and The Unnamable* (New York: Grove Press, 1965), p. 67.
17. Arthur Schopenhauer, *Selections*, ed. Dewitt H. Parker (New York: Scribners, 1928), p. 106.
18. Ibid., p. 107.
19. Ibid.

20. Ludwig Wittgenstein, *Wittgenstein: Lectures and Conversations on Aesthetics, Psychology and Religious Belief,* ed. Cyril Barnett (Berkeley: University of California, 1967), p. 27.

21. The reference to Hegel's phrase appears in Gunter Anders, "Being Without Time: On Beckett's Play *Waiting for Godot,*" rpt. in Esslin, *Samuel Beckett,* p. 146.

Part One, Chapter Two
1. Friedrich Nietzsche, *Twilight of the Idols,* trans. V. Crutchwell (Harmondsworth, Eng.: Penguin Books, 1968), p. 29.

2. Samuel Beckett, *Endgame* (New York: Grove Press, 1958), p. 53.

3. Samuel Beckett, *All that Fall* in *Krapp's Last Tape and Other Dramatic Pieces* (New York: Grove Press, 1957), p. 57.

4. Samuel Beckett, *Happy Days* (New York: Grove Press, 1961), p. 11.

5. Samuel Beckett, *How It Is* (New York: Grove Press, 1958), p. 34.

6. John Fletcher, *Samuel Beckett's Art* (London: Chatto and Windus, 1967), p. 12.

7. Michael Robinson, *The Long Sonata of the Dead: A Study of the Novels of Samuel Beckett* (New York: Grove Press, 1969).

8. Friedrich Nietzsche, *The Birth of Tragedy and the Genealogy of Morals,* trans. F. Golffing (New York: Doubleday, Anchor Press, 1960), p. 145.

9. Beckett, *Endgame,* p. 18.

10. Samuel Beckett, *Watt* (New York: Grove Press, 1959), p. 48.

11. Beckett, *All that Fall,* p. 88.

12. Michel Montaigne, *Essays,* trans. Charles Cotton (Chicago: University of Chicago Press, 1958), p. 529.

13. Samuel Beckett, *Stories and Texts for Nothing* (New York: Grove Press, 1967), p. 60.

14. Boethius, *The Consolation of Philosophy,* trans. R. B. Green, (Indianapolis: Bobbs-Merrill, 1962), p. 16.

15. Israel Shenker, "Moody Man of Letters," *New York Times,* 6 May 1956, sec. 2, p. 1.

16. Marcus Aurelius, *Meditations,* in Moses Hadas, ed., *The Stoic Philosophers* (New York: Bantam Books, 1959), p. 147.

17. Diogenes Laërtius, *The Lives of the Philosophers,* ed. R. D. Hicks (Cambridge: Harvard University Press, 1927), p. 27.

18. Seneca in Hadas, *The Stoic Philosophers,* p. 86.

19. Cited by Montaigne in *Essays,* p. 34.

20. Marcus Aurelius in Hadas, *The Stoic Philosophers,* p. 151.

21. Diogenes Laërtius in Hadas, *The Lives of the Philosophers,* p. 33.

22. Jean Jacques Rousseau, *The Reveries of a Solitary,* trans. J. G. Fletcher (New York: Brentano's, 1937), p. 38.

23. Beckett, *Watt,* p. 43.

24. Rousseau, *Reveries,* p. 57.

25. *Watt,* p. 48.

26. Paul Kristeller, *Renaissance Thought II* (New York: Harper and Row, 1965), p.

27. Arthur Schopenhauer, *Parega and Paralipomena,* trans. T. B. Saunders, in Kuno Francke, ed., *The German Classics of the Nineteenth and Twentieth Centuries* (Albany: J. Blyon, 1913), Vol. 15, p. 79.

Notes

Part One, Chapter Three

1. Michel Montaigne, *Essays*, trans. Charles Cotton (Chicago: University of Chicago Press, 1958), p. 503.
2. Cited in Miguel de Unamuno, *The Tragic Sense of Life*, trans. J. C. Flitch (New York: Dover, 1954), p. 304.
3. Boethius, *The Consolation of Philosophy*, trans. R. B. Green (Indianapolis: Bobbs-Merrill, 1962), p. 16.
4. Joris Karl Huysmans, *Against the Grain*, trans. R. Baldick (Harmondsworth, Eng.: Penguin Books, 1975), p. 329.
5. Arthur Schopenhauer, *Parega and Paralipomena*, trans. T. B. Saunders, in Kuno Francke, ed., *The German Classics of the Nineteenth and Twentieth Centuries* (Albany: J. Blyon, 1913), Vol. 15, p. 79.
6. Cited in E. M. Butler, *The Tyranny of Greece over Germany* (Boston: Beacon Press, 1958), p. 188.
7. Karl Gierow cited in Melvin Friedmann, ed., *Samuel Beckett Now* (Chicago: University of Chicago Press, 1970), p. 30.
8. Montaigne, *Essays*, p. 529.
9. Schopenhauer, *Parega and Paralipomena*, p. 82.
10. Fyodor Dostoevsky, *Notes from Underground*, trans. C. Garnett (New York: Dell, 1960), p. 35.
11. Louis Ferdinand Céline, *Journey to the End of the Night*, trans. John P. Marks (New York: New Directions, 1960), p. 288.
12. Albert Camus, *The Stranger*, trans. S. Gilbert (New York: Vintage Books, 1954), pp. 142–43.
13. Tom Driver, "Beckett by the Madelaine," in *Columbia University Forum*, 4, No. 3, (Summer 1961), 21–25.
14. Albert Camus, *The Myth of Sisyphus*, trans. J. O'Brien (New York, Random House, 1955), pp. 89–90.
15. Giacomo Leopardi, *Poems and Prose*, ed. and trans. Iris Origo and John Heath-Stubbs (New York: New American Library, 1960), p. 93.
16. Jules Renard, *The Journals of Jules Renard*, ed. and trans. Louise Bogan and Elizabeth Roget (New York: George Braziller, 1964), p. 67.
17. Friedrich Nietzsche, *Twilight of the Idols*, trans. V. Crutchwell (Harmondsworth, Eng.: Penguin Books, 1968), p. 30.
18. Samuel Beckett, "Whoroscope," rpt. in *Poems in English by Samuel Beckett* (New York: Grove Press, 1961), p. 15.
19. George von Lichtenberg, *The Lichtenberg Reader*, ed. and trans. by Franz Mautner and Henry Hartfield (Boston: Beacon Press, 1959), p. 55.
20. See David Hayman, "Molloy or the Quest for Meaninglessness: A Global Interpretation," rpt. in Melvin Friedmann, ed., *Samuel Beckett Now* (Chicago: University of Chicago, 1970), and G. C. Barnard, *Samuel Beckett: A New Approach* (New York: Dodd, Mead, 1970), p. x1.
21. Ionesco cited in Martin Esslin, *The Theatre of the Absurd* (Garden City, N. Y.: Doubleday, 1969), p. 307.
22. Friedrich Nietzsche, *Beyond Good and Evil*, trans. Walter Kaufmann (New York, Vintage Books, 1966), pp. 129–30.
23. Sextus Empiricus, *Outlines of Skepticism*, trans. J. B. Bury (Cambridge: Harvard University Press, 1927), p. 9.
24. G. S. Kirk and J. E. Raven, eds., *The Presocratic Philosophers* (London: Cambridge University Press, 1957), p. 193.

25. Cited in J. Glenn Gray, *Hegel and Greek Thought* (Evanston, Ill.: Harper and Row, 1941), p. 89.

26. Sextus Empiricus, in *Outlines of Skepticism*, p. 7.

27. Samuel Beckett, *Murphy* (New York: Grove Press, 1957), p. 39.

28. Beckett to Harold Hobson, cited in Hugh Kenner, *Samuel Beckett: A Critical Study* (New York: Grove Press, 1960), p. 100.

29. Ibid.

30. Miguel de Unamuno, *The Tragic Sense of Life*, ed. J. Flitch (New York: Dover, 1954), p. 3.

Part One, Chapter Four

1. Lawrence E. Harvey, *Samuel Beckett: Poet and Critic* (Princeton: Princeton University Press, 1970), p. 249.

2. Friedrich Nietzsche, *Philosophy in the Tragic Age of the Greeks,* trans. Marianne Cowan (Chicago: Henry Regnery, 1962), p. 84.

3. Martin Heidegger, "Nietzsche as Metaphysician," trans. John Stambaugh in Robert Solomon, ed., *Nietzsche: A Collection of Critical Essays* (Garden City, N. Y.: Anchor Books, 1973), p. 109.

4. Maurice Nadeau, cited in John Fletcher, *The Novels of Samuel Beckett* (London: Chatto and Windus, 1964), p. 99.

5. Hugh Kenner, *Samuel Beckett: A Critical Study* (New York: Grove Press, 1961), p. 35.

6. Northrop Frye, "The Nightmare Life in Death," in J. D. O'Hara, ed., *Twentieth Century Interpretations of Molloy, Malone Dies, and The Unnamable* (Englewood Cliffs, N. J.: Prentice-Hall, 1970), p. 29.

7. Ibid.

8. Harvey, *Samuel Beckett*, p. 222.

9. Frye, "The Nightmare Life in Death," p. 34.

10. R. M. Adams, *Nil* (New York: Oxford Press, 1966), p. 3.

11. Plato, *The Apology,* trans. Hugh Tredennick in *The Collected Dialogues of Plato*, ed. E. Hamilton and Huntington Cairns, (New York: Random House, 1964), p. 25.

12. Samuel Beckett, *Stories and Texts for Nothing* (New York: Grove Press, 1967), p. 25.

13. See Kenner, *Samuel Beckett*, p. 132 for the intellectual system (Newtonian); G. C. Barnard, *Samuel Beckett: A New Approach* (New York: Dodd, Mead, 1970), treats Beckett's heroes as paradigmatic schizophrenics.

14. Giacomo Leopardi, *Poems and Prose*, ed. and trans. Iris Origo and John Heath-Stubbs (New York: New American Library, 1960), p. 84.

15. See Kenneth Rexroth, "The Point Is Irrelevance," in R. Kostalanetz, ed., *On Contemporary Literature* (New York: Avon Books, 1964), p. 422; Gunter Anders, "Being Without Time: On Beckett's Play *Waiting for Godot*," in *Samuel Beckett: A Collection of Critical Essays*, Twentieth Century Views (Englewood Cliffs, N. J.: Prentice-Hall, 1965), p. 141; and Theodore Adorno, "Towards an Understanding of *Endgame*" in B. Gail Chevigny, ed., *Twentieth Century Interpretations of Endgame* (Englewood Cliffs, N. J.: Prentice-Hall, 1965), p. 19.

16. Leopardi, *Poems and Prose*, p. 60.

17. Friedrich Nietzsche, *Schopenhauer as Educator*, ed. E. Vivas (Chicago: Henry Regnery, 1965), p. 89.

18. Ibid.

19. Marcel Proust, *Remembrance of Things Past*, trans. F. A. Blossom (New York: Random House, 1934), II, 896.

20. Samuel Beckett, *Proust* (New York: Grove Press, 1970), p. 46.

21. Arthur Schopenhauer, *The World as Will and Idea*, in DeWitt H. Parker, ed., *Schopenhauer: Selections* (New York: Scribners, 1928), p. 236.

22. Samuel Beckett, *Stories and Texts*, pp. 66–67.

Part One, Chapter Five

1. Samuel Beckett, *Watt* (New York: Grove Press, 1959), p. 46.

2. Samuel Beckett, *Proust* (New York: Grove Press, 1960), p. 7.

3. Samuel Beckett, *Molloy, Malone Dies and The Unnamable* (New York: Grove Press, 1965), p. 130.

4. Ibid., p. 361.

5. R. Y. B. Scott, *The Way of Wisdom in the Old Testament* (New York: Macmillan Co., 1971), p. 122.

6. Cited ibid., p. 41.

7. Xenophanes cited in G. S. Kirk and J. E. Raven, eds., *The Presocratic Philosophers* (London: Cambridge University Press, 1957), p. 163.

8. Diogenes Laërtius, *The Lives of the Philosophers*, ed. R. D. Hicks (Cambridge: Harvard University Press, 1927), p. 27.

9. Ibid.

10. Diogenes Laërtius in Kirk and Raven, *The Presocratic Philosophers*, p. 187.

11. Samuel Beckett, *Stories and Texts for Nothing* (New York: Grove Press, 1967), p. 16.

12. Beckett, *Molloy*, p. 27.

13. Heraclitus in Kirk and Raven, *The Presocratic Philosophers*, p. 187.

14. Beckett, *Watt*, p. 46.

15. Samuel Beckett and Georges Duthuit, "Three Dialogues," *Transition 49*, rpt. in Martin Esslin, ed., *Samuel Beckett: A Collection of Critical Essays*, Twentieth Century Views (Englewood Cliffs, N. J.: Prentice-Hall, 1965), p. 19.

16. Kirk and Raven, *The Presocratic Philosophers*, p. 188.

17. Ibid., p. 212.

18. Ibid., p. 205.

19. For Heraclitus ideas about fire, see Phillip Wheelwright, *Heraclitus* (New York: Atheneum, 1971), pp. 37–57.

20. Samuel Beckett, *Murphy* (New York: Grove Press, 1957), p. 47.

21. Kirk and Raven, *The Presocratic Philosophers*, p. 231.

22. Ibid., p. 228.

23. Diogenes Laërtius, *The Lives*, p. 153.

24. Ibid., p. 165.

25. *Plato: The Collected Dialogues of Plato*, trans. Hugh Tredenick, Edith Hamilton and Huntington Cairns, eds., (New York: Bollingen, 1964), p. 66.

26. Ibid., p. 97.

27. W. C. K. Guthrie, *The Sophists* (Cambridge: Cambridge University Press, 1971), p. 89.

28. Cited in Richard Coe, *Samuel Beckett* (New York: Grove Press, 1964), p. 12.

29. Gabriel d'Auberde, "Waiting for Beckett," *Nouvelles Litteraires* (16 February 1961), pp. 1, 7.

30. Diogenes Laërtius, *The Lives*, p. 5.

31. Gorgias cited in Eduard Zeller, *Outlines of the History of Greek Philosophy*, 13th ed., trans. L. R. Palmer, rev. Wilhelm Nestle (New York: Meridian Books, 1960), p. 104.

32. Donald R. Dudley, *A History of Cynicism from Diogenes to the Sixth Century A. D.* (London: Methuen, 1937), p. 46.

33. Ibid., p. 32.

34. Diogenes Laërtius, *The Lives*, p. 33.

35. Ibid., p. 37.

36. Walter Kaufmann, *Nietzsche: Philosopher, Psychologist, Anti-Christ* (New York: Vintage, 1968), p. 350.

37. Ibid., p. 347.

38. Soren Kierkegaard, *The Concept of Irony*, ed. and trans. Lee M. Capel (Bloomington: Indiana University Press, 1965), p. 51.

39. W. C. K. Guthrie, *Socrates* (Cambridge: Cambridge University Press, 1971), p. 55.

40. Ibid., p. 173.

41. Dudley, *A History of Cynicism*, Chap. 1.

42. Guthrie, *Socrates*, p. 40.

43. Diogenes Laërtius, *The Lives*, p. 5.

44. Dudley, A History of Cynicism, p. 32.

45. Marcus Aurelius, *Meditations*, in Moses Hadas, ed., *The Stoic Philosophers* (New York: Bantam Books, 1959), p. 185.

46. Blaise Pascal, *Pensées*, trans. W. F. Trotter, ed. H. S. & E. B. Thayer (New York: Washington Square Press, 1965), p. 137.

47. Ibid., p. 41.

48. Ibid.

49. Ibid., p. 103.

50. Marande cited in Richard H. Popkin, *The History of Skepticism from Erasmus to Descartes* (New York: Harper and Row, 1964), p. 101.

51. Albert Einstein cited in Lincoln Barnett, *The Universe and Dr. Einstein* (New York: Bantam Books, 1968), p. 10.

52. Ibid.

53. Ibid., p. 108.

54. George von Lichtenberg, *The Lichtenberg Reader*, ed. and trans. Franz Mautner and Henry Hartfield (Boston: Beacon Press, 1959), p. 55.

55. Albert Tennyson cited in Miguel de Unamuno, *The Tragic Sense of Life*, ed. J. Flitch (New York: Dover, 1954), p. 33.

56. There are many allusions to Augustine; Beckett refers to Thomas à Kempis in *More Pricks than Kicks* (New York: Grove Press 1970), p. 37.

57. Boethius, *The Consolation of Philosophy*, trans. R. B. Green (Indianapolis: Bobbs-Merrill, 1962), p. 43.

58. Samuel Beckett, *Poems in English* (New York: Grove Press, 1961), p. 14.

59. Thomas à Kempis, *The Imitation of Christ*, ed. J. Pierce (Harmondsworth, Eng.: Penguin Books, 1968), p. 37.

60. Ibid., p. 39.

61. Ibid., p. 40.

62. Ibid.

63. Ibid., p. 55.

64. Ibid.

65. André Gide, *The Journals of André Gide*, ed. Justin O'Brien (New York: Vintage Books, 1957), I, 18.

66. Thomas à Kempis, *The Imitation of Christ*, p. 33.

67. Ibid., p. 142.

68. René Descartes, *Discourse on Method*, in *Philosophical Works of Descartes*, trans. and ed. E. Haldane and G. R. T. Ross (New York: Dover, 1955), Vol. 1, p. 86.

69. Rousseau cited in Georges Poulet, *Studies in Human Time*, trans. E. Coleman (New York: Harper and Row, 1959), p. 165.

70. Jean Jacques Rousseau, *The Reveries of a Solitary*, trans. J. G. Fletcher (New York: Brentano's, 1937), p. 56.

71. Ibid., p. 40.

72. Charles Baudelaire, *The Poem of Hashish*, trans. Norman Cameron, in P. Quennell, ed., *The Essence of Laughter and Other Essays, Journals, and Letters* (New York: Meridian Books, 1956), p. 100.

73. Charles Baudelaire cited in Georges Poulet, *Studies in Human Time*, trans. E. Coleman (New York: Harper and Row, 1959), p. 105.

74. Charles Baudelaire, *Flowers of Evil*, ed. J. Mathews (New York: New Directions, 1955), p. 4.

75. Ernst Cassirer, *Einstein's Theory of Relativity*, trans. W. C. and M. C. Swabey (New York: Dover Press, 1953), p. 371.

76. Richard Ellmann, *James Joyce* (Oxford: Oxford University Press, 1959), p. 179.

77. James Joyce, *Ulysses* (New York: Random House, 1961), p. 148.

78. Dudley, *A History of Cynicism*, Chap. 1.

79. Nathanael West, *The Dream Life of Balso Snell* in *Two Novels by Nathanael West* (New York: Noonday, 1963), p. 17.

80. Ibid., p. 7.

81. Ibid., p. 13.

82. Ibid., p. 25.

83. Ibid., p. 44.

84. Ibid., p. 17.

85. Ibid., p. 25.

86. Ibid., p. 24.

87. Ibid., p. 16.

88. André Breton cited in Richard Ellmann and Charles Feidelson, Jr., eds., *The Modern Tradition* (New York: Oxford University Press, 1965), p. 603.

89. Ibid., p. 602.

90. André Breton cited in Ferdinand Alquie, *The Philosophy of Surrealism* (Ann Arbor: University of Michigan Press, 1969), p. 113.

91. John Fletcher, *The Art of Samuel Beckett* (London: Chatto and Windus, 1967), p. 17.

92. André Breton cited in R. H. Wilenski, *Modern French Painters* (New York: Harcourt Brace Jovanovich, 1963), II, 147.

93. Louis Ferdinand Céline, *Journey to the End of the Night*, trans. John P. Marks (New York: New Directions, 1960), p. 220.

94. Ibid., p. 414.

95. Martin Esslin, ed., *Samuel Beckett: A Collection of Critical Essays*, Twentieth Century Views (Englewood Cliffs, N. J.: Prentice-Hall, 1965), p. 4.

96. Ibid., Introduction.

97. Soren Kierkegaard, *Journals*, ed. and trans. Alexander Dru (New York: Harper and Row, 1959), p. 40.

98. Soren Kierkegaard, *Repetition*, ed. Walter Lowrie (New York: Harper and Row, 1964), p. 11.

99. Kierkegaard, *Journals*, p. 50.

100. Ibid., p. 166.

101. Ibid., pp. 89–90.

102. Ibid., p. 97.

103. Ibid., p. 106.

104. J. de Espronceda cited in Miguel de Unamuno, *The Tragic Sense of Life*, ed. G. Flitch (New York: Dover, 1954), p. 241.

105. Kierkegaard, *Journals*, p. 143.

106. Ibid., p. 89.

107. Kierkegaard, *Repetition*, p. 38.

108. Kierkegaard, *Journals*, p. 107.

109. Ibid., p. 116.

110. Ibid., p. 192.

111. Ibid., p. 190.

112. Ibid., p. 172.

113. Ibid.

114. Ibid., p. 183.

115. Gabriel d'Auberde, "Waiting for Beckett," *Nouvelles Litteraires* (16 February 1961), pp. 1, 7.

116. Soren Kierkegaard, *Concluding Unscientific Postscript*, trans. D. F. Svenson and Walter Lowrie, in *Reality, Man and Existence: Essential Works of Existentialism*, ed. H. J. Blackham (New York: Bantam Books, 1963), p. 20.

117. Ibid., p. 23.

118. Ibid., p. 19.

119. Cited in Karl Jaspers, *Socrates, Buddha, Confucius, Jesus*, ed. and trans. R. Manheim (New York: Harcourt Brace, 1962), p. 25.

120. Ibid., p. 42.

121. Kierkegaard, *Repetition*, p. 34.

122. Germaine Brée, "The Strange World of Beckett's 'grand articules,' " rpt. in Melvin Freidmann, ed., *Samuel Beckett Now* (Chicago: University of Chicago Press, 1970), p. 80.

123. Samuel Beckett, *Play* in *Cascando and Other Short Dramatic Pieces* (New York: Grove Press, 1963), p. 45.

124. Edouard von Hartmann cited by Mitchell Ginsberg, "Nietzschean Psychiatry," in Robert Solomon, ed., *Nietzsche: A Collection of Critical Essays* (Garden City, N. Y.: Anchor Press, 1973), p. 304.

125. Lichtenberg, *The Lichtenberg Reader*, p. 50.

126. Samuel Beckett, *More Pricks than Kicks* (New York: Grove Press, 1970), p. 56.

Part Two, Chapter One

1. Israel Shenker, "Moody Man of Letters," *New York Times*, 6 May 1956, sec. 2, p. 3.

2. Samuel Beckett, *Proust* (New York: Grove Press, 1960), p. 7.

3. A. O. Lovejoy, *The Great Chain of Being* (New York: Harper, 1959), p. 208.

4. Richard Coe, *Samuel Beckett* (New York: Evergreen, 1964), p. 25.

5. Hugh Kenner, *Samuel Beckett: A Critical Study* (New York: Grove Press, 1961), pp. 42–44.

6. Beckett, *Proust*, "Foreword" (unnumbered page).

7. Marcel Proust, *Remembrance of Things Past*, trans. C. K. Scott Moncrieff (New York: Random House, 1934), II, 221.

8. Samuel Beckett, *Watt* (New York: Grove Press, 1959), p. 46.

9. Friedrich Nietzsche, *Schopenhauer as Educator*, ed. E. Vivas (Chicago: Henry Regnery, 1965), p. 2.

10. Friedrich Nietzsche, *The Birth of Tragedy and The Genealogy of Morals*, trans. F. Golffing (New York: Doubleday, Anchor Press, 1960), p. 145.

11. Friedrich Nietzsche, *The Will to Power*, ed. and trans. Walter Kaufmann (New York: Vintage Books, 1958), Bk. I, Chap. 1.

12. Nietzsche, *Schopenhauer*, p. 1.

13. Beckett may be thinking of the chapter on "Friendship" in *Thus Spake Zarathustra*, trans. Walter Kaufmann, in Kaufmann, ed., *The Portable Nietzsche* (New York: Viking, 1954), pp. 167–76.

14. Nietzsche, *The Will to Power*, Bk. I, Chap. 1.

15. Ibid.

16. Ibid.

17. Ibid.

18. Ibid.

19. Beckett, *Proust*, p. 5.

20. Soren Kierkegaard, *Repetition*, ed. Walter Lowrie (New York: Harper and Row, 1964), p. 78.

21. T. E. Hulme, *Speculations*, ed. Herbert Read (New York: Harcourt Brace, 1936), p. 47.

Part Two, Chapter Two

1. Marcel Proust, *Remembrance of Things Past*, trans. C. K. Scott Moncrieff and F. A. Blossom (New York: Random House, 1934), II, 999.

2. Ibid., I, 366.

3. Ibid., p. 36.

4. Ibid., II, 683.

5. Ibid., I, 20.

6. Ibid., II, 230.

7. Ibid., I, 170.

8. Ibid., II, 572.

9. Ibid., I, 1003.

10. Donald R. Dudley, *A History of Cynicism from Diogenes to the Sixth Century A. D.* (London: Methuen, 1937), p. 11.

11. Proust, Remembrance of Things Past, Vol. II.
12. Ibid., p. 1029.
13. Ibid.
14. Ibid., p. 479.
15. Ibid., p. 342.
16. Ibid., p. 554.
17. Ibid., p. 582.
18. Dudley, *A History of Cynicism*, p. 26.
19. Proust, *Remembrance of Things Past*, II, 12.
20. Ibid., p. 992.
21. Ibid., I, 35.
22. Ibid., II, 19.
23. Ibid., I, 125–26.
24. Ibid., p. 127.
25. Ibid., p. 29.
26. Ibid., II, 968.
27. *Webster's Seventh New Collegiate Dictionary* (Springfield: G. C. Merriam, 1970), p. 2.
28. Proust, *Remembrance of Things Past*, II, 698.
29. Ibid., I, 767.
30. Ibid., II, 995.
31. Ibid., p. 805.
32. Arthur Schopenhauer, Dewitt H. Parker, ed., *Schopenhauer: Selections* (New York: Scribners, 1928), pp. 173, 249.
33. Proust, *Remembrance of Things Past*, I, 66.
34. Ibid., p. 293.
35. Schopenhauer, *Selections*, p. 122.
36. Arthur Schopenhauer, *Parega and Paralipomena*, trans. T. B. Saunders, in Kuno Francke, ed., *The German Classics of the Nineteenth and Twentieth Centuries* (Albany: J. Blyon, 1913), Vol. 15, p. 93.
37. Proust, *Remembrance of Things Past*, I, 130.
38. Schopenhauer, *Selections*, p. 122.
39. Ibid., p. 235.
40. Ibid., pp. 235–6.
41. Ibid., p. 231.
42. Arthur Schopenhauer, *Selections from the Philosophy of Schopenhauer*, ed. G. Erdmann (New York: Modern Library, 1950), p. 264.
43. Proust, *Remembrance of Things Past*, vol. I, p. 130.
44. Ibid., p. 8.
45. Schopenhauer, *Selections*, p. 180.

Part Two, Chapter Three
1. Arthur Schopenhauer, Dewitt H. Parker, ed., *Schopenhauer: Selections* (New York: Scribners, 1928), p. 4.
2. Ibid.
3. Ibid. p. 96.
4. Richard Coe, *Samuel Beckett* (New York: Evergreen, 1964), p. 26.
5. Friedrich Nietzsche, *The Birth of Tragedy and the Genealogy of Morals*, ed. Francis Golffing (New York: Doubleday, Anchor Press, 1960), p. 254.

6. *A Handbook of Christian Theology,* ed. M. Halverson and A. Cohen (Cleveland: Meridian Books, 1958), p. 366.

7. William Barrett, *Irrational Man* (Garden City: Doubleday, 1962), p. 247.

8. S. Radhakrishnan and Charles A. Moore, *A Sourcebook in Indian Philosophy* (Princeton: Princeton University Press, 1957), p. 272.

9. Ibid., p. 274.

10. Ibid., p. 272.

11. Samuel Beckett, *Proust* (New York: Grove Press, 1960), pp. 3–4.

12. Radhakrishnan and Moore, *Indian Philosophy,* p. 272.

13. Ibid.

14. Samuel Beckett, *Murphy* (New York: Grove Press, 1957), p. 113.

15. Radhakrishnan and Moore, *Indian Philosophy,* p. 340.

16. Ibid.

17. Madame Guion cited in Schopenhauer, *Selections,* p. 340.

18. Radhakrishnan and Moore, *Indian Philosophy,* p. 340.

19. Beckett, *Proust,* p. 32.

20. Samuel Beckett, *Waiting for Godot* (New York: Grove Press, 1954), p. 29.

21. Cited in Karl Jaspers, *Socrates, Buddha, Confucius, Jesus,* ed. and trans. R. Manheim (New York: Harcourt and Brace, 1962), p. 29.

22. Beckett, *Proust,* p. 56.

23. Ernst Cassirer, *Substance and Function and Einstein's Theory of Relativity,* trans. W. C. and M. C. Swabey (New York: Dover Publications, 1953).

24. Leibniz cited in Lincoln Barnett, *The Universe and Doctor Einstein* (New York: Bantam Books, 1968), p. 46.

25. Nicholas Rescher, *The Philosophy of Leibniz* (Englewood Cliffs, N.J.: Prentice-Hall, 1967), p. 20.

26. Beckett, *Murphy,* p. 181.

27. Samuel Beckett, *Molloy, Malone Dies, and The Unnamable* (New York: Grove Press, 1965), p. 12.

28. Ibid., p. 90.

29. Gottfried Willhelm von Leibniz, *Monadology,* in G. Montgomery and A. Chandler, eds., *The Rationalists* (Garden City, N.Y.: Doubleday, 1968), p. 46.

30. See the concluding stanzas of "Ode on a Grecian Urn" and "Ode to a Nightingale."

31. Samuel Beckett and Georges Duthuit, "Three Dialogues," *Transition 49,* rpt. in Martin Esslin, ed., *Samuel Beckett: A Collection of Critical Essays,* Twentieth Century Views (Englewood Cliffs, N.J.: Prentice-Hall, 1965), p. 19.

32. Rescher, *The Philosophy of Leibniz,* p. 25.

33. Ibid., p. 158.

34. Leibniz, *Monadology,* p. 457.

35. Ibid.

36. George Berkeley, *The Principles of Human Knowledge and Three Dialogues between Hylas and Philonous,* ed. G. J. Warnock (Cleveland: Meridian Books, 1963), p. 66.

37. Ibid., p. 77.

232   *Samuel Beckett and the Pessimistic Tradition*

38. J. Glenn Gray, *Hegel and Greek Thought* (New York: Harper, 1941), p. 90.

39.. Soren Kierkegaard, *Concluding Unscientific Postscript*, trans. D. F. Svenson and Walter Lowrie, in H. J. Blackham, ed., *Reality, Man and Existence: Essential Works of Existentialism* (New York: Bantam Books, 1963), p. 20.

40. Gray, *Hegel and Greek Thought*, p. 5.

41. Ibid.,

42. Ibid., p. 6.

43. Beckett, *Molloy*, p. 36.

44. Soren Kierkegaard, *The Concept of Irony*, ed. and trans. Lee M. Capel (Bloomington: Indiana University Press, 1965), p. 59.

45. Soren Kierkegaard, *Repetition*, ed. Walter Lowrie (New York: Harper and Row, 1964), p. 41.

46. Soren Kierkegaard, *Either/Or*, in Robert Bretall, ed., *A Kierkegaard Anthology* (Princeton: Princeton University Press, 1946.

47. Friedrich Nietzsche, *The Will to Power*, ed. and trans. Walter Kaufmann (New York: Vintage, 1958), pp. 266–67.

48. See Arthur Danto, "Nietzsche's Perspectivism," in Robert Solomon, ed., *Nietzsche: A Collection of Critical Essays* (New York: Doubleday, Anchor Press, 1973), p. 38.

49. Beckett, *Proust*, p. 47.

50. Marcel Proust, *Remembrance of Things Past*, trans. C. K. Scott Moncrieff and F. A. Blossom (New York: Random House, 1934), I, 442.

51. Ibid., II, p. 448.

42. Ibid., p. 718.

Part Two, Chapter Four

1. Jean Paul Sartre, *Nausea*, trans. Lloyd Alexander (New York: New Directions, 1964), p. 79.

2. Mallarmé cited in R. M. Adams, *Nil* (London: Oxford University Press, 1966), p. 163.

3. Samuel Beckett, *Watt* (New York: Grove Press, 1959), p. 21.

4. Samuel Beckett, *Waiting for Godot* (New York: Grove Press, 1954), p. 39.

5. Leibniz cited in Nicholas Rescher, *The Philosophy of Leibniz* (Englewood Cliffs, N.J.: Prentice-Hall, 1967), p. 127.

6. Samuel Beckett, *Proust* (New York: Grove Press, 1960), p. 41.

7. Richard Coe, *Samuel Beckett* (New York: Evergreen, 1964), p. 17.

8. Parmenides cited in G. S. Kirk and J. E. Raven, eds., *The Presocratic Philosophers* (London: Cambridge University Press, 1957), pp. 273, 275.

9. Cited in Eugene Webb, *Samuel Beckett: A Study of His Novels* (Seattle: University of Washington Press, 1970), p. 38.

10. Ibid.

11. Marcel Proust, *Remembrance of Things Past*, trans. C. K. Scott Moncrieff and F. A. Blossom New York: Random House, 1934), I, 489.

12. Ibid., II, 718.

13. Ibid., I, 489.

14. St. Augustine, *The Confessions of St. Augustine*, trans. R. S. Pine-Coffin, (Harmondsworth, Eng.: Penguin Books, 1961), p. 198.

15. Beckett, *Proust*, pp. 5–6.

16. St. Augustine, *Confessions*, p. 267.

17. Ibid., p. 269.

18. Ibid., p. 264.

19. Ibid., p. 272.

20. Leibniz cited in Rescher, *The Philosophy of Leibniz*, p. 135.

21. St. Augustine, *Confessions*, p. 273.

22. Coe, *Samuel Beckett*, p. 52.

23. Georges Poulet, *Studies in Human Time*, trans. E. Coleman (New York: Harper, 1959), p. 83.

24. Ibid., p. 16.

25. Boileau cited ibid.

26. Ibid.

27. Samuel Beckett, *Poems in English* (New York: Grove Press, 1961), p. 59.

28. Ibid., p. 14.

29. René Descartes, *The Philosophical Works of Descartes* (New York: Dover Press, 1959), I, 168.

30. See the discussion of Occasionalism in Hugh Kenner, *Samuel Beckett: A Critical Study* (New York: Grove Press, 1961), pp. 83–84.

31. Jean Jacques Rousseau, *The Reveries of a Solitary*, trans. J. Fletcher (New York: Brentano's, 1927), p. 113.

32. Ibid., p. 173.

33. Schopenhauer cited in R. Ellmann and Charles Feidelson, Jr., eds., *The Modern Tradition* (New York: Oxford University Press, 1965), p. 546.

34. Ibid.

35. Ibid.

36. Poulet, *Studies in Human Time*, p. 132.

37. Ibid., p. 143.

38. Ibid., p. 141.

39. Charles Baudelaire, *Paris Spleen*, trans. L. Varese (New York: New Directions, 1970), p. 5.

40. Ibid., p. 6.

41. Ibid.

42. Ibid.

43. Ibid., p. 7.

44. John Fletcher, *The Art of Samuel Beckett* (London: Chatto and Windus, 1964), p. 195.

45. Jean Paul Sartre, *Literary and Philosophical Essays*, trans. Annette Michelson (New York: Collier, 1967), p. 28.

46. Ibid., p. 29.

47. Jean Paul Sartre, *Being and Nothingness*, trans. H. Barnes (New York: Citadel, 1966), pp. 36–37.

48. Ibid., p. 94.

49. Vladimir Nabokov, *Pale Fire* (New York: Lancer Books, 1964), p. 38.

50. Coe, *Samuel Beckett*, p. 17.

234   *Samuel Beckett and the Pessimistic Tradition*

51. Sartre, *Being and Nothingness,* p. 94.

52. Ibid.

53. Ibid., p. 95.

54. Richard H. Popkin, *The History of Skepticism from Erasmus to Descartes* (New York: Harper and Row, 1964), p. 204.

55. Lincoln Barnett, *The Universe and Doctor Einstein* (New York: Bantam Books, 1968), p. 48.

56. Sartre, *Being and Nothingness,* p. 83.

57. Ibid., p. 86.

58. Ibid.

59. Soren Kierkegaard, *Journals,* ed. and trans. Alexander Dru (New York: Harper and Row, 1959), p. 143.

60. Coe, *Samuel Beckett,* p. 18.

61. Poulet, *Studies in Human Time,* p. 16.

62. Sartre, *Being and Nothingness,* p. 184.

63. Friedrich Nietzsche, *The Birth of Tragedy and The Genealogy of Morals,* trans. F. Golffing (New York: Doubleday, Anchor Press, 1969), p. 145.

64. James Mill cited in William James, *Principles of Psychology* (New York: Henry Holt, 1890), p. 605.

65. Proust, *Remembrance of Things Past,* II, 943; Samuel Beckett, *Molloy, Malone Dies and The Unnamable* (New York: Grove Press, 1970), p. 57.

66. David Hume, *An Inquiry Concerning the Human Understanding,* in Isaiah Berlin, ed., *The Age of Enlightenment,* (New York: New American Library, 1956), p. 258.

67. Ibid., p. 260.

68. David Hume, *An Inquiry Concerning the Human Understanding,* (New York: Liberal Arts Press, 1959), pp. 58, 60.

69. Proust, *Remembrance of Things Past,* II, 408.

70. Ibid., I, 39.

71. Ibid.

72. Ibid., II, 676.

73. Ibid., vol. II.

74. Ibid., II, 112.

75. Ibid., p. 1023.

76. Ibid., I, 509.

77. Ibid., p. 281.

Part Two, Chapter Five

1. Marcel Proust, *Remembrance of Things Past,* trans. C. K. Scott Moncrieff and F. A. Blossom (New York: Random House, 1934), II, 111.

2. Ibid., p. 112.

3. Henri Bergson cited in R. Ellmann and Charles Feidelson, Jr., eds., *The Modern Tradition* (New York: Oxford University Press, 1965), p. 725.

4. Proust, *Remembrance of Things Past,* II, 1122–1123.

5. Ibid.

6. Ibid.

7. Ibid., p. 1124.

8. Soren Kierkegaard, *Journals,* ed. and trans. Alexander Dru, (New York: Harper and Row, 1959), p. 143.

9. Proust, *Remembrance of Things Past,* vol. II.

10. Ibid., II, 929.

11. Ibid., p. 763.

12. Ibid., I, 800.

13. Ibid., II, 992.

14. The Marquis de Sade, *Philosophy in the Bedroom,* trans. A. and R. Wainhouse (New York: Grove Press, 1965), p. 346.

15. Samuel Beckett, *More Pricks than Kicks* (New York: Grove Press, 1970), p. 22.

16. Ibid., p. 136.

17. Arthur Schopenhauer, Dewitt H. Parker, ed., *Schopenhauer: Selections,* (New York: Scribners, 1928), pp. 98–99. ˙

18. Ibid., p. 106.

19. Samuel Beckett, *Proust,* (New York: Grove Press, 1960), p. 69; and his *Murphy,* (New York: Grove Press, 1957), p. 21.

20. Schopenhauer, *Selections,* p. 327.

21. Ibid., pp. 327–28.

22. Ibid., p. 328.

23. Ibid.

24. Ibid., pp. 280–81.

25. Samuel Beckett and Georges Duthuit, "Three Dialogues," *Transition 49,* rpt. in Martin Esslin, ed., *Samuel Beckett: A Collection of Critical Essays, Twentieth Century Views* (Englewood Cliffs, N. J.: Prentice-Hall, 1965), p. 18.

26. Ibid., p. 21.

27. Ibid.

28. Ibid.

29. Ibid.

30. Ibid.

31. Ibid.

32. Ibid., p. 22.

33. Ibid., p. 21.

34. Ibid.

Bibliography

Adams, Robert M. *Nil*. New York: Oxford Press, 1966.

Alquie, Ferdinand. *The Philosophy of Surrealism*. Ann Arbor: University of Michigan, 1969.

Auerbach, Erich. *Mimesis*. New York: Doubleday, Anchor Press, 1957.

Augustine, Saint. *The Confessions of St. Augustine*. Trans. R. S. Pine-Coffin. Harmondsworth, Eng.: Penguin Books, 1961.

Barnard, G. C. *Samuel Beckett: A New Approach*. New York: Dodd, Mead, 1970.

Barnett, Lincoln. *The Universe and Doctor Einstein*. New York: Bantam Books, 1968.

Barrett, William. *Irrational Man*. Garden City, N.Y.: Doubleday, 1962.

Baudelaire, Charles. *The Essence of Laughter, and Other Essays, Journals and Letters*. Ed. Peter Quennel. New York: New Directions, 1970.

–––––– *Flowers of Evil*. Ed. J. Mathews. New York: New Directions, 1955.

–––––– *Paris Spleen*. Trans. Louise Varese. New York: New Directions, 1970.

Beckett, Samuel. *Cascando and Other Short Dramatic Pieces*. New York: Grove Press, 1963.

–––––– "Dante . . . Bruno. Vico . . . Joyce." In *Our Exagmination round His Factification for Incamination of Work in Progress*. London: Faber and Faber, 1929.

–––––– *Endgame*. New York: Grove Press, 1958.

–––––– *First Love and Other Shorts*. New York: Grove Press, 1974.

–––––– *Happy Days*. New York: Grove Press, 1961.

–––––– *How It Is*. New York: Grove Press, 1958.

–––––– *Krapp's Last Tape and Other Dramatic Pieces*. New York: Grove Press, 1957.

–––––– *The Lost Ones*. New York: Grove Press, 1972.

–––––– *Mercier and Camier*. New York: Grove Press, 1974.

_____ *Molloy, Malone Dies and The Unnamable.* New York: Grove Press, 1965.

_____ *More Pricks than Kicks.* New York: Grove Press, 1970.

_____ *Murphy.* New York: Grove Press, 1957.

_____ *Poems in English.* New York: Grove Press, 1961.

_____ *Proust.* New York: Grove Press, 1960.

_____ *Stories and Texts for Nothing.* New York: Grove Press, 1967.

_____ *Waiting for Godot.* New York: Grove Press, 1954.

_____ *Watt.* Grove Press, 1959.

Beckett, Samuel and Duthuit, Georges. "Three Dialogues." *Transition 49.* Rpt. in Esslin, Martin. *Samuel Beckett: A Collection of Critical Essays.* Englewood Cliffs, N. J.: Prentice-Hall, 1965.

Berkeley, George. *The Principles of Human Knowledge and Three Dialogues Between Hylas and Philonous.* Ed. G. J. Warnock. Cleveland: Meridian Books, 1963.

Blackham, H. J. (ed.) *Reality, Man and Existence: Essential Works of Existentialism* (New York: Bantam Books, 1963).

Boethius. *The Consolation of Philosophy.* Trans. R. B. Green, Indianapolis: Bobbs-Merrill, 1962.

Butler, E. M. *The Tyranny of Greece over Germany.* Boston: Beacon Press, 1958.

Camus, Albert. *The Myth of Sisyphus.* Trans. Justin O'Brien. New York: Random House, 1955.

_____ *The Stranger.* Trans. Stuart Gilbert. New York: Random House, 1954.

Cassirer, Ernst. *Substance and Function and Einstein's Theory of Relativity.* Trans. W. C. Swabey and M. C. Swabey. (New York: Dover Publications, 1953).

Céline, Louis Ferdinand. *Journey to the End of the Night.* Trans. John P. Marks. New York: New Directions, 1960.

Chevigny, B. Gail (ed.). *Twentieth Century Interpretations of Endgame.* Englewood Cliffs, N.J.: Prentice-Hall, 1965.

Coe, Richard. *Samuel Beckett.* New York: Grove Press, 1964.

d'Auberde, Gabriel. "Waiting for Beckett." *Nouvelles Litteraires,* 16 February 1961, pp. 1, 7.

Descartes, René. *Philosophical Works.* Trans. E. Haldane and G. R. T. Ross. New York: Dover, 1955.

Diogenes Laërtius. *The Lives of the Philosophers.* Trans. R. D. Hicks. Cambridge: Harvard University Press, 1927.

Dostoevsky, Fyodor. *Notes from Underground.* Trans. Constance Garnett. New York: Dell, 1960.

Driver, Tom. "Beckett by the Madelaine." *Columbia University Forum,* 4, no. 3 (summer 1961), 21–25.

Dudley, Donald R. *A History of Cynicism from Diogenes to the Sixth Century A.D.* London: Methuen, 1937.

Ellmann, Richard. *James Joyce*. Oxford: Oxford University Press, 1959.

Ellmann, Richard, and Feidelson, Charles, Jr. *The Modern Tradition*. New York: Oxford University Press, 1965.

Esslin, Martin. *The Theatre of the Absurd*. Garden City, N.Y.: Doubleday, 1969.

―――― *Samuel Beckett: A Collection of Critical Essays*. Englewood Cliffs, N.J.: Prentice-Hall. 1965.

Federman, Raymond. *Journey to Chaos: Samuel Beckett's Early Fiction*. Berkeley: University of California, 1963.

Fletcher, John. *The Novels of Samuel Beckett*. London: Chatto and Windus, 1964.

―――― *The Art of Samuel Beckett*. London: Chatto and Windus, 1967.

Friedman, M.J. *Samuel Beckett Now*. Chicago: University of Chicago Press, 1970.

Gide, André. *The Journals of André Gide*. Ed. and trans. J. O'Brien. New York: Vintage Books, 1957.

Gray, J. Glenn. *Hegel and Greek Thought*. Evanston, Ill.: Harper and Row, 1941.

Guthrie, W. K. C. *Socrates*. Cambridge: Cambridge University Press, 1971.

―――― *The Sophists*. Cambridge: Cambridge University Press, 1971.

Hadas, Moses (ed.). *The Stoic Philosophers*. New York: Bantam Books, 1959.

Halverson, M., and Cohen, A. (eds.). *A Handbook of Christian Theology*. Cleveland: Meridian Books, 1958.

Harvey, Lawrence. *Samuel Beckett: Poet and Critic*. Princeton: Princeton University Press, 1970.

Hindus, Milton. *The Proustian Vision*. Carbondale: Southern Illinois University Press, 1954.

Hume, David. *An Inquiry Concerning Human Understanding*. New York: Liberal Arts Press, 1959.

Huysmans, J. K. *Against the Grain*. Trans. R. Baldick. Harmondsworth, Eng.: Penguin Books, 1975.

James, William. *The Principles of Psychology*. New York: Henry Holt, 1890.

Jaspers, Karl. *Socrates, Buddha, Confucius, Jesus*. Trans. R. Manheim. New York: Harcourt Brace, 1962.

Joyce, James. *Portrait of the Artist as a Young Man*. New York: Viking Press, 1968.

―――― *Ulysses*. New York: Random House, 1961.

Kaufmann, Walter. *Nietzsche: Philosopher, Psychologist, Anti-Christ*. New York: Vintage, 1968.

Kenner, Hugh. *Samuel Beckett: A Critical Study*. New York: Grove Press, 1961.

Kierkegaard, Soren. *A Kierkegaard Anthology*. Ed. Robert Bretall. Princeton: Princeton University Press, 1946.

———. *The Concept of Irony*. Bloomington: Indiana University Press, 1965.

———. *Journals*. Tranns. Alexander Dru. New York: Harper and Row, 1959.

———. *Repetition*. Trans. Walter Lowrie. New York: Harper and Row, 1964.

Kirk, G. S., and Raven, J. E. *The Presocratic Philosophers*. London: Cambridge University Press, 1957.

Kostalanetz, Richard, ed. *On Contemporary Literature*. New York: Avon Books, 1964.

Kristeller, Paul. *Renaissance Thought II*. Harper and Row, 1965.

Leibniz, Gottfried Willhelm von. *Monadology*. In *The Rationalists*. Ed. G. Montgomery and A. Chandler. Garden City, N.Y.: Doubleday, 1968.

Leopardi, Giacomo. *Poems and Prose*. Trans. Iris Origo and John Heath-Stubbs (New York: New American Library, 1960).

Lichtenberg, George von. *The Lichtenberg Reader*. Trans. F. Mautner and H. Hartfield. Boston: Beacon Press, 1959.

Lovejoy, A. O. *The Great Chain of Being*. New York: Harper and Row, 1959.

Montaigne, Michel Eyquem, seigneur de. *Essays*. Trans. Charles Cotton. Chicago: University of Chicago Press, 1958.

Nabokov, Vladimir. *Pale Fire*. New York: Lancer Books, 1964.

Nietzsche, Friedrich. *Beyond Good and Evil*. Trans. Walter Kaufmann. New York: Vintage Books, 1966.

———. *The Birth of Tragedy and the Genealogy of Morals*. Trans. Francis Golffing. New York: Doubleday, Anchor Press, 1960.

———. *Philosophy in the Tragic Age of the Greeks*. Trans. Marianne Cowan. Chicago: Henry Regnery, 1965.

———. *The Portable Nietzsche*. Ed. Walter Kaufmann. New York: Viking, 1954.

———. *Schopenhauer as Educator*. Trans. E. Vivas. Chicago: Henry Regnery, 1965.

———. *The Twilight of the Idols*. Trans. V. Crutchwell. Harmondsworth, Eng.: Penguin Books, 1968.

———. *The Will to Power*. Trans. W. Kaufmann. Cleveland: Meridian Books, 1966.

O'Hara, J. D. *Twentieth Century Interpretations of Molloy, Malone Dies, and The Unnamable*. Englewood Cliffs, N.J.: Prentice-Hall, 1970.

Pascal, Blaise, *Pensées*. Trans. W. F. Trotter. New York: Washington Square Press, 1965.

Plato. *The Collected Dialogues of Plato.* Ed. Edith Hamilton and Huntington Cairns. New York: Random House, 1963.

Popkin, Richard H. *The History of Skepticism from Erasmus to Descartes.* New York: Harper and Row, 1964.

Poulet, Georges. *Studies in Human Time.* Trans. E. Coleman. New York: Harper and Row, 1959.

Pronko, L. C. *Avant-Garde: The Experimental Theatre in France.* Berkeley: University of California Press, 1969.

Proust, Marcel. *Remembrance of Things Past.* Trans. C. K. Scott Moncrieff and F. A. Blossom. New York: Random House, 1934.

Radhakrishnan, S., and Moore, C. *A Sourcebook in Indian Philosophy.* Princeton: Princeton University Press, 1957.

Renard, Jules. *The Journals of Jules Renard.* Trans. Louise Bogan and Elizabeth Roget. New York: Braziller, 1964.

Rescher, Nicholas. *The Philosophy of Leibniz.* Englewood Cliffs, N.J.: Prentice-Hall, 1967.

Robinson, Michael. *The Long Sonata of the Dead.* New York: Grove Press, 1969.

Rousseau, Jean Jacques. *Reveries of a Solitary.* Trans. J. G. Fletcher. New York: Brentano's, 1927.

Sade, Marquis de. *Philosophy in the Bedroom.* Trans. A. and R. Wainhouse. New York: Grove Press, 1965.

Sartre, Jean Paul. *Being and Nothingness.* Trans. H. Barnes. New York: The Citadel Press, 1966.

———*Literary and Philosophical Essays.* Trans. Annette Michelson. New York: Collier, 1967.

———*Literature and Existentialism.* New York: Citadel Press, 1959.

———*Nausea.* Trans. Lloyd Alexander (New York: New Directions, 1964).

Schopenhauer, Arthur. *Schopenhauer: Selections.* Ed. Dewitt Parker. New York: Scribner's, 1928.

——— *Selections from the Philosophy of Schopenhauer.* Ed. G. Erdmann. New York: Modern Library, 1950.

Scott, R. Y. B. *The Way of Wisdom in the Old Testament.* New York: Macmillan and Company, 1971.

Sextus Empiricus. *Outlines of Skepticism.* Trans. J. B. Bury. Cambridge: Harvard University Press, 1927.

Shenker, Israel. "Moody Man of Letters." *New York Times,* 6 May 1956, sec. 2, p. 1.

Solomon, Robert (ed.) *Nietzsche: A Collection of Critical Essays.* Garden City, N.Y.: Anchor Books, 1973.

Thomas à Kempis. *The Imitation of Christ,* Ed. J. Pierce. Harmondsworth, Eng.: Penguin Books, 1968.

Tindall, W. Y. *Samuel Beckett*. New York: Columbia University Press, 1964.

Unamuno, Miguel de. *The Tragic Sense of Life*. Ed. J. Flitch. New York: Dover, 1954.

Voltaire. *Candide*. Trans. R. M. Adams. New York: Norton, 1966.

Webb, Eugene. *Samuel Beckett: A Study of His Novels*. Seattle: University of Washington, 1970.

West, Nathanael. *Two Novels by Nathanael West: The Dream Life of Balso Snell and A Cool Million*. New York: Noonday, 1963.

Wilenski, R. H. *Modern French Painters*. New York: Harcourt Brace Jovanovich, 1963.

Wittgenstein, Ludwig. *Wittgenstein: Lectures and Conversations on Aesthetics, Psychology and Religious Belief*. Ed. Cyril Barnett. (Berkeley: University of California, 1967).

Zeller, Eduard. *Outlines of the History of Greek Philosophy*. New York: Meridian Books, 1955.

Index

A.E. (George William Russell), cited,
95–96
absurd, the, 5, 11–12, 154, 163, 192;
beauty of, 13–14; consolation and,
214, 219–20; habit and, 194–95;
morality and, 52, 209; obligation
and, 21; realism and, 59; skepticism and, 54; surrealism and, 97;
symmetry and, 108–109
Acts Without Words (Beckett), 62
Adams, R. M., cited, 63, 214
Adler, Alfred, 38, 135
Adolphe (Constant), 133
aesthetics, 11; of futility, 10–11, 49,
164, 214, 215–19; generalization
in, 61, 63, 68, 100, 204; passivity
and, 25, 26–27, 67, 97–98, 106; of
Proust, 8, 128, 140–41, 142, 162,
196, 204, 210, 211, 216; reality perceptions and, 9–10, 12–15, 16, 18,
31, 53, 58, 106, 138–39, 164, 170,
188, 195–96, 211–12; simplicity
and, 6–8, 9–10, 39; symmetry and,
55–56, 106; tragedy and, 67–68,
195–96
Albertine (Proust character), 133,
158, 172, 175, 195
ambiguity, 24, 57; nullifying alternatives and, 59–60, 63–64, 106–
10, 215, 217–18, 220
Amiel, Henri Frédéric, 128, 206
"Ancient Sage, The" (Tennyson),
88–89
animals, 32–33
Antisthenes the Cynic, 83–84, 95;
quoted, 29, 86, 140
anxiety, 26–27, 52; death and, 64, 65;
discontinuity and, 155, 156, 173,
177, 180, 181, 182, 192–93, 195,
199–200, 201, 204; nothingness

and, 214, 215, 216–17
apathy, 60–61, 65, 72–73, 75, 105–
106; asceticism and, 86, 89, 90, 92,
144–45, 146; Buddhist, 158, 160;
cruelty and, 208; French philosophy and, 93, 94, 97; insanity and,
27, 98, 220; insult and, 69, 140; of
Molloy, 110–13, 127, 202; of Socrates, 74, 80, 81, 83; time and, 114,
115, 116, 166, 182–83, 184–85
Apollonius of Tyana, 96
Apology (Plato), 31, 64. *See also* Socrates
Aristippus, 85
Aristophanes, 85, 86
Aristotle, 82–83, 118
Arsene (character), 10, 71, 74, 110; on
desire, 27; on knowledge, 30, 78,
127; on optimism, 26
asceticism, 26–27, 83, 168; Christian,
74, 89–92, 93, 160; exultation of,
86, 160; of Kierkegaard, 101;
Proust and, 138, 143, 144, 146
Atlas Mountains, 77
Augustine, Saint, 55, 74, 89, 90, 91;
Rousseau on, 93; time and, 177–
79, 180, 181, 183, 184, 190, 191
automatic writing, 97–98, 99

Barmadu (Céline character), 44–46,
47
Baudelaire, Charles, 74, 92, 95, 173,
187, 190, 191; quoted, 94, 153, 184,
185, 186
"Beast in the Jungle, The" (James),
214
beauty, 9–10, 13, 107; apathy and,
106; religious, 88. *See also* aesthetics
being: art and, 12–13, 14–15, 16, 58,

being (*continued*)
97–98, 138–39, 195–96; "form" of,
58, 77, 88, 211; Gorgias on, 83;
immediacy of, 175–76, 178–79,
180, 181–82, 183, 187, 188–89,
190, 191, 192–93, 200, 201; ordering of, 53–54, 77, 166–67; "recovery" of, 202–203; relations within,
154, 155–57, 158–60, 161, 164–65,
169, 184, 199, 213, 216; unity of,
155–56, 157–58, 169, 211; wisdom
and, 74–75, 80, 81, 127; of Worm,
18
Being and Nothingness (Sartre), 187
Bellacqua (character), 206, 208, 210
Bergson, Henri, 190; quoted, 200
Berkeley, George, 154, 168; quoted,
166–67
Bible, The, 74, 75–76
Blake, William, 26, 79
Boethius, Anicius Manlius Severi-
nus, 24–32, 37, 38–39, 89; Camus
and, 46
Boileau-Despréaux, Nicolas, quoted,
181, 191
boredom, 109–10; habit and, 197–
98; time and, 152, 157, 174, 185–
86, 190
bourgeoisie, the, 13
Brahma, 71, 124, 214
Breath (Beckett), 58
Brée, Germaine, quoted, 112
Breton, André, 92, 97, 99; quoted, 98
Britain, 15, 129
Buddhism, 54, 104, 156–58, 159–60,
168, 214

Calderón de la Barca, Pedro, 67, 167;
quoted, 37, 145
Camus, Albert, 92, 95, 164, 187;
quoted, 46–47, 49–50
Candide (Voltaire), 33, 120
Candle of Vision, The (Russell),
95–96
capitalism, 66
Carlyle, Thomas, quoted, 113, 125
Cassirer, Ernst, cited, 161
causality, 157, 161, 213; habit and,
193, 194, 196
Celia (character), 55, 72, 96, 105, 164,
213
Céline, Louis Ferdinand, 44–46, 47,
74, 92, 112; quoted, 99

Cervantes Saavedra, Miguel de, 120
Charlus (Proust character), 144
Chateaubriand, François René de,
128, 206
Christianity: asceticism of, 74,
89–92, 93, 160; "crucified thieves"
metaphor in, 55–56; pessimism
and, 21, 105; Trinitarian, 156, 160,
219
circularity, 16, 18, 56, 106, 108; Augustine on time and, 178–79;
monadic, 161–62, 169; universals
and, 62, 63. *See also* futility
Clov (character), 7, 65
Cocteau, Jean, 128
Coe, Richard, 83, 125, 155; quoted,
175, 180, 188
comedy: apathy and, 112, 208; death
and, 70, 183, 184; form and, 108–
109; generalizations and, 57–58,
59; pessimism and, 20, 22, 25, 27,
33–34, 47, 50–51, 60, 118–20, 163,
208–10; the sages and, 72–73, 75,
77, 79, 99, 118; unreason and, 10,
13, 17, 194, 195
Come and Go (Beckett), 6, 58, 219
Concept of Irony (Kierkegaard), 169
Confessions (Augustine), 90, 91,
177–79
Confessions (Rousseau), 29, 93–94
Confucius, 104
Conrad, Joseph, 33
consciousness, *see* contemplation;
self, the
consolation, 19–35, 75, 101, 114, 199;
aesthetic, 211–12, 217, 218, 219–
20; Christian, 91–92, 93; death as,
45–46, 47, 64, 86, 96, 197, 214,
215; of insanity, 98–99; memory
as, 199–201, 203; pessimism as,
37–44, 47–48, 49, 50–51, 53, 96,
118–19, 208, 218, 220; *Proust*
(Beckett) on, 128, 202, 205; skepticism as, 52–56, 103, 104, 127;
Stoic, 87; of tolerance, 148, 206,
219
Consolation of Philosophy (Boethius), 24–32, 37, 38–39
Constant, Benjamin, 92, 128, 133
contemplation, 71–120; emotional
colors of, 56, 127, 138–39, 155,
159–60, 168, 169, 171; habit and,
196; interior monologue of, 58–59,
60–61, 187; joy of, 8, 11, 14, 15, 16,

17, 43, 48, 55, 144–45, 160, 202;
time and, 114–18, 187, 189, 191,
201, 211–12
Conversion (Nock), 89
"craft," of Socrates, 81
Crime and Punishment (Dostoevsky), 202
criticism: Beckett attitudes in, 125–
35, 137–45, 153, 205–206, 210–
11; Beckett on, 6–7; surrealists
and, 97, 98. *See also* aesthetics;
judgment
cruelty, 13, 207, 219; boredom and,
110; Céline on, 45–46; critical,
125, 128–29; pessimism and, 22,
32–33, 41–42, 44, 119, 126, 208–
10; Proust on, 142–43
Curtius, Ernst Robert, 128, 133
Cynic philosophers, 74, 83–87, 93;
Joyce and, 95

Dans le labyrinthe (Robbe-Grillet),
187
Dante Alighieri, 148, 210
"Dante and the Lobster" (Beckett),
32–33, 208, 210
death, 40, 45, 46–47, 62, 63–66, 70,
93, 109; Buddhism and, 156–57,
158, 159, 160, 162; Camus on, 95;
contemplation of, 196, 214, 218;
desire for, 86, 111, 197; Leibniz
on, 161–62; Proust on, 137, 197,
202–203; time and, 173, 177, 183,
184, 186, 202, 207
Democritus, 76, 181
Descartes, René, 74, 92, 95, 151, 165,
184, 190, 191; quoted, 93, 181–82;
Baudelaire on, 185, 186; on God,
194; Proust and, 145, 204; Sartre
on, 189
Descartes (character), 52
Des Esseintes (Huysmans character),
39
desire, 62, 146, 168, 171–72; Augustine on, 178; pleasures and, 30,
149–51, 152, 156–57, 159–60, 166,
180, 183, 185, 186, 188; poverty of,
113, 116; skepticism and, 54–55;
spiritual, 91; wisdom and, 26–27,
71–73, 80, 81, 86, 89, 90, 105, 106,
115, 144–45
Dialogues with Duthuit (Beckett and
Duthuit), 8, 48, 164, 170, 188; on
nothingness, 215; on occasion, 216

didacticism, 73–74, 76, 81–82, 105,
132; amoral, 85, 209; of Kierkegaard, 102–103; of Proust,
142–44; of *Proust*, 125, 207, 208; of
West, 96
dilemma, 155, 164, 165–66, 171. *See
also* anxiety; desire; time
Diogenes the Cynic, 28, 83–84, 85,
86; cosmopolitanism and, 96;
Joyce and, 95
Don Quixote (Cervantes), 120
Dostoevsky, Fyodor, 46, 47, 95, 112;
quoted, 42, 43, 44; modernity and,
52; Proust and, 145, 202
"Double Room, The" (Baudelaire),
185
Dream Life of Balso Snell, The
(West), 96
Dreyfus Affair, 139
Duthuit, Georges, *see Dialogues
with Duthuit* (Beckett and
Duthuit)

Ecclesiastes, 21, 26, 49, 76, 103; Beck-
ett parody, 75, 106; Buddhism
and, 157; on desire, 62, 146; on
wisdom, 51–52, 131–32
Egypt, 76
Einstein, Albert, 161; quoted, 88, 189
Either/Or (Kierkegaard), 105, 170
Ellman, Richard, cited, 95
emotion, 138–39. *See also* anxiety;
apathy; desire; pessimism
Empedocles, 76
End, The (Beckett), 23, 68–69
Endgame (Beckett), 7, 65, 105
Endon (character), 86
English language, 192
English philosophy, 15, 129
ennui, *see* boredom
Essay on Man (Pope), 26
Essays (Montaigne), 93
Esslin, Martin, quoted, 99–100
Estragon (character), 6, 7, 61, 167
Etranger, L' (Camus), 187
evil, 40, 124, 168; animals and,
32–33; human nature as, 90–91,
94; knowledge of, 30–31, 38, 52,
53; nihilist "sickness," 131; Proust
and, 142–43, 144
Existentialism, 15, 169, 190, 213
Expelled, The (Beckett), 66, 77
experience, 154, 164; cruelty and,
207–208; knowledge and, 212;

experience (*continued*)
memory and, 199–201, 203–204;
of nothingness, 214; reason and,
205–206; time and, 178, 181, 187,
188, 189, 190, 191, 192, 202–203,
213, 216

faith, 88–89, 90, 91, 135; dilemma
and, 155–56; Hell and, 92; Socratic ignorance and, 103. *See also* religion
Film (Beckett), 29–30, 153, 166, 167,
213, 217
Finnegan's Wake (Joyce), 6
Fletcher, John, quoted, 21, 98, 187,
192
flux, 156–57. *See also* time
forgetting, 170, 171–72, 203; Proust
on, 176–77, 200–201
France, Anatole, 133
France, 192; meditative literature of,
74, 88, 92–93, 99, 180, 182, 187
freedom, 19, 25, 110; as attitude, 46,
60, 61, 69, 89–90, 169; in skepticism, 54; tragic, 196; unattain-
ability of, 63, 81, 87; wisdom as,
80, 86–87. *See also* will, the
French language, 192
Freud, Sigmund, 16, 48, 49, 200
friendship, 130, 170
Frye, Northrop, 63, 155; quoted, 58,
59
futility, 5, 10–11, 16–17, 48–51, 95,
104, 123–24, 199; of action, 59–60,
62, 66, 71–72, 80, 102, 105–106,
129, 135, 151, 164, 165–66, 213,
215; of apathy, 27, 61, 74–75, 110,
113, 114, 202, 220; of art, 49, 164,
214, 215–19; death and, 64, 214; of
faith, 91, 160; of insanity, 99; of
love, 45, 46, 115, 116, 146, 171–72;
of melancholy, 206; of memory,
200; *Proust* (Beckett) on, 126–27,
129, 130, 131, 135, 149–50, 210;
Sartre on, 154, 189–90; of self-
knowledge, 29, 87, 116–17, 212,
213; of speech, 21, 25, 77, 78, 83,
100–101, 103, 117, 118, 188, 189,
190, 191

Gaber (character), 34, 41
Galls (character), 62–63
Germany, 154, 160, 170
Geulinex, Arnold, 74, 95, 182;
quoted, 83

Gide, André, 128–29, 130; quoted,
91; Nietzsche and, 132–33
Gierow, Karl, quoted, 41
God, 154, 182; the atomic instant
and, 193, 194; Augustine and, 178,
179, 191; Berkeley and, 167; Leibniz on, 165, 166; Original Sin and,
184
Goethe, Johann Wolfgang von, 7;
quoted, 95
Gorgias, 83
Greece, pre-Socratic, 74, 76–80,
82–83, 95, 156
grief, Proust on, 138. *See also* death;
pessimism
Guermantes, Duc de (Proust character), 139
guilt, 24–25, 33, 92, 147; Dostoevsky
on, 42; Ionesco on, 52; Proust on,
143–44, 148–49; time and, 191;
violence and, 208, 209
Guion, Madame, quoted, 158
Gulliver's Travels (Swift), 33

habit, 48, 49, 106–107, 117; apathy
and, 111, 114, 202; Augustine on,
177–78; Kierkegaard on, 104; mo-
rality and, 128–29, 130, 131, 133,
142, 148, 197–98; Nietzsche on,
129–30; rhetorical structures and,
109, 110; self and, 193–94
Hackett (character), 110
Hamlet (Shakespeare), 52, 64
Hamm (character), 7, 65
Happy Days (Beckett), 9, 23, 48, 174;
style of, 129
Hardy, Thomas, 33
Hecataeus, 77
Hegel, Georg Wilhelm Friedrich,
quoted, 16, 54, 168–69
Heidegger, Martin, quoted, 58
Hell, 92, 148
Heraclitus, 76, 219; quoted, 53, 77,
78, 79; Surrealists and, 97
Hesiod, 77
Hinduism, 54, 74, 155–56, 157, 160
Hippasos the Akousmatic, 79
holism, 26, 37
homosexuality, 141, 142–43, 144
How It Is (Beckett), 20, 28, 31, 41,
219; on death, 64; the sage in, 73,
104, 105, 127, 165
Huet, Daniel, 189
Hulme, T. E., quoted, 135
humanitarianism: of Camus, 49–50;

political, 13, 68–70
Hume, David, quoted, 193, 194
humor, *see* comedy
Huysmans, Joris-Karl, 39
hypochondria, 146

idealism, 168–69, 201; aesthetics
   and, 14–15, 140, 211–12, 216
ignorance, 105, 123–24, 127, 210;
   aesthetic values of, 5–18, 19, 25,
   218; Augustine and, 179–80, 190;
   Baudelaire on, 94, 185; of death, 31,
   64, 66; inattention and, 201; joys of,
   31, 43, 51, 52; Karma and, 159–60;
   Socratic, 11, 53, 64, 80, 81–82, 88,
   96–97, 103–104; Tennyson on,
   88–89
Imagination Dead Imagine (Beckett),
   6, 58, 219
Imitation of Christ, The (Thomas à
   Kempis), 21, 90, 91, 92
Immoralist, The (Gide), 132
impotence, 49–50, 174, 215; morality
   and, 24–25, 31, 38, 50, 52–53, 75,
   130, 208; pessimism and, 40–41,
   127, 131. *See also* futility
inattention, 54, 201–202
incuriousness, *see* ignorance
indolence, 185, 186. *See also* futility,
   of action
indecorum, 119
India, 155, 156–57, 214
inferiority complex, theory of the, 38,
   135
insanity, 27, 98–99, 101, 127, 162,
   195. *See also* absurd, the
intellection, *see* contemplation;
   knowledge
Intermittences of the Heart, The
   (Beckett), 177
internationalism, 96
Ionesco, Eugene, quoted, 52
Ireland, 95, 96
"Ireland, Land of Saints and Sages"
   (Joyce), 95
irony, 84, 212; of knowledge, 71–72,
   77–78, 117; pessimism and, 33–34,
   41, 50, 220

James, Henry, 214
James, William, 99; quoted, 192
Jerusalem, 157
Job, 76, 101
Journals (Kierkegaard), 99, 100–101,
   205

Journey to the End of the Night
   (Céline), 44–46, 99
Joyce, James, 6, 10, 15, 95
Judaism, 157
judgment, 34–35, 51, 56, 60, 132;
   moral, 141–44, 147–49; skeptic's
   evasion of, 52, 54–55, 88, 128, 134
justice, 28, 38, 145; political, 13,
   66–67, 69

Kafka, Franz, 52
Kant, Immanuel, 154, 161
Karma doctrine, 155, 159–60
Keats, John, 162; quoted, 16, 168
Kenner, Hugh, 55, 125, 165; quoted,
   58
Kierkegaard, Søren, 99, 190; on communication, 100–101, 102; on dis-
   content, 134–35; on futility, 105; on
   grace, 205; on Hegel, 168–69; on
   Leibniz, 161; on memory, 170; on
   Socrates, 11, 84–85, 103–104
Knott (character), 109, 159, 174; porridge of, 180–81
knowledge, 14–15, 51, 88; of death,
   64, 93; of evil, 30–31, 38, 52, 53;
   futility of, 10–11, 16–17, 71–72,
   74–75, 78, 83, 87, 95, 100, 102, 104,
   105, 113, 116, 117–18, 123–24,
   131–32, 154, 160, 165, 189, 202,
   212, 213; Karma and, 159–60;
   Logos of Heraclitus and, 77–78;
   Pythagorean, 79–80; time and, 192,
   204–205. *See also* contemplation;
   ignorance
Krapp (character), 114–18
Krapp's Last Tape (Beckett), 29,
   114–18, 164, 190
Kristeller, Paul, quoted, 32

ladder image, 169
Lambert (character), 117
La Rochefoucauld, François, duc de,
   139
Leibniz, Gottfried Wilhelm von, 22,
   128, 130; quoted, 175, 179; rel-
   ativism of, 160–62, 164–65;
   Schopenhauer and, 153, 154
Léonie (Proust character), 195, 205–
   206
Leopardi, Giacomo, 71, 74, 124;
   quoted, 50, 66, 67
Leventhal, A. J., cited, 83
Lichtenberg, Georg Christoph;
   quoted, 2, 52, 88, 118

Logos concept, 77–78
London, England, 96
Lost Ones, The (Beckett), 65, 73, 105, 129, 219
love: as consolation, 45, 46, 146; time and, 102, 115, 116, 171–72, 175, 183
Lovejoy, A. O., quoted, 124, 138n3
Lucky (character), 118, 159, 167
Lucretius, 28
Lynch family (characters), 209

Madhyamika school, 156, 157
Malebranche, Nicolas de, 182
Mallarmé, Stéphane, 173
Malone (Beckett), 17
Malone (character), 17, 61, 72, 82; on being, 181; death and, 23, 28, 65, 74, 81, 191; misanthropy of, 47
Malone Dies (Beckett), 33, 93, 105, 117, 127, 219
Marcus Aurelius, quoted, 26, 28–29, 31, 87
Marriage of Heaven and Hell, The (Blake), 26
Mayoux, Jean-Jacques, quoted, 58
meaning, 5–18, 19, 154, 214, 218, 219; habit and, 195; Lost Ones on, 129; profitable, 75; skepticism and, 55–56, 123; time and, 114; universals, 57, 62–63, 100, 131
Measure for Measure (Shakespeare), 119
Meditations (Descartes), 93
melancholy, 206
memory, 102, 114–18, 170, 171–72; involuntary, 125, 128, 134, 140, 150, 162, 176, 177, 189, 190, 197, 199, 200, 201, 203–204, 207, 211
Mercier and Camier (Beckett), 209
Meursault (Camus character), 46–47, 95
Mill, James, 192
misanthropy, 44–46, 47, 90, 95, 119, 219; of Diogenes, 84, 85; generalization and, 71; of Heraclitus, 77; of Kierkegaard, 101; Nietzsche on, 129; in Proust, 124, 126, 127, 128, 130, 132, 135, 140, 149, 206–207; of Rousseau, 93; of Schopenhauer, 148, 149
Molloy (Beckett), 9, 10–12, 17, 33, 34, 41, 80, 110–13, 150; Christianity and, 89; conclusion of, 59–60, 104, 217; on habit, 193, 202; inspiration of, 82, 104, 105; plot of, 127, 164;

time in, 180
Molloy (character), 15, 48, 63, 81, 85, 110, 208, 219; on contemplation, 60–61, 72; Heraclitus and, 77; hope and, 26, 27, 40, 50, 64, 92, 164; on ignorance, 9, 10, 11, 12, 13, 14, 16, 17, 18, 19, 43, 51, 53, 66, 82, 127, 185, 212; indifference of, 6, 110–13, 119, 158; on intercourse, 59, 111; Leibniz and, 161; on memory, 203; skepticism of, 51, 54–55; on solitude, 16–17; speech style of, 126; "They" of, 99; on waking, 176
monad, doctrine of the, 161–62; Waiting for Godot and, 162–63, 164
Montaigne, Michel de, 37, 53, 74, 92; quoted, 22–23, 41, 93; Céline on, 44; Rousseau on, 93
morality, 154; didacticism and, 73–74 (See also didacticism); Diogenes on, 85; habit and, 128–29, 130, 131, 133, 142, 148, 197–98; impotence and, 24–25, 31, 38, 50, 52–53, 75, 130, 208; nihilism and, 131, 132, 135, 214; of Proust, 141–44, 148–49, 197, 206; reason and, 13, 15, 31, 32, 33, 123–24; of Schopenhauer, 148; skepticism and, 72, 105; time and, 187, 191
Moran (character), 32, 34, 59–60, 70, 85, 164, 208, 219; on anxiety, 27; bees of, 14, 15, 82, 118, 212; on contemplation, 11, 30, 74, 75, 81, 171; on death, 47, 64, 86; "fiends" of, 99; on freedom, 63; on guilt, 25; on perseverence, 48, 49, 50, 104, 114, 126; on pessimism, 19, 40, 41; on silence, 117; skepticism of, 51, 127
More Pricks than Kicks (Beckett), 30, 32, 90, 93, 132, 206; time in, 176, 182, 193
Murphy (Beckett), 7, 16, 85, 158; on chaos, 53–54; on creative action, 164; pessimism of, 20, 27, 101–102, 127, 169, 212; sages in, 72, 79, 83, 86, 95, 96, 98–99, 105–106, 110, 127, 159, 166, 214; symmetries in, 106–108
Murphy (character), 21–22, 108, 110, 213; guile of, 85; mind of, 16–17, 27, 31, 54, 55, 96, 100, 101–102, 158, 159, 170, 182; monadism and, 161; pleasures of, 48, 54, 105–106, 107, 158, 159
Myth of Sisyphus, The (Camus), 164

Nabokov, Vladimir, quoted, 173
Nagarjuna, quoted, 156–57, 158, 159–60
nature, 42, 65, 66, 161, 182; cycles of, 26, 62, 63; Proust and, 138; Stoics and, 86, 90
Nausea (Sartre), 12, 14; on time, 173, 174, 187
Neary (character), 54, 72, 79, 108
Newton, Isaac, 161
Nietzsche, Friedrich, 50, 128, 156, 162, 170; on beauty, 9; on being, 58; on cynicism, 84; on habit, 129–30; nihilism of, 130–33, 135; on pessimism, 19, 22, 51; on politics, 67; on Schopenhauer, 191; on silence, 57; on skepticism, 52–53
nihilism, 75–76, 124, 130–33, 135; Buddhist, 156–57, 158, 159, 214; of Gorgias, 83; of Robbe-Grillet, 13–14; style and, 63, 214
Nil (Adams), 63, 214
Nirvana, 157–58, 159, 162, 214
Nobel Prize, 41, 77
Nock, A. D., cited, 89
Notes from the Underground (Dostoevsky), 42–44, 95
nothingness, 214–17, 218. *See also* death; nihilism; Nirvana
Not I (Beckett), 114
Nouvelle Revue Française (periodical), 125

obscurity, 6–8, 17; aesthetics of, 9–10, 11, 97. *See also* ignorance
occasionalism, 182, 216
"Ode on a Grecian Urn" (Keats), 16
"Ode to a Nightingale" (Keats), 168
Odette (Proust character), 146
Oedipus figure, 156
Original Sin doctrine, 90, 94, 178, 184

Pale Fire (Nabokov), 173
paranoia, 99
Paris, France, 96, 97, 99
Paris Spleen (Baudelaire), 187
Parmenides, 95, 156; quoted, 175–76
Pascal, Blaise, 74, 89, 92, 191; quoted, 37, 39, 41, 87, 180
perception, 54, 146, 168; Berkeley on, 166–67; habit and, 195, 196; Hume on, 194; James on, 192; language and, 188; Leibniz on, 162, 166; memory and, 201, 203; Schopenhauer on, 211, 213, 216, 218;

tragic, 196–97
Periander of Corinth, quoted, 58
pessimism, 8, 19–35, 64, 75–76, 105; apathy and, 60, 61, 75, 114, 166; Buddhism and, 159–60; as consolation, 37–44, 47–48, 49, 50–51, 53, 96, 118–19, 120, 208–209, 218, 220; generalization and, 61, 66, 99, 138, 199; misanthropy and, 44–46, 47, 119, 124, 126, 130, 132, 149, 219; politics and, 66–67, 68; Proust and, 123, 125, 128, 130, 133, 137–39, 145, 146, 148, 149–50, 152, 192, 196–98, 199, 201, 205, 206, 211; of Sartre, 187–88, 189–90; skepticism and, 51–56, 62, 86–87, 118, 123, 127, 168; of Voltaire, 123, 161
Phaedo (Plato), 80
philosophy, 71–120; emotional sources of, 138–39. *See also* contemplation; knowledge; *and see specific philosophers*
Pim (character), 65, 85
Ping (Beckett), 11, 219
Plato, 14, 15, 31, 64, 82–83, 211; on knowledge, 74, 80; on unity, 156, 157, 160
Play (Beckett), 57, 64, 65, 112
pleasure, 48–49, 50, 86, 91, 152; Buddhism and, 159–60; Leibniz on, 166; Proust and, 138, 143–44, 146, 149–50, 197–98; time and, 180, 183, 185–86, 188
politics, 13, 66–67, 134, 139; Kierkegaard and, 101
Pope, Alexander, 26; quoted, 199
Poulet, Georges, on time, 180, 181
power, 24–25, 31, 40–41, 49; Nietzsche on, 132; prudence and, 75; of reason, 28–29, 38. *See also* impotence
Pozzo (character), 39–40, 41, 174
problematic, the, *see* dilemma
Proust, Marcel, 8, 74, 92, 160, 168, 170, 175, 188, 189, 190, 210; quoted, 5, 67, 138–46 *passim*, 148, 152, 158, 171, 172, 176, 177, 194–95, 196–97, 200, 207, 216; continuation anxiety of, 155, 156, 173, 177, 180, 193, 195, 199–200, 201, 204; on death, 137, 197, 202–203; Leibniz and, 162; on passivity, 184; pessimism of, 123, 125, 128, 130, 133, 137–39, 145, 146, 148, 149–50, 152, 192, 196–98,

Proust, Marcel (*continued*)
   199, 201, 205, 206, 211; political
   material and, 67–68, 134, 139; tolerance and, 141–44, 148–49, 197,
   206, 207, 219
Proust (Beckett), 9, 25, 37, 40, 53, 81,
   123–35, 137–52; on Baudelaire,
   184; on Calderón, 167; on contemplation, 171, 196, 212; on death,
   63–64, 202–203, 207; on desire,
   26–27, 71–72, 86, 105, 144, 149–
   51, 156–57, 160, 166; on habit, 48,
   128–29, 130, 133, 193, 196, 202; on
   Leibniz, 128, 130, 153, 161, 164–
   65; on memory, 170, 190, 201,
   202–203, 207; on Schopenhauer,
   14, 39, 132, 145–46, 147–48, 151,
   153–54, 170; on style, 58, 210, 216;
   on time, 114, 149, 155, 157, 173,
   175, 176, 180, 183, 186, 187, 188,
   190, 201, 202–203, 205, 213
prudence, 75
psychic automatism, 97–98, 99
Pythagoras, 76, 77, 79–80

quiescence, 157–58, 160. *See also*
   apathy

race, Nietzsche on, 52–53
rationalism, 13, 137, 205–206; biblical, 75–76; Christian, 92; critical,
   98; of Leibniz, 164–65; optimism
   and, 22–23, 28–29, 30–31, 32, 38,
   46, 48, 128, 138; rhetorical absurdity and, 54; of the sages, 86–87,
   124
realism, 58, 59, 69; of Proust, 138, 146
reality, *see* being
relativism, 153–72, 189; art and,
   216–17, 218; desire and, 149–51,
   152, 156–57, 158; Nietzsche and,
   130; Proust and, 133, 158, 188;
   Schopenhauer and, 183, 184, 190,
   211–12, 213
relativity theory, 161, 189
religion, 88–89, 99, 155–58, 191;
   Hulme on, 135; Kierkegaard on,
   105, 205. *See also* Buddhism;
   Christianity; Judaism
Remembrance of Things Past
   (Proust), 67, 138, 139, 140; time
   "recovered" in, 202–203. *See also*
   Proust, Marcel
Renaissance, the, 92

Renan, Ernest, 133
Renard, Jules, quoted, 50
Repetition (Kierkegaard), 169
Republic, The (Plato), 31, 81
responsibility: futility of, 48–49, 154;
   guilt and, 24–25, 37, 42, 191; skep-
   ticism and, 72
Reveries (Rousseau), 29, 93
Robbe-Grillet, Alain, 13–14, 187, 192
Robinson, Michael, 48; quoted, 22
romanticism, 163, 197
Roquentin (Sartre character), 12–13,
   191
Rousseau, Jean-Jacques, 30, 74, 92,
   184, 190, 191; quoted, 29, 93,
   182–83; Baudelaire on, 94
Russell, George ("A. E."), 95–96

Sade, Donatien Alphonse, comte de,
   163; quoted, 208
sadism, *see* cruelty; violence
Sages, The, 71–120, 124, 127, 131–
   32, 154, 219. *See also specific
   philosophers*
Sartre, Jean-Paul, 12–13, 14, 92, 213;
   quoted, 154, 187, 188, 189–90;
   Buddhism and, 156; on freedom,
   25; time and, 173, 174, 177, 187–
   89, 190, 191, 192
Schiller, Johann Christoph Friedrich
   von, quoted, 40
Schopenhauer, Arthur, 10, 54, 124,
   153, 197; on happiness, 68; on
   nothingness, 214–15; on pain, 33,
   40, 42; on perception, 211, 213,
   216, 218; on rationalism, 137; as
   sage, 39, 74, 83, 132, 145, 154, 170;
   time and, 173, 183–84, 186–87,
   188, 190, 191, 211; the will and,
   14–15, 135, 146, 147, 149, 150,
   151, 152, 158, 168, 211, 212, 213,
   214, 216
Secret Agent, The (Conrad), 33
self, the, 29–30, 38, 154, 202, 212;
   death and, 66, 70, 95, 156–57; evil
   and, 90–91; habit and, 193–94,
   195, 196; Heraclitus on, 79; insanity and, 98–99; memory and,
   176–77, 195, 200–201, 204;
   Nietzschean, 128, 129; Proust on
   morality and, 143–44, 206; skepticism and, 54; Socrates on, 80; stoicism and, 87, 93–94; time and,
   115, 125, 173, 181–82, 183, 187,

188, 189–90, 191, 192; universals and, 71, 78; will and intellect interaction in, 213, 216

Seneca, 28

Sextus Empiricus, 93; quoted, 53, 54

sexuality, 21, 55; apathy and, 111, 115, 116; homosexual figures, 141, 142–43, 144; Sartre and, 13, 14; West and, 96

Shakespeare, William, 52, 53, 64, 119

silence, 63, 75, 101, 117, 214

simplification, 39, 153

Sisyphus myth, 49–50, 104, 114, 126

skepticism, 18, 51–56, 62, 66, 127–28, 139, 210; relativism and, 130, 133, 154, 168; the "sage mentality" and, 72, 74, 82, 83, 84, 86, 88–89, 92–93, 103–104, 118, 123

society: Proust and, 67–68, 130, 134, 138–41, 142, 143, 197, 198, 203–205, 206; Schopenhauer on, 148

Socrates, 31, 74; on Hades, 65; on ignorance, 11, 53, 64, 80, 81–82, 88, 96, 103–104; subversion charges against, 84, 85

solipsism, 16–17, 54, 154–55; of Quixote, 120. *See also* self, the

solitude, 140–41, 171, 204, 206. *See also* self, the

space, 161, 191; in causality, 196, 213

spite, 5, 101; apathy and, 111, 140; in critical attack, 128–29, 130, 133, 134, 135; pessimism and, 41–42, 44, 50–51, 126, 127, 148, 149

Staël, Anne Louise Germaine, Baronne de Staël-Holstein, quoted, 123

Stephen Dedalus (Joyce character), 10, 15, 95

stoicism, 26–27, 28–29, 37–38, 74, 86–89; comedy and, 112; French philosophy and, 92, 93, 94. *See also* asceticism

Stranger, The (Camus), 46–47

Surrealism, 16, 74, 97–98, 170

Swann (Proust character), 139, 146

Sweden, 41

Swift, Jonathan, 33

Symbolist poets, 16

symmetry, 13, 33, 54–56, 106–109

Tantalus myth, 105, 147, 150

Tennyson, Alfred, Lord, quoted, 88–89

Texts for Nothing (Beckett), 25, 191, 215

Thales, 76

Thomas à Kempis, Saint, 33, 74, 89; quoted, 90–91, 92

thought, *see* contemplation; perception; philosophy; rationalism

Thrasymachus, 81

time, 102, 149; apathy and, 114, 115, 116, 166, 182–83, 184–85; art and, 216; Baudelaire and, 173, 184–86, 190; being and, 156–57, 171–72, 175–76, 178, 180, 183–84, 188–89, 190, 192, 213; in causality, 196; contemplation and, 114–18, 187, 189, 211–12; Proust and, 125, 139, 152, 155, 173, 175, 177, 178, 180, 188, 190, 199–200, 201, 202–203, 204–205, 206, 211

Tractatus (Wittgenstein), 169

tragedy, 40, 49, 67–68, 118–20; habit and, 195, 196–97; *Proust* on, 153, 171, 196

tragicomedy, 208–10, 217, 219; defined, 118–20. *See also* comedy; tragedy

transition (periodical), 98

Trinity doctrine, 156, 160, 219

Ulysses (Joyce), 95

Unamuno y Jugo, Miguel de, quoted, 56

Unconscious, The, 16, 58–59, 97–98; memory and, 200–201, 203–204

Underground Man (Dostoevsky character), 42–44, 47, 52, 95

understanding, *see* knowledge

uniqueness, 9–10, 11, 12, 15. *See also* being; self, the

United States, 96

universals, 57–70, 71, 99, 100; Heraclitus on, 77–78; nihilist, 131; society and, 204

Unnamable, The (Beckett), 64, 75, 105, 114, 215, 219; contradictions of, 127, 151

Unnamable (character), 17, 27, 58, 85, 112; "college of tyrants" and, 99, 186; on communication, 101; on consolations, 23, 28, 29, 30, 55, 87, 158; immortality of, 65, 104, 162; jar of, 97; style of, 126, 210; on time, 114, 174, 176; on Worm, 18, 99

Van Velde, Bram, 8, 10, 215, 217, 218

Vida es sueño, La (Calderón), 67, 167

Vinteuil (Proust character), 142–43

violence, 21, 85, 163; pain and, 32–33; symmetry and, 13, 33; tragicomic, 119–20, 208–210

Vladimir (character), 6, 39–40, 55–56, 65, 174; dog poem of, 162–63; Estragon's dream and, 167, 168

Voltaire, 33, 120, 123, 161; quoted, 19

Waiting for Godot (Beckett), 6, 39–40, 61, 80, 118; on Berkeley, 166, 167; on Christianity, 92; monadism and, 162–63, 164; time in, 174; as tragicomedy, 119

Watt (Beckett), 6, 9, 26, 33, 99, 103, 105, 160, 212, 219; birds in, 119; cataloguing in, 59, 108–109, 110, 209, 214–15; Christianity and, 89; on desire, 27; ending of, 34–35; *exempla* in, 74; on humor, 10; Knott's house in, 159, 174, 180–81; ladder in, 169; madness in, 127; piano-tuning in, 62–63; Russell and, 95, 96

Watt (character), 57, 174

Werther (Goethe), 7

West, Nathanael, 96

"Whoroscope" (Beckett), 52, 90, 181

will, the, 37, 106; Camus on, 49–50; memory and, 200; Nietzsche on, 131, 132; pessimism and, 24–25, 123; Proust and, 141–42, 144, 146, 148; Schopenhauer on, 14–15, 135, 146, 147, 149, 150, 151, 158, 168, 211, 212, 213, 214, 216. *See also* desire

Winnie (character), 174

wisdom, *see* contemplation; knowledge

wisdom literature, 75–76, 90, 124; Hindu, 155–56

wit, *see* comedy

Wittgenstein, Ludwig, 169; quoted, 15

work-ethic, 197

World as Will and Idea, The (Schopenhauer), 145

Worm, 99; ignorance of, 18

Wylie (character), 79

Xanthippe, 80

Xenophanes, 76, 77

Yeats, Jack B., 61

Youdi (character), 34

Zeno, 76, 114, 156, 171; on magnitudes, 176; Sartre and, 191

Zeno the Eleatic, 83, 133, 190